The
Greening
of
Literary
Scholarship

The Greening of
Literary Scholarship
Literature, Theory,
and the Environment

edited by STEVEN ROSENDALE

foreword by SCOTT SLOVIC

UNIVERSITY OF IOWA PRESS Iowa City

University of Iowa Press, Iowa City 52242
Printed in the United States of America
Design by Richard Hendel
http://www.uiowa.edu/~uipress

A version of Michael P. Branch's "Saving All the Pieces: The Place of
Textual Editing in Ecocriticism" was first published in *Interdisciplinary
Literary Studies* (November 2001). Portions of James D. Lilley's "Of
Whales and Men: The Dynamics of Cormac McCarthy's Environmental
Imagination" were published in the *Southern Quarterly* 38:2 (Winter
2000).

The publication of this book was generously supported by the University
of Iowa Foundation.

Printed on acid-free paper

Library of Congress
Cataloging-in-Publication Data
The greening of literary scholarship: essays on literature, theory, and the
environment / edited by Steven Rosendale; foreword by Scott Slovic.
     p.   cm.
   Includes bibliographical references and index.
   ISBN 0-87745-802-2 (cloth), ISBN 0-87745-803-0 (pbk.)
   1. Ecocriticism.   2. Nature in literature.   3. Literature, Modern—
History and criticism.   I. Rosendale, Steven.

PN98.E36 R67 2002
809'.93355—dc21   2002016008

02 03 04 05 06 C 5 4 3 2 1
02 03 04 05 06 P 5 4 3 2 1

CONTENTS

III. RETHINKING REPRESENTATION AND THE SUBLIME

FOREWORD SCOTT SLOVIC

"Please come home, Scott. There's been an accident. Sally didn't make it, she's gone." The other day, while I was at my office meeting with a student and discussing his upcoming project, our dogs escaped from the yard at home, and two were hit by a truck, one of them killed instantly. My fiancée, Susie, left the frantic and despairing message on my answering machine, while I chatted about environmental writing in the other room. Of course, there's nothing I could have done about the accident, even if I had been at home that morning. But as I replay those words in my mind, "didn't make it, she's gone," I find myself drifting from the specific pronoun referent, the sweet and clueless little yellow dog we called Sally, to other things that might be going, going, gone. I imagine some being saying, "Well, I'm afraid Earth just didn't make it — it's gone." Or, more likely, "Those humans — they didn't make it. They're gone."

I'm trying to figure out why it is that many of today's talented students and literary scholars are doing what we call "ecocriticism." What's the purpose of this zealous activity — what's the hope? What brings me into the office every day? Perhaps it's the unwillingness to have the cosmos ringing with some equivalent of the phrases, "They didn't make it. They're gone. Never knew what hit them, never saw it coming."

In 1992 I published a book titled *Seeking Awareness in American Nature Writing*, arguing that one of the central purposes of nonfiction nature writing (and perhaps environmental writing in all genres) is the exploration of the psychological phenomenon of consciousness and, in some cases, the stimulation of self-awareness and environmental awareness in readers. Six years later, I gave a talk called "Reaching Out to the Great Unwashed: Ecocritics, Environmental Writers, and Their Audience(s)" as the opening presentation at the American Literature Association's symposium on environmental literature and ecocriticism in Puerto Vallarta, and I began with the premise that "we are sufficiently aware. We, as members of an industrialized, information-oriented society, are already saturated with environmental consciousness. . . . The processes we deplore — the usual litany of planetary degradations — have continued virtually unchecked, despite our accrual of awareness." My friends and colleagues worried that

I was suffering from "ecodespair" and urged me to lighten up. Some of them did so with copious free margaritas. I soaked myself in camaraderie, sunlight, and salty air, and I felt better by weekend's end.

Ecodespair notwithstanding, I continue to spend my days talking with students, friends, and colleagues about their writing projects, their career plans, their notions of ecocriticism and green literature. This is a daily activity for me — and it's fun, even sometimes heartening. When it's not my own students here in the office, I'm fielding inquiries about University of Nevada, Reno's Literature and Environment Program over the Internet, or sometimes coaching German students about doing ecocriticism on campuses where their advisers don't sanction this newfangled approach to criticism, or agreeing to take a look at a Taiwanese student's ecocritical master's thesis. Submissions to *ISLE: Interdisciplinary Studies in Literature and Environment* stream in at a rate of several per week — earnest, thoughtful, and often intricately argued studies. I have next to me on the desk an advance copy of the latest issue of *ISLE*, offering ten new ecocritical articles on subjects ranging from science fiction treatments of population issues to urban ecocritical theory, from nineteenth-century American literature to experimental films about cities. The community of ecocritics and environmental writers, it seems to me, is thriving — the theoretical sophistication of the environmental humanities is growing in leaps and bounds, the range of topics under consideration in history, cultural studies, philosophy, literary scholarship, and other neighboring fields is rapidly expanding.

But I do think it's wise and reasonable to step back occasionally and ask big questions — to ask what this is all for. When I urged nature writer David Quammen to consider writing a manuscript for Milkweed Editions' Credo Series back in 1998, he made the following comment to me in an E-mail: "[A]mong the firmest of my professional convictions is that a writer who wants to influence how humans interact with landscape and nature should strive to reach as large an audience as possible and NOT preach to the converted. That means, for me, flavoring my work with entertainment-value, wrapping my convictions subversively within packages that might amuse and engage a large unconverted audience, and placing my work whenever possible in publications that reach the great unwashed" (May 28, 1998).

My partner in the series, Milkweed publisher Emilie Buchwald, quickly urged me to write back to David and let him know that that's our goal, too:

to engage a large, unconverted audience. I found myself fretting and musing, though — if this is really our goal, what are our chances of achieving it? Who are "the great unwashed"? (I suspect that many of my ecocritic and nature-writer friends would love to be classified in this way.) What do the "unwashed" read? Do they read — or listen or watch? How could I justify luring David away from devoting his energies to writing sharp-eyed, learned book reviews and articles for the immense audiences of the *New York Times* and *Outside*?

Most of us who call ourselves ecocritics or nature writers publish our words for much smaller, narrower audiences. A moderately successful ecocritical book might sell 2,000 copies. Even an extraordinarily successful work of nature writing, like Terry Tempest Williams's *Refuge*, has sold only about 140,000 copies in its first decade. To the extent that those of us involved in this work maintain idealistic visions about the social efficacy of our thoughts and words, we must affirm these visions with notions of the "ripple effect" and "trickle down communication" — we have indirect access, at best, to "the great unwashed."

Nonetheless, the enterprise of ecocriticism and green literary pedagogy forges ahead eagerly, thoughtfully, and hopefully. Despite the environmental backsliding that's resulted already from the 2000 American presidential election, despite the cancerous proliferation of Barnes & Noble and Borders at the expense of independent booksellers, and despite the dour pronouncements about public literacy and literary scholarship in recent years (such as Harold Bloom's assertion, "I do not believe that literary studies as such have a future" [226]) — despite all reasons for gloom and doom — the teachers and scholars who represent what Steven Rosendale calls "the greening of literary scholarship" make it clear that intellectual vigor and an authentic love of art and ideas continue to thrive in the world today and make it clear, further, that humanistic approaches to environmental topics are viable, powerful contributions to scholarship. In their 2000 collection titled *Earth, Air, Water, Fire: Humanistic Studies of the Environment*, Jill Ker Conway, Kenneth Keniston, and Leo Marx argue: "If we are to understand and devise effective solutions for today's environmental threats, we must locate them within their larger historical, societal, and cultural setting" (3).

Much of this contextualizing work is exemplified in *The Greening of Literary Scholarship* as well. The present collection restructures the history of nature writing, offers new exploration of literary theories and critical practices that have not (or have seldom) been applied to environmental writing, and applies environmental-literary scholarship to particular authors and texts (and sometimes larger literary traditions) that have not commonly been examined in this context. All of this is clearly and convincingly explained in Steven Rosendale's excellent introduction. I find the goals of this project to be significant and challenging, and I'm genuinely impressed with the quality of the individual essays gathered here and with the cumulative power of the assembled material.

I cannot think of the title of this new book without recalling Charles A. Reich's 1970 publication, *The Greening of America*, with its eager pronouncement: "There is a revolution coming. It will not be like revolutions of the past. It will originate with the individual and with culture, and it will change the political structure only as its final act. It will not require violence to succeed, and it cannot be successfully resisted by violence. . . . Its ultimate creation will be a new and enduring wholeness and beauty — a renewed relationship of man to himself, to other men, to society, to nature, and to the land" (2).

Some would say "the revolution" has been a long time in coming — others today would scoff at the need for any social change or the plausibility of a radically modified economic system or body of environmental policy and law. But embedded in the scholarly phrasing and academic arguments of the essays in this collection is the subtle spirit of revolution. The murmured refrain in the hallways of every ecocritical conference is something like this: "Let's do something new and important. Let's make this more than just another academic trend." This was true in 1992 when the Association for the Study of Literature and Environment was founded, and it remains true today, at least in my experience.

I'm not sure the articles in this book will be of much direct use to David Quammen's "great unwashed." Literary scholarship is an acquired taste, a taste that will remain unfamiliar to the average reader or television watcher or SUV driver. Some critics and writers will take heart in the ripple effect of these essays, by which this scholarship will affect what teachers do in their classrooms, which will in turn reach broad groups of students, who will in turn become teachers themselves or move out into the world and carry with them faint hints of the ideas represented here.

As the rain forests burn and the oil drillers prepare to move into the Arctic National Wildlife Refuge or other sacred places, I take heart in the evidence presented here that literary studies, directly or indirectly, can still function as society's conscience. Our society's actions today, however harmful and shortsighted, will not pass without resistance, critique, and remembrance. Going, going, . . . Maybe so — but it's impressive to see the vigorous historical and cultural contextualization of our environmental ideas taking place in these pages. Without this sense of context — of causes and values and language — there's no possibility of advancing the green revolution.

ACKNOWLEDGMENTS

The idea for this book was in part the result of a conference called Representing Place, held at Northern Arizona University in 1998. I would like to thank the scholars and writers who participated in that conference as well as my co-organizers, Jane Woodman, Paul Ferlazzo, Geoff Chase, and Susan Fitzmaurice. Thanks are also due the many people who have provided encouragement and helpful comments on the project as it developed, including Michael Branch, John Elder, Sibylle Gruber, and Scott Slovic. I would also like to express appreciation to Lori Thomas and Robert Burchfield for their able assistance in the preparation of the manuscript.

Special thanks are reserved for my students in the various seminars on literature and the environment I have taught in recent years: their enthusiasm and sense of purpose have been a source of delight. As with most things in my life, this project has been lived as well as witnessed by Laura A. Gray-Rosendale, to whom I dedicate this book.

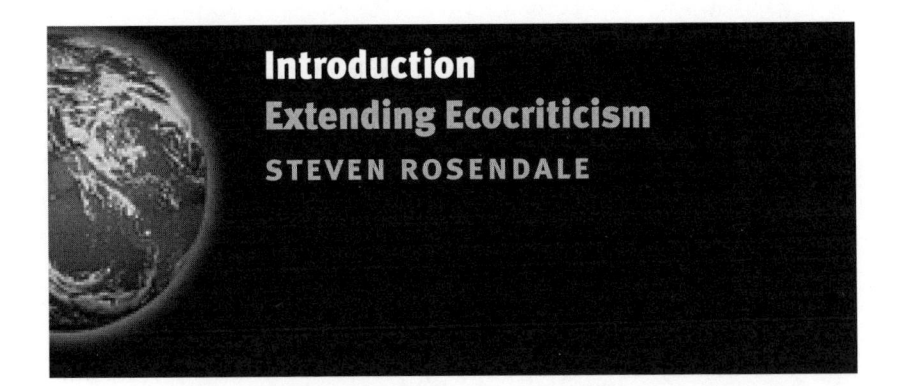

Introduction
Extending Ecocriticism
STEVEN ROSENDALE

Environmental literary criticism is at something of a crossroads: once the province of a tiny coterie of literary professionals, it is on the verge of becoming an important subfield of literary scholarship at American universities. Supported by a large national organization (Association for the Study of Literature and Environment [ASLE]) and a number of publishing outlets, ecocriticism may not yet be in the mainstream, but it has become one of the more publicly visible currents in literary study today.[1] The demand for classes in literature and the environment is growing (the ASLE Web site, for example, provides links to over 150 university classes), and the number of university composition courses and programs built around environmental themes increases annually. Several universities now offer graduate training in literature and the environment, and a growing number of scholars are emerging from Ph.D. work with dissertations on literature and the environment in hand. Environmental literary criticism, it appears, has a chance of establishing a lasting presence in American universities.

How ecocriticism arrived at its present institutional condition is a story that has been summarized elsewhere (for example, Glotfelty, "Introduction," xv–xxiv), but several elements of that story deserve additional emphasis here. From its origins, ecocriticism was methodologically and theoretically eclectic, encompassing a wide variety of literatures and critical practices, some of them already well established in literary studies. But the movement's identity today — its status as a distinctive, recognizable critical enterprise — derives less from the ecumenical reality of the entire field than from the more oppositional and even revolutionary emphasis of early endeavors to establish environmental criticism in the academy.

Glen A. Love's ecocritical manifesto "Revaluing Nature: Toward an Eco-logical Criticism" provides a typical example of environmental literary criticism's oppositional mode. Rightly lauded as an influential declaration of ecocritical purpose, it is an important document in the history of eco-criticism's movement into the academy. Love's argument begins with a hy-pothesis that has and must continue to underlie the project of ecocriti-cism — that human-caused environmental catastrophe is imminent and must be urgently addressed. Giving proper priority to this exigency, for Love, entails not a minor but a radical adjustment of critical practices. Ar-guing that literary scholars have largely "placed self-interest above public interest, even, irrationally enough, in matters of common survival" (202), he decries our profession's "narrowly anthropocentric view of what is con-sequential in life" (205). Instead, he advocates for an "eco-centric" criti-cism that radically rejects the anthropocentric concerns that have charac-terized literary study. For Love, the project of replacing "anthro"- with "eco"-oriented criticism entails three specific shifts: (1) the elevation of western American and nature-writing texts over ostensibly more human-centered canons, (2) the restoration of realism over "poststructuralist ni-hilism" as the dominant mode for the revaluation of nature, and (3) the supplanting of nationalist with global, ecological critical perspectives.

"Revaluing Nature" is, of course, a manifesto, and the particular exi-gencies of Love's rhetorical task probably require such an aggressive and unequivocal statement of aims. Ecocritics might well debate the merits of the particular practical program of action Love sets forth, but the basic ag-onistic strategy that he employs — the distinction between eco- and an-thropocentric criticisms — has proven a dominant strain in ecocriticism's struggle to establish itself and has had two consequences that largely command the ecocritical enterprise today. The first is the necessary em-phasis on bringing nature-writing texts into the fold of acceptable objects for literary study, a task that has proven difficult despite the publication of such notable anthologies as Robert Finch and John Elder's *Norton Book of Nature Writing*. The second is a general reliance on the critique of ostensi-bly anthropocentric critical modes and concerns, from which ecocriti-cism often seeks in various ways to distinguish itself.

The two most frequently practiced (and the most recognizably ecocrit-ical) environmental-literary-critical approaches respond to these con-cerns. The first considers the environmental implications of the represen-tation of nature, whether in nature-writing texts or in other literatures.

The second major current in ecocriticism has complicated the absolute anti-anthropocentric thrust of Love's argument and has sought to distinguish environmentally useful emphases on the human component of the human-nature relationship from a merely anthropocentric and harmful focus on the human. A wide variety of studies, for instance, have been devoted to probing the psychology of the nature writer as a means of investigating possible relationships to the natural world (for example, Slovic; Buell).

These are important issues and will likely continue to occupy the center of literary-environmental scholarship as identifiably, uniquely ecocritical approaches to literature. But in a problematic, ecocritical replay of traditional scholarship's division of "major" and "minor" literatures, a variety of other ecocritical emphases and modes have received less attention. A growing number of scholars are clearly interested in expanding the purview of ecocritical practice by widening the canon of texts for ecocritical investigation and placing environmental criticism in a more productive relation with other, perhaps suspiciously humanistic, theoretical perspectives and critical practices. This body of "auxiliary" environmental-literary scholarship has in recent years begun to gain mass and presents an important challenge to ecocriticism today.[2] Must environmental-literary scholarship be grounded in a scrupulous differentiation of ecocriticism from most other literary-critical practices? Is the rigorous separation of ecocentric "sheep" from anthropocentric "goats," so important in the early struggle to establish environmental-literary criticism's identity, still a productive way to think about the ecocritical enterprise?

The essays in *The Greening of Literary Scholarship* suggest that it is not. An emphasis on mutually enriching dialogue between environmental criticism and the anthropocentric concerns of established literatures and critical perspectives is a keynote of each essay in this volume. What the outcome of this effort within ecological literary criticism will be is uncertain, but several broad trends are indicated by the scholarship collected in this text.

Essays in the first section of this volume, "Remapping Literary Histories," exemplify efforts to reconfigure the literary history of nature writing, revisit neglected theories and critical practices to evaluate their usefulness for ecocriticism, and consider how environmental-literary scholarship might usefully impact our sense of the value of American literary traditions other than nature writing.

Michael Branch's "Saving All the Pieces: The Place of Textual Editing in Ecocriticism" and Gordon Sayre's "Le Page du Pratz's Fabulous Journey of Discovery: Learning about Nature Writing from a Colonial Promotional Narrative" both argue in different ways that the canon of nature-writing texts itself needs to be expanded to include colonial and other older texts. Both scholars point to environmental-literary studies' too exclusive focus on post-Thoreauvian nature writing and advocate for the recovery of more texts that predate our usual nature-writing canon.

For both Branch and Sayre, the project of recovering these vital elements of environmental-literary history entails the simultaneous recovery of critical practices that are increasingly neglected by ecocritics and by literary scholars generally. Instead of a new movement into the critical future, Branch and Sayre demonstrate the usefulness of a recovery of texts and practices from our cultural and our critical pasts.

Branch argues that ecocritics must engage in the traditional practices of textual editing — preparing previously unpublished materials for publication, recovering the text of previously corrupted editions of a work, or presenting a particularly inaccessible work in a scholarly edition that makes it useful to a general audience. Branch cites four reasons for ecocriticism's neglect of textual editing: its emphasis on modern texts and genres of nature writing that require little textual editing, like the personal "nature essay"; a lack of training in methodologies of textual editing; the academy's failure to provide incentives for textual editors; and ecocriticism's own neglect of older texts that seem "too alien in their generic forms or rhetorical conventions, or too unsympathetic in their ideological approaches to nature." Challenging these disincentives to textual editing, Branch examines one work from each of the past five centuries in order to illustrate the value of textual editing to ecocritical scholarship — Álvar Núñez Cabeza de Vaca's *La Relación* (1542), William Wood's *New England's Prospect* (1634), Cotton Mather's *The Christian Philosopher* (1721), Susan Cooper's *Rural Hours* (1850) and *John Muir's Last Journey: South to the Amazon and East to Africa* (written in 1911–1912 but never published until Branch's edition appeared in 2001). For each work, Branch provides a brief recovery history and demonstrates the potential each restored text has to substantially alter the way critics understand literary representations of the American land.

Sayre's essay also combines a plea for ecocritical attention to neglected practices like textual editing (as well as translation) with an argument

about the potential significance of a neglected text — in this case, a previously untranslated episode from Le Page du Pratz's 1758 *Histoire de la
Louisiane*. In the newly translated episode, du Pratz claims to have under-
taken a voyage of discovery on the Great Plains with the goal of finding
valuable commodities no one else had seen. Although, as Sayre acknowledges, "[a] colonial text employed for such goals as these might seem to
be the least attractive object for green literary studies," a close study of du
Pratz's narrative actually raises questions of urgent concern for ecocritics.
First, the narrative conventions of the colonial promotional tract disturbs
the implied contract between historians and the texts they analyze in
ways that highlight the need for rhetorically astute, genre-sensitive attention to older texts. Even more important, Sayre's analysis of du Pratz's narrative reveals a pattern of representation (what Sayre calls the "'topo-
graphic fallacy,' the tendency to confuse land with writing") that has
disturbing echoes in modern genres that purport to describe nature.

Essays by Helena Feder, myself, and Alison Byerly take related approaches to the expansion of the ecocritical canon. These scholars also
argue for an enlargement of the body of literatures that ecocritics
study, contending like Branch and Sayre that texts usually neglected by
environmental-literary scholars might bring important contributions to
the ecocritical project. In addition, each essay demonstrates the mutually
beneficial impact that ecocritical and other critical perspectives can have
upon each other.

Helena Feder's essay, "Ecocriticism, New Historicism, and Romantic
Apostrophe," argues that ecological literary criticism isn't merely an alternative to new historicism's recent dominance of the critical landscape:
it is a natural companion of new historicist thought, emphasizing the importance of both material reality and contexts to their fullest extent by focusing attention on the complex interconnection of Earth systems. In an
extended analysis of a single romantic trope, the apostrophe, Feder examines the critical and literary heritage of ecocriticism, demonstrating the
relationship between nature writing, literary form, ecology, and the key
tenets of new historicist thought. Apostrophe, she argues, may be understood as a form that manifests a number of assumptions that ecocriticism
and new historicism hold in common. The poet's sympathetic address to
objects in the material world (the defining characteristic of romantic apostrophe), for example, often develops a view of the object that acknowledges that the speaker's perspective, interests, and agenda inevitably color

perception, while also expressing a desire for connection with the object and acknowledging that consciousness itself is a form of reciprocity and interdependence with the material world. Feder closes by proposing that these basic natural affinities between ecocriticism and new historicism mandate a further reexamination of the usual segregation of ecocriticism from mainstream critical practices.

My essay, "In Search of Left Ecology's Usable Past: *The Jungle*, Social Change, and the Class Character of Environmental Impairment," focuses on another literary tradition that has received scant attention from environmental-literary critics — the urban literature of the American literary Left. I begin by challenging the conceptual basis of ecocriticism's frequent failure to address the issues of class and social justice that have long underlain traditional distinctions between Right and Left politics. Noting the growing body of scholarship devoted to recovering theoretical precedents for a coordination of Left and green concerns, I assert that the literatures of the American Left might serve as a usable cultural past for political ecology today. Through an analysis of how nature representation functions in Upton Sinclair's *The Jungle*, I point out the unexpected way in which the novel articulates a rudimentary political ecology that illustrates how the human experience of environmental devastation differs according to class, the close linkage between environmental and social values, and the insufficiency of models of social change that fail to provide for a radical revision of the technical basis of production itself. Although most critics have seen the political optimism of Sinclair's closing chapters as an unrealistic break with the determinism of the early parts of the novel, I argue that an ecocritical approach to the text actually reveals a more useful understanding of this notorious novel, in which *The Jungle*'s structural "break" indicates Sinclair's attempt to focus intently on the need for radical social change and the need for a radical revision of production's environmental consequences. Thus ecocriticism not only offers a view of this important novel's environmental implications but also challenges a critique of the novel's structure that has been an entrenched part of American literary criticism for nearly a century.

In "Rivers, Journeys, and the Construction of Place in Nineteenth-Century English Literature," Byerly makes a powerful argument for enlarging the environmental-literary canon to include a variety of nineteenth-century British novels, travel accounts, and scenic set pieces that demonstrate the simultaneous rise of "scenic entertainments" and the convention of the literary panorama. The most popular subjects of panoramas were river journeys that provided a sense of access into foreign lands by allowing the viewer to "travel" down the Nile, the Rhine, or the Mississippi. Although hardly nature writing in the usual sense, these panoramas are important for ecocritics to study, Byerly asserts, because of the challenge they present to the dream of an innocent and objective representation of "place" itself. Although they superficially appear to be place-centered, eighteenth- and nineteenth-century representations of the river journey, Byerly suggests, actually encode powerful political anxieties, subtly treating the river journey as a metaphor for the movement of British culture abroad. In providing an image that simultaneously raised anxiety about political boundaries (rivers often mark borders) and quelled anxiety by suggesting a predetermined outcome (one moves downstream, inevitably), Byerly argues that the representation of river journeys participated in what Mary Louise Pratt has called "anti-conquest," the "strategies of representation whereby European bourgeois subjects seek to secure their innocence in the same moment as they assert European hegemony." While these representations of the river journey are thus not laudable models of place-literature, Byerly contends, they are clearly worthy objects for ecocritics, who need to be increasingly aware of the potential political inflections of the construction of place and who can learn much from historical examples.

Like the research described above, the essays in the second section, "Expanding the Subject in Ecocriticism," insist that ecocritical practice has much to gain from engaging with the insights of established literary theories. The common theme of this group of essays is their intent focus on the issue of "the subject." This topic has long been an important one for environmental-literary scholarship that addresses the psychology of particular nature writers. These studies have delineated useful models for human-nature interrelation and illuminated some of the sources of the power of major nature-writing texts. However, their emphasis on general concepts like "modes of awareness" needs to be supplemented by perspectives that are more sensitive to how other subjective categories construct the human experience of the environment. The essays in this section contribute to a minority tradition in environmental-literary scholarship that has applied the insights of psychoanalytic and poststructuralist theory in order to further specify these categories, including race, ethnicity, gender, and the body. Although other essays in the collection also take up these concerns, each of the essays in this section does so by scrutinizing the relationship between identity and place in literary texts.

James Tarter's essay, "Locating the Uranium Mine: Place, Multiethnicity, and Environmental Justice in Leslie Marmon Silko's *Ceremony*," maintains that Silko's novel delineates a relationship between ethnicity, place, and coalition politics that has been missing from both mainstream multiculturalism and current forms of ecocriticism. Tarter discusses the deep interpenetration of individual identity, place awareness, social relationships, and animism in the Laguna-Pueblo sense of "place" articulated in *Ceremony* and shows that this understanding of place differs in crucial ways from the Western notion of environment that fuels much environmental-literary criticism. As Silko herself has argued before him, Tarter's analysis of "radioactive colonialism" in *Ceremony* demonstrates the value of a deep engagement with native cultural understandings of place, which in this case appear as though they might serve as an exceptionally useful tool for addressing the subtle and flagrant forms of environmental racism that have characterized human life on the land in North America.

Following the lead of critics like Annette Kolodny, whose 1975 *The Lay of the Land: Metaphor as Experience and History in American Life and Letters* pioneered a theoretically sophisticated approach to ecofeminist criticism, essays by Andrea Blair and Eleanor Hersey address the relevance of gender to ecocritical perspective. Blair's "Landscape in Drag: The Paradox of Feminine Space in Susan Warner's *The Wide, Wide World*" offers a thought-provoking negotiation of competing theories regarding "feminizations of place," like the metaphor of land-as-woman. Unlike so many treatments of the topic, Blair argues that this metaphor need neither be wholly embraced nor rejected. Tackling the issue of whether such gendered concepts for place derive from ultimately intractable psychological and corporeal realities or are better understood as mutable social constructions, Blair escapes the impasse by proposing a subversively "paradoxical" approach to gendered landscape. Like the self-conscious reappropriation of marginalizing concepts like "queer" and "nigger" by homosexual and African American groups, respectively, Blair argues, the metaphor of land-as-woman may be susceptible to uses that counter the negative effects for women and land alike that Kolodny enumerated in *The Lay of the Land*. Blair's analysis of Warner's *The Wide, Wide World* locates an example of subversive gendering of landscape, surprisingly enough, in a kind of text that rarely receives ecocritical notice — a nineteenth-century novel of domesticity.

Eleanor Hersey's "'Space Is a Frame We Map Ourselves In': The Feminist Geographies of Susan Howe's *Frame Structures*" uses a study of postmodern poet Susan Howe as a point of departure for her discussion of the relationship between environmental criticism, feminism, and postcolonial theory. In a provocative analysis of Howe's essay "Frame Structures," Hersey proposes that Howe's emphasis on landscapes as sites of colonial oppression might function as a model for retheorizing the political and gendered dimensions of place. In contrast to the static conceptions of identity, time, and place that inform many beloved nature-writing bulwarks, Hersey advocates for an alternative "feminist cartography" based on a disjointed, multidimensional, unstable model of relationship to place that is exemplified in Howe's work. Extending and challenging the research of contemporary feminist geographers, Hersey demonstrates the need for ecocriticism to develop more complicated models of relationship to place and fruitfully challenges some of the unexamined assumptions about identity and place that underlie much of the nature-writing canon.

While numerous works of environmental-literary criticism have been devoted to the processes of mind, James D. Lilley's "Of Whales and Men: The Dynamics of Cormac McCarthy's Environmental Imagination" takes up an issue that has only recently come to the fore in environmental philosophy — the status of the material body. Using an analysis of Cormac McCarthy's fiction as a springboard, Lilley argues that nature writing, like any interaction with nature, assumes the presence of an embodied observer and that the human-environment relation cannot be understood apart from an understanding of what it means to have a body. In McCarthy's fiction, Lilley finds an invaluable exploration of embodiment, in which static models of the body-environment interface are continuously dislocated and reconfigured in instructive ways. Like Neil Everndon, whose *The Social Creation of Nature* advocated intersubjective consciousness in which the concept of "self" is diffused and identified with the environment, Lilley's noteworthy analysis of McCarthy elucidates a body-environment frontier that is fluid and penetrable — a "borderland" where the embodied self and environment intermingle.

The final essay in this section, Louis H. Palmer III's ominously titled "Articulating the Cyborg: An Impure Model for Environmental Revolution," advances an even more radically fluid model of human subjectivity and its relation to both social and natural worlds. Palmer argues that eco-criticism's attempts to evade poststructuralism's critique of the Enlightenment concepts of humans and autonomous ego (not incidentally, key assumptions in much nature writing) are untenable. Instead, he suggests the need for a radical shift in the critical model of the subject that ecocritics employ. The challenge to Enlightenment models, Palmer notes, raises a question about how we might "develop new ways of knowing ourselves and our environment that will cause us to stop doing harm without falling back on essentialist or elitist models of the human in the world." He finds the initial outlines of an answer to this question in Donna Haraway's "cyborg theory," which allows us to understand the subject's "part in the system as something like integration or articulation into the environment—we become part of a cyborg, already attached." The figure of the cyborg, a socially constructed organism "continually integrated with machines in a series of informational connections," offers a model of subjectivity that has close parallels with models proposed in other essays in this collection. The cyborg-subject harmonizes well with ecology's emphasis on the interconnectedness of natural systems, precisely because it utterly destabilizes familiar "nature/culture" boundaries and radically refuses to hierarchize between self and other, original and the artificial. Although the effects of such a theory are, as Palmer notes, dizzying, he maintains that the practice of "thinking according to such tropes helps us to see who we are as part of a larger system rather than as transcendental and separate from where we are."

This trend toward an intensive ecocritical engagement with theory is also reflected in the final section, "Rethinking Representation and the Sublime," which addresses the implications of the concept of the sublime for an understanding of literary representations of the environment. More than an outworn philosophical category, the sublime emerges in these essays as a concept uniquely capable of focusing contemporary ecocritical attention upon the quandaries of representation itself and their environmental implications. Since most notions of the sublime include a recognition of the strictly unrepresentable elements of the human experience of the environment, the sublime might, these essays suggest, prove a particularly powerful concept for thinking about the limits, purposes, and potential of nature writing.

The sublime, as Rick Van Noy notes in "Surveying the Sublime: Literary Cartographers and the Spirit of Place," is an especially meaningful concept for ecocritics to address precisely because it deals with the intersection between a striking experience of place and representation itself. His study of exploration narratives by Henry David Thoreau and two directors of the U.S. Geological Survey, Clarence King and John Wesley Powell, reveals the surprising degree to which the concept of the sublime colors and constructs even the scientific project of representing the environment through mapping. Yet Van Noy suggests that mapping and the sublime are apparently contradictory: the sublime deals with measureless emotion, what can't be mapped or represented, while surveying precisely measures and strives for comprehensive representation. By teasing out the implications of this unusual contradiction, Van Noy also shows how the frequently criticized "colonizing" components of historic exploration and cartography projects can be tempered with an attitude of "environmental humility" derived from aesthetic response.

Aaron Dunckel's "'Mont Blanc': Shelley's Sublime Allegory of the Real" also proceeds from an acknowledgment of a potential contradiction between sublimity and representation. This essay sketches a theory for reading the relationship between literature and the environment through an interpretation of a frequent object of romantic ecocriticism — "Mont Blanc," Percy Shelley's poem about the highest mountain peak in Europe. Although the poem is a familiar one to ecocritics, Dunckel's analysis develops a line of thinking that carries momentous implications for a critical, widely held, a priori assumption of environmental-literary criticism — the very basic idea that literature "represents" the environment. Dunckel acknowledges that literature strives to "represent" nature, but he also argues that literature's main value is that it moves beyond a purely mimetic concept of the inscription of nature. He demonstrates that Shelley's poem, for example, is finally a "deictic" poem, pointing outside itself to what is strictly unrepresentable in nature. Drawing upon the work of such diverse theorists as William Howarth, Paul de Man, and Slavoj Zizek, Dunckel proposes a critical emphasis on literature's deictic qualities (specifically, its ability to indicate a world that escapes attempts at representation) as an alternative to the mimetic concepts of literature's representation of nature that currently dominate ecocritical thought. In contrast to critics like Palmer and Lilley, who argue for a critical emphasis on the interpenetration of self and environment, Dunckel provocatively suggests that it is precisely literature's deictic qualities — its ability to point to a nature that cannot be textually appropriated — that makes the literary a crucial resource for environmentalism.

In the final essay of the collection, philosopher James Kirwan also focuses intently on the resources for environmental thought presented by specifically literary texts. His essay, "Vicarious Edification: Radcliffe and the Sublime," maintains that the notion of sublimity, so often at play in environmental discourse, is an essentially literary concept, developed and best understood through literary models. Kirwan examines how the "fictionality" of literature impacts the representation of landscape in Ann Radcliffe's work and how the model of representation offered in literature can provide insights into human understanding of nature itself. He begins his essay with an incisive look at the philosophical precedents for the concept of the sublime at work in Radcliffe's novel *The Mysteries of Udolpho*. Kirwan goes on to assert that Radcliffe's novel can serve as an exemplary model for understanding how the concept of sublimity constructs the human-nature relationship. Specifically, Kirwan argues that the human-nature relationship created by sublime experience is doubled in an ironic way that only literary fiction can adequately delineate. Radcliffe's novel points to the sublime response to nature as a transcendent moment for human consciousness, in which nature can reveal suprahuman truths. But precisely by representing sublime landscapes — that is, by casting the sublime in terms available to ordinary human consciousness — *The Mysteries of Udolpho* also undermines the very transcendence of human consciousness that the sublime is by definition supposed to confer. Thus Kirwan's analysis of Radcliffe illustrates a fundamental paradox that carries immense implications for the project of valuing the environment and evaluating our relation to it through writing. Kirwan's closing words admonish us that the difficulties of the ecocritical project itself cannot be solved by refusing to address the conundrums of representation. Instead, it is primarily through the literary model that an accurate sense of our relation to the environment can be conceived:

> It is impossible to take Wordsworth's advice to shut up our books and turn to nature, for what we will find on the other side of this border between books and nature is that very self that we thought would, at this point, lie behind us. Human beings never can shut up their books, in

the sense of escaping human culture. What we call "nature" is ineluctably a story, one we have known since childhood, and the knowing
of it since childhood is another story. It is, indeed, the literary, the very
site, now traditional, of the celebration of nature, that must always reveal this.

THE FUTURE OF ENVIRONMENTAL-LITERARY CRITICISM

The essays in this book do much more than urge us simply to integrate
environmental concerns into literary studies. They manifest the developing demand among ecocritics for a careful consideration of just what such
an integration ought properly to entail. Elevation of nature-writing texts
to positions of esteem remains an important goal, but it is recognized that
our received nature-writing canon and the relatively small arsenal of critical approaches that have been applied to it have been too narrowly limited.
To extend the title metaphor of Michael Branch's essay a bit, the essays in
this collection demonstrate that "saving all the pieces" of our ecocritical resources will involve considering a potentially very wide variety of texts,
some of which present objectionable assumptions about nature and many
of which are drawn from genres and traditions alien to nature writing as
it is usually conceived. It will also require an increasingly sophisticated
concentration on mainstream literary theories and methods that until now
have been largely marginalized in environmental-literary scholarship.

Extending the horizons of ecocriticism in this way may change the
identity of the movement, but it also has the potential to revitalize radically the larger field of literary studies as well. In his book *The Rise and Fall
of English*, Robert Scholes notes that the transcendental justification that
"professing literature" used to carry has largely died, in the public imagination and in institutional reality, along with the death of the quasi-sacred
status of literature itself. Arguing that the profession must take steps to
acknowledge and deal with that fact, Scholes proposes a general restruc-
turing of literary studies. Instead of clinging to outworn justifications for
literary training, Scholes advocates that the discipline institutionalize a
concentration upon four areas: history (the contexts in which texts are situated), production (how to compose texts), consumption (how to read
texts), and theory (the canon of methods used to study the other three as-

pects of textuality). This is not the place for an extended discussion of the merits of Scholes's specific proposal (which does not address environmental criticism directly), but there is a certain convergence between his schema for a revitalization of literary study and the general approach evident in the essays collected in *The Greening of Literary Scholarship* that is worth noting here.

The Greening of Literary Scholarship offers a wealth of evidence for the significance of literature without making any appeal to discredited notions of literature's transcendent status. In a time when literary scholars find it difficult to define the value of their profession, the essays in this book offer robust arguments for the profound importance of deep and informed engagements with the literary, not as a mere cultural adjunct to more important forms of environmental activism but as the primary location where human relationship to the environment can be understood and perhaps altered. This unusually strong formulation of literature's importance has much to offer a beleaguered discipline that is increasingly seen as irrelevant to public concerns.

Finally, the scholarship collected in this volume represents an ongoing transformation in ecocriticism's concept of itself — a transformation that provides a useful pattern for the more general reconstruction of literary studies proposed by Scholes. Moving toward a more comprehensive sense of how to situate environmental-literary texts (history), focusing on the implications of familiar and recovered texts for the writing of nature today (production), intensively attentive to the practices of reading (consumption), and insistent upon a sustained attention to the methods used to understand textuality itself (theory), the ecocritical perspectives represented in this volume point the way to a vital and sophisticated practice that must continue to reform literary scholarship in our time.

NOTES

1. Witness, for example, the increasingly frequent appearance of periodical features like Jay Parini's "The Greening of the Humanities" and Gregory McNamee's "Wild Things: Forget Deconstruction — Today's Hippest Literary Critics Have Gone Green."

2. Part of the reason for this challenge may be found in the emerging institutional situation of environmental-literary criticism. Most of the growing group of scholars working in the field do so under conditions that call for an articulation of ecocritical and more established critical practices, canons, and theories. In this re-

gard, I am perhaps a typical example: hired to teach university courses in American naturalism, modernism, and literary theory, I can devote only one course in three semesters exclusively to a topical investigation of "literature and the environment." My professional life has thus required that I continually think through the relationship between, say, my scholarship and teaching in American naturalism and environmental issues. Although some might prefer to focus exclusively on nature writing, I do not. Indeed, the necessity of putting my ecocritical interests in relation to my work on various American literary traditions and to my understanding of literary theory has been an exciting engagement.

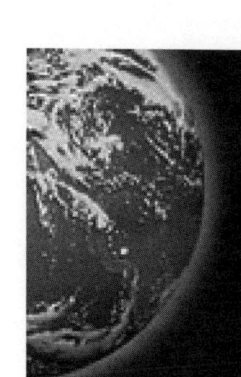

PART ONE

Remapping Literary Histories

1. Saving All the Pieces
The Place of Textual Editing in Ecocriticism
MICHAEL P. BRANCH

> *[W]ho but a fool would discard seemingly useless parts? To keep every cog and wheel is the first precaution of intelligent tinkering.*
> —Aldo Leopold, Round River

THE VALUE OF TEXTUAL EDITING TO ECOCRITICISM

When ecologists and conservation biologists theorize the study, alteration, or restoration of natural ecosystems, they often begin with the maxim that it is imperative to "save all the pieces" — that however else humans might alter the patterns of nature, we should be certain that our intervention does not result in the extinction of a plant or animal that may ultimately prove vital to the healthy functioning of the ecosystem. This essay argues that a full understanding of the American land and its various literary representations will require that scholars of environmental literature dedicate themselves to the preservation and restoration of the many rare, corrupted, or otherwise "endangered" texts upon which that full understanding may ultimately depend. In the first part of the essay, I speculate upon why ecocritics have not widely recognized the value of textual editing, and I suggest a number of reasons why textual editing should receive more attention in ecocritical studies. In order to make more clear how the practical work of textual editing contributes to the ecocritical enterprise, I devote the second part of the essay to five short case studies — one from each of the past five centuries — of textually edited books that significantly enhance our understanding of the North American landscape and its various cultural and literary representations.

By "textual editing," I mean the scholarly work of preparing unpublished materials for publication, recovering the texts of works that have appeared in corrupted editions, or presenting particularly obscure or inaccessible works in editions that make the work comprehensible and useful to a nonspecialist audience. Although "textual editing" is the older and more expansive term, "documentary editing" is sometimes preferred by those wishing to distance themselves from the substantial editorial liberties taken by many early textual editors, while "historical editing" or "literary editing" is favored among those wishing to identify their work primarily according to the discipline in which it occurs. I prefer the term "textual editing" for its inclusiveness while nevertheless avoiding the troubling generality of the term "scholarly editing." By my operational definition, then, textual editors are those scholars who discover, recover, and clearly present previously unknown, unavailable, or unusable documents.

Textual editing has long been understood as central to the project of literary and cultural studies, especially in such areas as medieval and Renaissance literature, where the rarity of many texts renders their proper preservation and presentation essential to the scholar's enterprise. Indeed, the past century has seen remarkable advances in the technologies and techniques of textual editing, such that Fredson Bowers, who was among the first American literary scholars to draw attention to the need for textual editing and to articulate explicitly a set of principles by which it should be done, could in 1976 claim that "when the history of scholarship in the twentieth century comes to be written, a very good case should be made for calling it the age of editing" (Kline xvi). Major projects in American textual editing began as early as the 1830s and gained momentum after the Civil War. By 1934, Congress had created the National Historical Publications Commission, and by the late 1940s the first variorum and genetic texts were being produced by Bowers and other mid-twentieth-century editors of American literature. By 1963, the Modern Language Association had created the Center for Editions of American Authors (succeeded in 1976 by the Center for Scholarly Editions), an influential institution that, with funding support from the National Endowment for the Humanities, went on to publish its *Statement of Editorial Principles* (1967) and to encourage and certify the proper editing of literary texts (Kline 3–8). Meanwhile, the formation of the Association for Documentary Editing in 1978 created a scholarly community for textual editors in all disciplines. The next generation of textual editing technology may be suggested by the Electronic Text Center at the University of Virginia, established in 1992, which uses recent technologies to make full texts of literary works available electronically and which tries to offer layered hypertext constellations in which edited texts are augmented by manuscript, typescript, or textual variants, as well as enhanced by illustrative images and sound and appropriate critical, historical, and biographical works (Electronic Text Center, homepage).

Despite the prominence and importance of textual editing — and the wide recognition of its value in many specialties of literary studies — scholars of environmental literature have been slow to recognize the need for and importance of textual editing. While the reasons for this ecocritical lacuna are many, we might consider several of the more important. First, our working definition of nature writing has, as the contents of *The Norton Book of Nature Writing* perhaps suggest, until recently been limited to the nonfiction personal essay that sympathetically describes nature and the authorial response to it — a quite modern literary subgenre that has thus required relatively little textual editing. Indeed, the assumption that nature writing should respond to immediate environmental problems has forced ecocritical attention not only toward the twentieth and twenty-first centuries but toward the handful of well-known contemporary environmental writers whose work appears to address most directly the current crisis.

Second, few ecocritics are adequately trained in methodologies of textual editing. While most literary scholars receive years of instruction in the myriad ways of taking a text apart analytically, very few are trained in the painstaking techniques necessary to put a text together literally — or put it back together when it has been corrupted by a complicated textual history. No graduate degree exists for those wishing to receive scholarly training as textual editors, and even advanced courses in the subject are rare. Although the past decade has seen the publication of a number of book-length guides to the practice and principles of textual editing — those by Kline, Sharpe and Gunther, and Stevens and Burg are especially helpful — many scholars remain understandably intimidated by an enterprise that Arthur Plotnik describes as "an excruciating act of self-discipline, mind-reading, and stable cleaning" (34).

Third, those American works least known to ecocritics and most in need of textual editing are often from the precolonial, colonial, and Revolutionary periods — periods traditionally underrepresented in ecocritical

studies. Unfortunately, ecocritics often find these older works too historically dense or theologically inflected, too alien in their generic forms or
rhetorical conventions, or too unsympathetic in their ideological approaches to nature. However, if ecocritics are to construct a more complete
and accurate understanding of how landscapes are understood and depicted in literature, it is essential that we broaden our thinking to imagine
nature writing as a category that includes sermons, settlement narratives,
and government reports — as well as personal essays — and that we recover and examine the works of earlier writers who may be overlooked
because their understanding of the natural world is predicated upon ideological or aesthetic assumptions different from our own.

Finally, the academy has often failed to provide adequate incentive or
reward for textual editing, leaving too many textual editors to pursue their
work without necessary support from the institutions within which they
work. Until recently, the profession has tended to value a critical article
published in a narrowly read academic journal over a restored, reintro-
duced text that might substantially inform our understanding of how the
landscapes of North America have been engaged and represented in the
literature of the past five centuries. While part of this institutional attitude
stems from our culture's Emersonian preference for work that is clearly
identifiable as the fruit of individual genius — that is, writing is seen as
one's own work while editing may be seen as tinkering with the product of
someone else's genius — it is more often the case that the apparently ar-
cane work of the textual editor is simply not understood and, until better
understood, cannot be valued more highly.

Despite the various and compelling disincentives to ecocritical textual editing, the arguments for the value and use of such editing are yet more
compelling. Before offering several practical examples of textually edited
books that are vital to the ecocritical enterprise, I wish to suggest several
important ways ecocriticism can benefit from a greater recognition of the
value of textual editing.

As I have suggested, the circumscription of ecocritical attention to post-
Thoreauvian nature writing deprives us of a full understanding of American attitudes toward and descriptions of the land. Textual editing can help
to recover and reintroduce the many now obscure texts upon which
Thoreau and his literary descendants both consciously and unconsciously

based their work. By "saving all the pieces" — or saving as many of the pieces as are extant and recoverable — we will increase the likelihood that our scholarly reconstruction of America's literary environmental history will be complete and accurate. In using textual editing to cultivate this deeper appreciation for early American literary representations of the land, our work will also establish historical context within which the post-Thoreauvian literature of nature may be better understood.

Ecocriticism will also be enriched by new attention to works in genres other than the nonfiction essay. Textual editing can help make more accessible American environmental writing in such less familiar rhetorical forms as the exploration account, settlement narrative, promotional tract, spiritual autobiography, sermon, diary, letter, or scientific report. Because the nonfiction personal essay has, like all literary genres, developed a set of conventions that privilege certain assumptions about the author and the world — in this case, assumptions such as the availability of leisure time, the primacy of personal experience, the inherent value of philosophical reflection, and the beneficence of nature — it tends to offer a deep but rather narrow view of how writers have perceived and represented American environments. Because textual editing invites and encourages the careful study of documents in a number of literary and nonliterary rhetorical forms, it promotes a salutary widening of the ecocritical focus.

Ecocriticism also needs to look more closely at works that express what seems an anthropocentric or even a destructively instrumentalist approach toward nature. By restoring and contextualizing works that represent the land in ways we now find ideologically offensive, textual editing can help reveal the origins of ideas that have often resulted in the degradation of American environments. We need to study literary representations that may offend precisely because their thorough theologizing of landscape may be alien to our modern secular sensibility, or because their scientific understanding of nature is by our own standards so fatally flawed, or because their mercantilist interpretation of the landscape appears so reductive in its ignorance of the aesthetic and spiritual value of the natural world. Only in this way might we begin to transcend the inevitable limitations of our own vision in order to catch glimpses of this land from the points of view of those who came before us — and only in this sympathetic engagement of other perspectives can we fully understand the roots of our own environmental assumptions and values, however different from those of our predecessors.

Finally, in its effort to identify the roots of a sustainable land ethic, ecocriticism must also continue to search for a marginalized tradition of American literature in which love of the land finds expression. Textual editing can help us discover works that — precisely because of their iconoclastic or unpopular celebration of nature — have been suppressed, corrupted, or lost. The aphorism that "the winners write the histories" suggests the predicament of the American environmental historian or ecocritic, for the dominant American environmental ethic has long been one of instrumental valuation, capitalist utility, and short-term profit. This dominant, utilitarian ethic has ensured that, until fairly recently, the attention and resources of publishers, funding sources, and paying audiences have been directed primarily toward writing that maintains the status quo while refusing to ask challenging questions about the sustainability and wisdom of this dominant environmental ethic. Thus textual editing is particularly valuable in helping us discover and restore otherwise obscure texts whose environmental sympathy or advocacy may have caused them to meet with resistance at all levels of cultural production and dissemination.

FIVE EXAMPLES OF ECOCRITICAL TEXTUAL EDITING

By "ecocritical textual editing," I refer not to a specific editing methodology but rather to any work of documentary editing that contributes to a more complete understanding of our environmental literary history. In this part of the essay, I have chosen one primary text from each of the past five centuries to illustrate the value of textual editing to ecocritical scholarship. In each case the work in question has remained practically inaccessible until relatively recently, and in each case the work has, since its editing and republication, substantially influenced the way we understand literary representations of the American land. In a very brief discussion of each of these exemplary works, I explain how the text was initially corrupted or lost, how it was recovered and restored by the textual editor(s), and how its accessibility contributes to our understanding of environmental values and landscape representations in the literature of its period.

**Álvar Núñez Cabeza de Vaca, *La Relación* (1542),
translated and edited by Cyclone Covey in 1998
as *Adventures in the Unknown Interior of America***

First published in 1542, Cabeza de Vaca's *La Relación* is among the most fascinating and valuable sixteenth-century accounts of New World exploration. In it, the author describes his epic eight-year journey across the then unknown wilderness of what is now the American Gulf Coast and Southwest. As one of only four survivors of the disastrous three hundred–person Narváez expedition of 1527, Cabeza de Vaca managed — by courage, resourcefulness, perseverance, and luck — to survive shipwreck, storms, hunger, thirst, exposure, illness, injury, enslavement, and attacks by Native Americans. He lived to tell the story of his six thousand–mile walk across what is now Florida, Texas, New Mexico, Arizona, and northern Mexico. By turns adventure story, autobiography, travel narrative, anthropological tract, and nature writing, *La Relación* describes the land and its native inhabitants and narrates Cabeza de Vaca's remarkable personal transformation from conquistador to castaway to merchant to slave to faith healer.

Although it is now among the best-known and most widely appreciated sixteenth-century accounts of New World exploration, *La Relación* has had a long and complicated textual history. First published in 1542, the book was followed by a second edition, misleadingly retitled *Naufragios* (Shipwrecks), in 1555. This second edition, prepared by a different publisher, introduced chapter titles and made other substantial structural changes to the original text. In addition to these two editions, there existed a rare, earlier document called the *Joint Report*, prepared by Cabeza de Vaca and two of his fellow survivors in Mexico City in 1536. Although the original of this document did not survive, a 1539 copy of it was included in Gonzalo Fernández de Oviedo y Valdés's important book *Historia General y Natural de las Indias . . .* (General and natural history of the Indies . . .), published in several volumes throughout the mid-sixteenth century. Because the *Joint Report* includes information that is essential to a full understanding of the events described in *La Relación*, it constitutes an indispensable part of Cabeza de Vaca's story.

Although an English paraphrase of *La Relación* appeared in the 1613 edition of the famous compilation *Purchas His Pilgrimes*, the only full English translations of the book were the Smith edition of 1851 and the Bandelier edition of 1905. In 1961, Cyclone Covey at last met the daunting chal-

lenge of assembling an accurate, accessible edition of Cabeza de Vaca's remarkable book. In his edition of *La Relación*, which he titled *Adventures in
the Unknown Interior of America*, Covey carefully collated the 1542 and
1555 editions of *La Relación* and the *Joint Report* to create the first coherent, complete, and readable English edition of the narrative. His edition,
which was cross-checked against various Spanish versions and English
translations of the original text, is also annotated to include information —
which came to light only as a product of anthropological research con-
ducted during the 1930s — regarding the likely route of Cabeza de Vaca's
journey through the Southwest. Now in its ninth printing, Covey's edition
of Cabeza de Vaca's epic narrative has introduced thousands of readers to
one of the most important sixteenth-century descriptions of the New
World landscape (Covey 15–17).

Because it contains the earliest known extant descriptions of the geography, flora, and fauna of the American Southwest, *La Relación* is of special value to ecocritics. Cabeza de Vaca is among the first Europeans to
record his impressions of the North American wilderness, which, after
landing in Florida, he calls "a difficult and marvelous country of vast
forests, the trees astonishingly high" (38). Cabeza de Vaca is the first European explorer to describe that "vast river," the Mississippi (52). He is
also the first to witness and record the impressive movements of that great
beast, the buffalo, and is likewise the first to describe other wild American
animals, "including one which carries its young in a pouch on its belly until they are big enough to find food by themselves" — the opossum (40).
Indeed, his observations are sufficiently astute to allow him to distinguish
among three kinds of mosquitoes he encounters during his travels. Of the
landscapes he encounters near the end of his journey, he writes apprecia-
tively that "this land, in short, lacks nothing to be regarded as blest" (129).

Cabeza de Vaca is also the first European to record the existence and
customs of many nations, tribes, and groups of Native Americans. His account proves that precolonial North America was widely, if sparsely, populated, and it offers valuable information regarding the lifeways and land-
use patterns of sixteenth-century Native Americans. Ecocritics will be
especially interested in the book's often detailed descriptions of Native
American hunting and fishing practices, medicinal wild plant prepara-
tions, and rituals of religious devotion to landscape features, plants, and
animals. Yet more remarkable is the way Cabeza de Vaca's attitude toward
Native Americans changes over the course of his eight-year journey. At

first ethnocentric in his assumption of European superiority, he is slowly transformed by near-daily contact with various Native Americans during his years of wandering. Eventually he comes not only to appreciate the natives but to join with them and, ultimately, to minister to them as a spiritual healer who earns the devotion of thousands of followers. Rather than use his power to amass personal wealth by exploiting their labor, he devotes himself to advancing the peace and prosperity of the natives; indeed, he becomes so devoted to Native American welfare and freedom that his objections to Spanish enslavement of Native Americans eventually results in his arrest by the Spanish.

Thus Cyclone Covey's collated, restored, and annotated edition of Cabeza de Vaca's classic sixteenth-century expedition narrative enhances our understanding of the literature of exploration by demonstrating that at least one early European voyager learned to view the New World landscape and its native inhabitants with attention and respect. It also contributes to our understanding of the American nature-writing tradition by making available one of the earliest and richest literary accounts of the flora and fauna of the pre-European Southwest. Because documents such as Cabeza de Vaca's are so rare and because the insight they provide is so crucial to understanding the roots of a long tradition of literary responses to the North American landscape, Covey's work as a textual editor has made a substantial and permanent contribution to ecocritical scholarship.

William Wood, *New England's Prospect* (1634), edited by Alden T. Vaughan in 1977

Very little is known of Englishman William Wood, who spent four years in New England between 1629 and 1634. Indeed, we have no certain information about his birth and death years, training and education, vocation, or family background. It is probable, however, that Wood was a member of John Endecott's scouting party, sent to Salem to open the way for the settlement of the Massachusetts Bay Colony, which began under the leadership of Governor John Winthrop in 1630.

It is certain, however, that William Wood has left ecocritics one of the most unusual and valuable literary artifacts of the seventeenth century. First published in 1634, *New England's Prospect* carried the subtitle *A true, lively, and experimental description of that part of America, commonly called New England: discovering the state of that country, both as it stands to our new-come English planters; and to the old native inhabitants, laying down that which may both enrich the knowledge of the mind-traveling reader, or benefit the future voyager.* As his subtitle suggests, Wood was devoted to entertaining his readers, but he was also devoted (as many writers of his day were not) to accurate and detailed descriptions that were "experimental" — that is, derived from the author's personal experiences and observations. At a time when English readers were hungry for reports from the New World, Wood's book was the earliest comprehensive, firsthand description of New England geography, climate, flora, and fauna. *New England's Prospect* is of special value to ecocritical studies because its focus on nature is so unusually sustained and detailed; indeed, it was not until John Josselyn published *New England's Rarities Discovered* in 1672 that any book could challenge Wood's for the honor of being the most complete natural history of colonial New England.

Well received upon its publication in 1634, *New England's Prospect* consequently went through a second edition in 1635 and a third in 1639. The fact that these subsequent editions came so quickly on the heels of the first — and that each was completely reset rather than simply reprinted — demonstrates the popularity of the volume. Appreciative references to Wood's book in Thomas Morton's *New English Canaan* (1637) and other seventeenth-century English documents confirm that *New England's Prospect* was considered an authoritative description of the New England wilderness. Nevertheless, the first American edition of the book was not published until more than a century later, in the Rogers edition of 1764, which replaced Wood's original prefatory material with a long essay by the editor. Another century passed before the second American edition was published by the Prince Society in 1865. A third edition, published in 1898 by Wood descendant Eben Moody Boynton, was an inaccurate version that modified the original text and introduced numerous errors (Vaughan 2–3, 11–13).

The textual history of *New England's Prospect* is unfortunate but not unusual. Of the three American editions published since the original editions of the 1630s, two were corrupted by inaccurate transcription, and none was based upon the authoritative 1635 edition, which is known to have been corrected by the author. Furthermore, all of these editions were published in very small print runs, and the book had remained out of print since 1898. Then, in 1977 Alden T. Vaughan published his Commonwealth edition of *New England's Prospect* through the University of Massachusetts Press. In addition to offering an expertly edited text, adding helpful an-notations, and modernizing Wood's archaic spelling and orthography, Vaughan's edition was based on Wood's corrected second edition of 1635, thus making it the first edition since 1639 to present an authoritative text. At last, readers and scholars had practical access to Wood's remarkable book as he wrote it (Vaughan 11–14).

New England's Prospect is of special value to ecocritics for a number of reasons. As the most complete natural history of New England written before the 1670s, it provides our most comprehensive view of the wild country of New England before its extensive settlement by Europeans; thus the book gives us glimpses of a lost world and establishes an environmental historical baseline against which later changes in New England ecology may be profitably measured. The book is also unusually accurate, for although written in an age when descriptions of the New World were often clouded by folk superstition or distorted by promotional rhetoric, Wood honors his pledge to correct the "scandalous and false reports past [*sic*] upon the country" by other writers, many of whom had never even seen the New World they pretended to describe (20). Perhaps most important, *New England's Prospect* is extremely rare as a surviving record of the New England landscape written from a secular point of view. Unlike better known literary New England colonists such as John Winthrop, William Bradford, and Cotton Mather, William Wood does not view nature through the providential filter of Puritan theology.

In a series of well-organized and clearly written chapters, Wood describes New England geography ("Of the Situation, Bays, Havens, and Inlets"), climate ("Of the Seasons of the Year . . ." and "Of the Climate . . ."), soil ("Of the Nature of the Soil"), plants and minerals ("Of the Herbs, Fruits, Woods, Waters, and Minerals"), terrestrial mammals ("Of the Beasts that Live on the Land"), aquatic mammals ("Beasts Living in the Water"), birds ("Of the Birds and Fowls . . ."), and fish ("Of Fish"). In these chapters, which are roughly structured according to the pre-Linnean taxonomy common to seventeenth-century natural histories, Wood demonstrates an appreciation for the ingenuity and beauty of the natural world that is most unusual in writers of his time and place. In addition to praising the fertility of its soil, the fecundity of its forests, and the healthfulness of its waters, Wood genuinely admires the New World for the strange and wonderful creatures he encounters there. Of the beaver, he writes that "the wisdom and understanding of this beast will almost conclude him a reasonable creature" (47). Of the hummingbird, which he declares "one of the wonders of the country," he writes that "for color, she is as glorious as the rainbow" (50). And of the now extinct passenger pigeon, he offers the wonderful relation that "I have seen them fly as if the airy regiment had been pigeons, seeing neither beginning nor ending, length or breadth of these millions of millions" (50). Wood's sympathy for the intellectual and aesthetic value of nature makes him an early forerunner of Henry Thoreau, who in 1855 enjoyed reading *New England's Prospect* in the American edition of 1764.

Without William Wood's *New England's Prospect*, there would simply be no early-seventeenth-century American text offering a comprehensive — and largely secular — description of the New England wilderness, and there would be no comparably enthusiastic document bearing witness to the wonders of nature in the New World. Alden Vaughan's work as a textual editor thus deepens our understanding of American environmental literary history by reintroducing a valuable text that provides a rare view of the seventeenth-century New England environment from the perspective of an interested observer whose view of nature was not conditioned by the dominant ideology of Puritanism.

Cotton Mather, *The Christian Philosopher* (1721), edited by Winton U. Solberg in 1994

Cotton Mather, Puritan theologian and author of more than 460 published works, is well known as one of the leading intellectuals of early-eighteenth-century America. A prominent member of the powerful Mather dynasty and a civic and religious luminary of unrivaled stature within New England culture, Cotton Mather was also responsible for helping to introduce Enlightenment thinking to colonial America. Although the early Puritan antipathy toward wild nature has been strongly emphasized by Roderick Nash and other environmental historians, Cotton Mather was a late Puritan who demonstrated genuine enthusiasm for the study of nature, albeit as a means to the end of achieving orthodox religious piety. Indeed, Mather believed strongly that the study of natural science should be understood as a form of religious devotion that would ennoble the individual soul while demonstrating and celebrating the infinite ingenuity of the Creator.

Far from repudiating natural science, as the stereotype of the Puritan minister might suggest that he would have, Mather in his later years studied natural science assiduously and was among the first colonials to embrace the revolutionary new scientific theories of that *"Perpetual Dictator of the learned World, in the Principles of Natural Philosophy,"* Sir Isaac Newton (65). As an author, Mather treated subjects in various fields of natural philosophy — what we now call "science" — including agriculture and animal husbandry, biology and medicine, astronomy and physics, zoology and botany, and geography and climatology. Among Mather's most important contributions to colonial American natural science is his "Curiosa Americana," a series of at least eighty-two letters describing American natural "curiosities," which he sent to the Royal Society in London between 1712 and 1724 and which earned him the coveted title of F.R.S., Fellow of the Royal Society (Solberg xl–xlii).

Cotton Mather's monumental contribution to the literature of American natural history is *The Christian Philosopher: A Collection of the Best Discoveries in Nature, with Religious Improvements,* completed in 1715 and published in London in 1720 (but bearing a 1721 imprint). Only about sixty copies of the first edition are extant, and until 1994 the book had been republished only twice: in the corrupted 1815 M'Kown edition (which omits entire segments of the text) and in a difficult-to-use 1968 facsimile reprint of the first edition. Mather's remarkable treatise, which has been justly called "the first comprehensive account of the physical and natural sciences written by an American" (Solberg xxi), is among the most important works of American natural history published during the eighteenth century. It is also among the most ambitious, erudite, derivative, allusive, and therefore least accessible American literary texts of the century. In attempting to provide a usable edition of the book, Winton U. Solberg recognized clearly that *The Christian Philosopher* was "too formidable for most readers." The book's "baroque style and learned allusions, its numerous Latin and biblical quotations, its pages of ornate prose, packed with names of authors and titles of books, recondite terms and concepts, seemed impenetrable. In due time, the work became a neglected American 'classic' — the title familiar to many, the contents known by few" (Solberg xxi). Rather than having been lost, forgotten, or corrupted — as is the case with so many books in need of textual editing — *The Christian Philosopher* demanded expert editing even to make it comprehensible to an audience of nonspecialist readers.

The preparation of his superb 1994 University of Illinois Press edition of *The Christian Philosopher* required that Solberg create an impressive scholarly apparatus for the text. First, he identified nearly all of the 415 authors whom Mather cites, and he included relevant biographical information on many of these figures in a 50-page "Biographical Register." Next, he methodically traced the sources of Mather's highly derivative text, reporting his findings in a "Recapitulation of Mather's Sources," which precisely documented the extent of Mather's borrowings in a chapter-by-chapter tabular format. Next, he researched the sources of Mather's citations and allusions to the Bible and included them in a comprehensive "Index of Biblical References." In editing the text itself, Solberg presented the 1721 first-edition text of Mather's book (with minor adjustments and corrections) and also included a full 60 pages of helpful explanatory notes. Finally, he composed a 134-page introduction — which itself contains over three hundred endnotes — to help readers understand the biographical, literary, historical, philosophical, and scientific significance of Mather's daunting but important work of natural philosophy. Few texts require such ambitious editorial apparatus, but Mather's treatise absolutely does; indeed, *The Christian Philosopher* remained effectively unreadable until Solberg's magisterial scholarly edition made comprehensible its vital place within the long tradition of natural philosophy and natural theology.

Though it presents a formidable challenge, *The Christian Philosopher* is essential to anyone who would understand the first stirrings of Enlightenment rationality and Newtonian science in the British colonies of America. Mather's book is a monument of intellectual history because it so clearly demonstrates a transition from the Puritans' providential worldview toward the positivist scientific paradigm that would ultimately displace it in the American intellectual and scientific tradition. Indeed, *The Christian Philosopher* was the first American book to systematically promote the argument from design — the assertion, derived from the work of then-prominent natural theologians including John Ray and William Derham, that the natural world can and should be studied as evidence of the Creator. Anticipating Ralph Waldo Emerson by more than a century, Mather believes strongly that natural science will produce spiritual insights, and he fervently hopes that his book will, as its opening sentence states, "demonstrate, that *Philosophy* [science] is no *Enemy*, but a mighty and wondrous *Incentive* to *Religion*" (7). In attempting to measure the spiritual value of the Creation and reconcile the insights of science with the divinity of nature, Mather plants a seed that will later blossom in the work of the notably unorthodox but equally inspired transcendentalists — a seed that is being admirably nurtured by nature writers of our own day.

The thirty-two chapters of *The Christian Philosopher* cover nearly every subject under consideration by natural scientists of the period, from heavenly bodies, comets, and lightning to the forces of light, gravity, and magnetism; to air, water, and soil; to plants and animals; and even to "MAN . . . a *Priest* for the rest of the Creation" (236). Perhaps most striking to the ecocritic is Mather's genuine enthusiasm for the wonder and beauty of the natural world — a world that even a generation before had been cast by Puritan patriarchs in the role of howling wilderness, moral vacuum, and place of exile. To Mather, all parts of the natural world become miraculous when inspected by the pious naturalist. Even of the lowly gnat, Mather avers that "the Story of his Proceedings would give you a thousand astonishments!" (169). And although, like most writers of his day, Mather adhered to the anthropocentric, hierarchical paradigm of the Great Chain of Being, he was capable of bringing humility and attentiveness to his study of nature. In responding to the legend of Saint Anthony preaching to the fishes, for example, he writes that "it will be a Discretion in me to make the reverse of the *Fable*, and hear the *Fishes* preaching to me, which they do many Truths of no small importance. As *mute* as they are, they are *plain* and *loud* Preachers; I want nothing but an *Ear* to make me a profitable Hearer of them" (191).

Without the monumental achievement of documentary editing that Solberg's edition of *The Christian Philosopher* represents, ecocritics would be denied practical access to one of the most important works of eighteenth-century American natural history, and they would miss the opportunity to glimpse the roots of our modern literary environmental sensibility in the work of one of the leading American intellectuals of the century — the man who wrote the first American book arguing that "the whole *World* is indeed a *Temple* of GOD, *built* and *fill'd* by that Almighty *Architect*" (7).

Susan Fenimore Cooper, *Rural Hours* (1850), edited by Rochelle Johnson and Daniel Patterson in 1998

Susan Fenimore Cooper was the eldest daughter of novelist James Fenimore Cooper, who was among the most successful — and remains among the best-known — American authors of the mid-nineteenth century. Susan Cooper, by contrast, has remained relatively obscure, though she published several books, including the 1850 nature-writing classic, *Rural Hours*. Like much of her father's work, *Rural Hours* is set in New York's Lake Otsego country and is largely concerned with the character of and changes in the Otsego landscape. Unlike her father's fictional treatment of the Otsego region, however, Susan Cooper's nonfiction book demonstrates a formidable knowledge of natural history and provides an attentive, detailed record of her rambles and studies in her home landscape. Published four years before Henry Thoreau's *Walden*, with which it may be profitably compared, *Rural Hours* is an eloquent and engaging regional literary natural history that also contains one of the earliest explicit calls for the preservation of American forests. Indeed, Cooper's *Rural Hours* is the first fully developed work of nonfiction nature writing published by an American woman.

Despite the literary value and historical importance of *Rural Hours*, the book has until recently received little scholarly attention. As is the case with many books written by nineteenth-century women, the relative obscurity of Cooper's book is due, in large part, to its textual history. The 1850 first edition of *Rural Hours* was widely praised and well received and sold well enough to send the book through six distinct editions by 1855, with a seventh edition published that year under the title *Journal of a Naturalist in the United States*. Although sales of the book slowed after the 1850s, it continued to be read — especially by those interested in natural history — and eighth and ninth editions followed in 1868 and 1876, respectively.

A decade after the ninth edition, in an effort to convince Houghton Mifflin to republish the book, Cooper created a severely abridged version, which was released in 1887. After 1887, *Rural Hours* was republished only once, in David Jones's edition of 1968, which unfortunately reprinted the 1887 abridgment rather than the longer and more successful original text. For more than a century, then, the text of *Rural Hours* known to most of those few readers who even knew of its existence was that of the 1887 edition — an altered text that, at little more than half the length of the original, inevitably compromised the book's structural integrity, weakened its narrative flow, and excised some of its finest passages. This long period of neglect at last ended when Rochelle Johnson and Daniel Patterson published their 1998 University of Georgia Press edition of *Rural Hours*, thus making the original text of Cooper's book available for the first time since 1876 and sparking a new wave of scholarly interest in her impressive literary accomplishments (Johnson and Patterson xv).

Rural Hours is of immense value to ecocritics and fully deserves the critical attention it has finally begun to receive. First, and perhaps most important, *Rural Hours* reminds us that American women were indeed writing literary natural history during the mid-nineteenth century. One of the most important women nature writers of the century, Cooper not only displays impressive literary talent but also demonstrates an unusual depth of knowledge in the natural sciences, an intellectual arena few American women of her day had entered. Cooper was an inquisitive and disciplined observer in the field, but she was also an accomplished student of natural history, as her familiarity with Linnean taxonomy and her many references to — and even corrections of — such prominent nineteenth-century American naturalists as Alexander Wilson, John James Audubon, and Thomas Nuttall suggest.

Susan Cooper is also of interest to ecocritics because she brings what we would now call a bioregional perspective to her study and celebration of the natural world. Like Thoreau, Cooper is devoted to cultivating a sense of place on her home ground — ground that, like the woods surrounding Walden Pond, had by midcentury become a mixture of the domestic, agricultural, and wild. Cooper walks, rides, and sleighs out into the meadows and forests in all seasons, and she returns with detailed, enthusiastic reports of the landscape, weather, fauna, and, especially, the flora of her native place. She organizes *Rural Hours* into journal form, allowing her to emphasize the organic revolutions of the days and the seasons while also placing a literary premium upon her personal experiences in the field. A celebration of the local that anticipates the bioregional movement by more than a century, *Rural Hours* is devoted to the understanding, engagement, description, and appreciation of one particular place.

Rural Hours is also valuable as one of the first American books to advocate explicitly for forest preservation. Insisting that the "noble gift" of the forests should cause us to feel "a debt of gratitude . . . for their utility and their beauty," Cooper insists that "no perfection of tillage, no luxuriance of produce can make up to a country for the loss of its forests" (125, 139). She encourages her neighbors to recognize the preciousness of the wood they so prodigally consume, she recommends sparing those forests growing on steep slopes and around watercourses, and she argues strongly for the preservation of old-growth forests. Of the practice of planting saplings after a timber harvest, she writes, "[t]his is very desirable, but it is only the first step in the track; something more is needed; the preservation of

fine trees, already standing, marks a farther progress, and this point we
have not yet reached" (133). Perhaps most impressive is Cooper's pre-
scient appreciation and celebration of the aesthetic, cultural, and spiritual
value of the natural world. "[I]ndependently of their market values in dollars and cents, the trees have other values," she writes, "they have their
importance in an intellectual and in a moral sense" (133).

Finally, Cooper's book also anticipates the nature writing of our own day
in its elegiac quality — its desire to measure, lament, and discourage the
exploitative land-use practices that result in the extermination of species.
Much of *Rural Hours* describes the increasing rarity of various plants and
animals in the Otsego landscape and sadly prognosticates the ultimate
cultural and ecological consequences of their loss. "[M]any of the species
will entirely disappear from our woods and hills, in the course of the next
century," she worries. "They have already become so rare in the cultivated
parts of the country, that most people forget their existence, and are more
familiar with the history of the half-fabulous Unicorn, than with that of
the American panther or moose" (314). Like later writers confronted with
substantial environmental degradation, Cooper feels a moral obligation
to document the loss she witnesses and to encourage the adoption of a
more responsible and sustainable environmental ethic.

Thanks to the Johnson-Patterson edition of *Rural Hours*, which expertly
restores and reintroduces Susan Cooper's original 1850 text, this important work by one of America's earliest and most gifted nature writers is
once again available for our study and appreciation. Thus a work of textual editing has reconnected us with a nineteenth-century literary environmentalist who, through her own aesthetic and spiritual valuation of
nature, attempted "to educate Americans about their natural world, to in-
still in them a pride of place based on this deeper knowledge, and finally
to convince them of a moral obligation to preserve their environment"
(Johnson and Patterson ix).

John Muir, *John Muir's Last Journey: South to the Amazon and East to Africa* (1911–1912), edited by Michael P. Branch in 2001

A gifted naturalist, mountaineer, preservationist, and nature writer,
John Muir is well known as one of America's preeminent environmental
advocates and writers. Muir demonstrated the glacial origins of Yosemite
Valley and discovered the first living glacier in the Sierra, and he completed solo ascents of many of the highest peaks in the West. He founded

the Sierra Club in 1892, serving as its president until his death in 1914. Muir also was instrumental in establishing Yosemite National Park in 1890 — which, although preceded by the creation of Yellowstone National Park in 1872, was the first national park established with wilderness protection as its primary goal. In his battles against environmental exploitation, best exemplified by his tireless efforts to save Yosemite's Hetch Hetchy Valley from damming, he set the agenda for the preservationist wing of the American environmental movement. Muir used his impressive literary gifts to encourage Americans to celebrate the aesthetic and spiritual value of wilderness and to resist the ravaging commercialism that posed an ever-increasing threat to America's wildlands.

The textual histories of many of Muir's books are complicated by the fact that he kept journals for more than a quarter century before publishing his first book. Thus his work exists in many forms, and one may sometimes find virtually the same Muir passage in a manuscript, letter, journal, newspaper article, magazine article, and book. Some published pieces also exist in variants, and thousands of pages of Muir's manuscripts remain unpublished. Only through the devotion of a number of gifted Muir scholars — chief among them William F. Badè, Linnie Marsh Wolfe, and Ronald H. Limbaugh — does Muir's literary legacy remain open for our study and appreciation. As a useful example, consider Muir's important book *A Thousand-Mile Walk to the Gulf*: written in 1867 as a journal describing Muir's epic walk from Indianapolis to the Gulf of Mexico, it was published only after his death, when in 1916 William F. Badè transcribed, edited, and published Muir's manuscript account of his journey.

Muir is justly famous as a literary celebrant and protector of American wilderness, as the father of the American national parks, and as the grand old man of the Sierra, which he affectionately called the "Range of Light." However, few readers are aware of Muir's lifelong interest in wildernesses outside America; while many know of his botanical excursions to Canada and Alaska, few know of his extensive travels to study the natural history of continents other than North America. Though Muir made a three-month trip to Europe in 1893, a full year's journey around the world in 1903–1904, and an eight-month, 40,000-mile voyage to South America and Africa in 1911–1912, little is known of this aspect of Muir's life and career because virtually no materials from these trips have been published. In focusing upon Muir primarily as an influential celebrant of American wilderness and the national park idea, we have unfortunately forgotten the John Muir whose passionate interests in global conservation, botany, and geology took him to every corner of the globe.

My own interest lies in the journals and correspondence from Muir's 1911–1912 journey to South America and Africa, which I have textually edited and recently published as *John Muir's Last Journey: South to the Amazon and East to Africa*. I find this journey particularly fascinating because it includes the fulfillment of Muir's dream of studying the tropical landscapes of the Amazon Basin. When Muir left Indianapolis in 1867 on his long walk to the Gulf, he had actually intended to continue his journey to South America, as he explains in *A Thousand-Mile Walk to the Gulf*: "I had long wished to visit the Orinoco basin and in particular the basin of the Amazon. My plan was to get ashore anywhere on the north end of the continent, push on southward through the wilderness around the headwaters of the Orinoco, until I reached a tributary of the Amazon, and float down on a raft or skiff the whole length of the great river to its mouth." However, Muir's poor health — and the difficulty he had in finding passage to South America — persuaded him to postpone the longer southern journey and instead seek the celebrated mountains and forests of California. "There," he wrote, "I shall find health and new plants and mountains, and after a year spent in that interesting country I can carry out my Amazon plans" (96).

The famous walk to the Gulf took place in 1867–1868. Forty-four years later, in 1911–1912, at the age of seventy-three and traveling alone, Muir at last fulfilled his long-held dream of visiting the Amazon. Indeed, there is a sense in which Muir's entire career as a writer and an environmentalist may be seen as having occurred during the long hiatus between his first and second attempts to reach the rich forests of South America. After visiting the Amazon in August and September 1911, Muir continued south along the Atlantic coast, then crossed the continent to study the forests of the high Andes. Returning to the east coast, he sailed to southern Africa (the long route, via the Canary Islands) to examine the baobab forests and the headwaters of the Nile River before sailing up the east coast of Africa, through the Indian Ocean, Red Sea, and Mediterranean, and finally back across the stormy North Atlantic to America. It was a remarkable journey, as Muir confirmed in his enthusiastic assertion that "on this pair of hot wild continents I've had the most fruitful time of my life" (159).

The 1911–1912 holograph journal of Muir's voyage, replete with field sketches, has survived in fairly good condition; also extant is Muir's typescript transcription of the journal, which he partially edited during 1912. However, creating a textual edition of the journal from these unfinished archival materials posed several special challenges, all of which bear on the question of authorial intent and on the editor's obligation to honor that intent to the greatest degree possible. First, it was necessary to establish the text of the book, which involved transcribing Muir's typescript, determining which of the editorial corrections to the typescript are Muir's own, correcting errors in the parts of the typescript not edited by Muir, incorporating appropriate editorial directions, and resolving ambiguities in the text, usually by comparison to the holograph manuscript. To provide contextualizing notes it was imperative to consult early-twentieth-century maps, cross-checking the place names Muir mentions in his journal against pre–World War I cartographic sources to determine where Muir was when he made the particular observations described in his journal. It was also necessary to edit Muir's scores of sketches by deciding which should be included in the published book and how they should be presented in relation to the text; some drawings were damaged and could not be reproduced, while others needed technical enhancements to be publishable. Finally, a text such as Muir's journal required a substantial critical introduction to place both the journey and the journal within the larger context of Muir's life and literary career.

The journal of these travels to South America and Africa enriches our understanding of Muir in a number of ways. In particular, it humanizes Muir, reminding us that although we often imagine him only as a solitary icon of American wilderness, he was also a man blessed with deep family connections and troubled by very human concerns. For example, his writing here reveals the older Muir — a figure rarely represented in his previously published books — as someone who, despite his fortunate vitality of body and spirit, has begun to meditate deeply on his own mortality. The journal also expands our understanding of Muir's literary style and aesthetic sensibility, for it contains field observations that are characterized by a spontaneous energy and insight sometimes lacking in the ornate prose of his more heavily revised and published books.

For ecocritics, Muir's 1911–1912 journal and correspondence offer especially rich views. Here we are able, for the first time, to examine Muir's perceptions and descriptions of tropical landscapes — and tropical seascapes that include whales, dolphins, flying fish, and storms and sunsets at sea. Among Muir's fascinating natural history observations in the tropics are many that link the glacially carved landscapes of South America and Africa — which he enthusiastically called "noble palmy ice land[s]" (81) — to the glaciated mountains of California and Alaska. This journal also makes clear for the first time that Muir was accomplished as a tropical botanist; his precise measurements, descriptions, and drawings of the flora he observed are remarkably detailed and accurate, and his ability to locate rare trees such as *Araucaria braziliana* and *Araucaria imbricata* was impressive even to professional botanists in the regions through which he traveled. Furthermore, Muir's condemnation of the "tree desolation" by which the forests of the Amazon Basin, the Andes, and south and central Africa "are being rapidly destroyed" demonstrates that he was a global conservationist whose concerns reached far beyond the Range of Light (114). This last of Muir's journals thus helps correct our narrow vision of Muir as the sage of the Sierra and reminds us that his address was not Yosemite, California, but rather — as he famously wrote on the flyleaf of his first journal — "John Muir, Earth-planet, Universe" (*Thousand* xv). It is my hope that *John Muir's Last Journey* will help ecocritics enlarge their understanding of John Muir as a person, writer, traveler, botanist, and advocate of global environmental protection.

SAVING ALL THE PIECES

The discussion of the five examples is intended not as a thorough analysis of particular works but as a reminder of how much ecocritics stand to gain from good textual editing and how much we stand to lose if we do not attend to the important work of preserving, restoring, and presenting texts accurately and in ways that make them accessible and useful. It may indeed be the case, as Arthur S. Link has argued, that textual editing is "the most important scholarly work being done in the United States, and, if well done, it will be the most enduring" (Kline xvi). If not for the work of textual editors, each of the books discussed above might have been literally or practically lost, leaving an unfortunate gap in our knowledge — a chapter missing from the story we are trying to write about the American land and how it has been encountered, engaged, and represented over the past half millennium. In addition to these texts, many more — each of genuine interest and value to ecocritics — remain endangered by rarity, obscurity, or textual corruption.

Though it would be irresponsible to equate the loss of a book with the more monumental loss of a species, there is a useful and fearful symmetry in the analogy. Even if we do not agree that all books are worth saving, who among us can know with certainty which texts will prove most valuable in helping us understand our environmental past and chart our environmental future? Until that impossible day when we can be sure which particular ideas about the human relation to the natural world will not be useful to us, it is vital that we recognize the value of textual editing as a means of saving all the pieces.

2. Le Page du Pratz's Fabulous Journey of Discovery
Learning about Nature Writing from a Colonial Promotional Narrative

GORDON SAYRE

Living in the Pacific Northwest and working as a scholar and teacher of colonial American literature, I have sometimes struggled to find the connections that so many academics cultivate between my studies and my extracurricular interests. In recent years, a focus on literature and the environment, or ecocriticism, has flourished among my students and colleagues at the University of Oregon, many of whom are active in environmental causes and share my passion for local forests, rivers, and mountains. Many of these colleagues study expressions of environmental philosophy in contemporary nature writing and poetry or in the works of western authors like John Muir or Mary Austin. But those writers and the emerging canon of green American literature all postdate my period of specialization. So while I have taken great interest in reading early exploration narratives of the Northeast, in vicariously visiting Niagara Falls, Cape Cod, or Hudson Bay as those places were in the 1600s, I am hard-pressed to find colonial literature that represents the landscape and native peoples of the Northwest.[1] However, I can share one brief but fascinating eighteenth-century text about the Pacific Northwest and proceed to a discussion of the ecocritical relevance of its little-known author, Antoine-Simon Le Page du Pratz, and his own narrative of western exploration.

Around 1725 this French colonist met a "native of the Yazoo Nation" named Moncacht-apé, a name he translated as "one who kills difficulties or fatigues." Moncacht-apé told of his lengthy journeys in search of evidence about the origins of his people, who according to their own legends had migrated to the lower Mississippi valley from the Northwest. In *The Journey of Moncacht-apé, an Indian of the Yazou Tribe, across the continent, about the year 1700*, Le Page du Pratz transcribed his narrative, which he compared to those of "the early Greeks, who traveled among the Eastern people to examine the manners and customs of the distant countries and then returned to communicate what they had learned to their country-men" (16).[2] Moncacht-apé told of his travels to the Northeast, where he first saw the ocean, was amazed by the tides, and visited Niagara Falls. But of greater interest is the subsequent account of a five-year-long voyage to the Northwest coast. He followed the "Beautiful River," from its headwaters north of the Missouri River down to the sea. At the mouth of this river, which could plausibly be the Columbia, he stayed with natives who ate plentifully upon large fish and shellfish but who had "always to be on the watch against the bearded men, who do all that they can to carry away the young persons" (26). These bearded men were white-skinned and always wore clothes, even in hot weather. On giant *pirogues* the bearded ones "came from where the sun sets to seek upon this coast a yellow and bad-smelling wood which dyes a beautiful yellow. That as they had observed that the bearded men came to carry off this wood each year when the cold weather had ceased, they had destroyed all these trees, following the advice of an old man, so that they came no more, because they found no more of this wood. In truth, the banks of the river, which were formerly covered, were then naked, and there remained of this wood in this country only a small quantity" (26–27).

This tale of the destruction of Northwest forests resonates with that currently being inflicted on the Port Orford Cedar (*Chamaecyparis lawsoniana*), whose wood is highly sought after for the lucrative Japanese lumber market and which is now also imperiled by a disease spread by logging trucks and other equipment. The species is at present confined to isolated roadless areas along the Oregon coast southward from the town of Port Orford. The smooth-grained, lightweight wood of Port Orford Cedar and of the related species Alaskan yellow cedar (*Chamaecyparis nootkatensis*, which is somewhat less threatened) were also highly prized by native peoples for building boats, paddles, and tools. The bark of the latter was favored for weaving waterproof clothing. Although cedar would not be described by most as "bad-smelling" and is not suitable for use as a dye, as Moncacht-apé suggested, the similarities are nonetheless striking. The idea that native peoples might purposely destroy these majestic trees in the name of saving their own culture is terrifying yet recalls the situation of timber towns such as Coos Bay, Oregon, which in the 1980s exported thousands of whole logs to Japan, a trade that decimated forests even as it provided minimal support for local workers. Because of his knowledge of European colonists in Louisiana, Moncacht-apé recognized these bearded invaders and offered to assist the locals in planning an attack upon them. Their retaliation was successful and killed eleven of the invaders. From his examination of the corpses, Moncacht-apé had the occasion to describe in greater detail their clothing, powder, and firearms, which he explained were different from those of the French, Spanish, and English.

The story of Moncacht-apé is so eerily familiar that it is easy to ignore the question of its authenticity. Certainly it would not have been impossible for a native individual to travel such a distance, and I believe that someone probably did. That Moncacht-apé was the great explorer and that he told his story to Le Page du Pratz I cannot be sure. The French writer could have invented the tale to suggest the existence of a practical transcontinental river route, which had been an obsession of European imperialism for centuries and would have enhanced the importance of controlling Louisiana and the Mississippi valley. The same imperial geopolitics inspired the mission of Lewis and Clark, who carried with them a copy of the English translation of Le Page du Pratz's book (Lawson-Peebles 191). But if the story is true, it offers a valuable corrective to the tendency of United States history to imagine its white forebears as the discoverers of the entire continent. In "'Are You an Environmentalist or Do You Work for a Living?': Work and Nature," Richard White has powerfully critiqued this myth of the "first white men [traveling] through lands untouched by humans," reminding us that native peoples knew all these lands (175). It is quite possible that American Indians like Moncacht-apé shared the European desire for exploration and embarked on long voyages among foreign peoples.

Regardless of the veracity of this episode, however, it suggests patterns for inquiry into the relationships between colonialism and ecological thought. Le Page du Pratz was quite sympathetic and grateful toward his informant. At this moment in his text, he was seeking confirmation of his theory that Native Americans "of the north," including the Yazou tribe, were descendants of people who had migrated across a land bridge from Asia, whereas an elite group of more sophisticated tribes "of the south," including the Aztecs and Natchez, were descended from people who had crossed the Atlantic from Europe. Another component of this theory of cultural classification emerges when we realize that the bearded invaders

of the Northwest, whose actions are little different from those of early explorers on the east coast of America, nonetheless are differentiated from
Le Page du Pratz and his French compatriots. He refers to them in mar-
ginal notations as "les Japonais," or the Japanese. The reader is invited to
take sympathy with Moncacht-apé and his defense of the trees and the native settlements, much as I and other Northwest environmentalists adopt
a proprietary stance toward the local forests, even though our status as locals dates back barely 150 years. Does the political defense of natural
resources such as the Port Orford Cedar imply a claim to appropriate it
for oneself and to assert a status as "native" that shoves aside indigenous
peoples? Is there a touch of anti-Japanese xenophobia in efforts to deny
this lumber to a market that pays top prices for it? Am I inclined to ignore
clues that point to the story as a fiction because it facilitates a cultural and
environmental appropriation? These are unsettling questions, and I believe that a reading of another episode from Le Page du Pratz's text reveals
that this ambivalence is not just one of the modern environmental movement but emerges from eighteenth-century colonialism and the conventions of writing about it.

Antoine-Simon Le Page du Pratz lived in Louisiana from 1718 to 1734, during the tumultuous early years of French colonization. Neither his date
nor his place of birth is known, although his name suggests a Dutch an-
cestry. He traveled to the New World as a soldier but soon acquired land
near Natchez, Mississippi, where he lived with a native woman and several slaves and farmed for at least eight years. Upon returning to France,
he published a series of articles about the colony in the *Journal Oeco-
nomique* in 1751 and 1752 and the three-volume *Histoire de la Louisiane* in
1758. This extraordinary text is little known today but is a delightful read
and an invaluable source of information about colonial Louisiana and the
cultures of its native peoples, particularly the Natchez. Just as in French
"histoire" means "story" as well as "history," the book far exceeds the purposes and conventions of history. It fits Peter Hulme's definition of the hybrid multigenres of colonialist writing in *Colonial Encounters: Europe and
the Native Caribbean, 1492–1797*: "methods of procedure and analysis,
and kinds of writing and imagery, normally separated out into the discrete areas of military strategy, political order, social reform, imaginative
literature, personal memoir and so on" (2). The imbrication of the book
with imperialist power is more than theoretical. In 1763, as a result of vic-

tory over France in the Seven Years War, the British acquired Louisiana and suddenly needed information about the vast lands of the Mississippi valley. That same year an English translation of *Histoire de la Louisiane* was published in London, with a new title that subordinated the territory to adjacent English colonies: *The History of Louisiana, or of the Western parts of Virginia and Carolina*. The English version abridged and rearranged the original French text, as if the words of a former enemy could not be ingested unaltered.[3] Even more than the original, the purpose of the translation was not historical but commercial. The preface by the unnamed translator/editor explained that by means of the book English readers "may now reap some advantages from those countries" that "by right always belonged to Great Britain . . . by learning from the experience of others, what they are likely to produce, that may turn to account" (ii–iii).

A colonial text employed for such goals as these might seem to be the least attractive object for green literary studies. After all, the projection of European desires upon America fostered exploitation of native peoples and disdain for the intrinsic value of nature. In the search for El Dorado or the Northwest Passage, European explorers demonstrated a tenacious capacity to ignore the true shape of the American landscape while sustaining a fantasy of fabulous wealth to be carried out of it. The harmful legacy of these notorious myths is all too obvious, but to reject and disavow them today is also hazardous, for we need to acknowledge the seduction of these myths and the ambivalence of the desire behind them. Myths of abundant natural resources reveal continuing connections between wilderness landscape, human desire, and the exploration literature that brought them together.[4] As Timothy Sweet has shown in his essay "Economy, Ecology and *Utopia* in Early Colonial Promotional Literature," colonial promotional tracts articulated fundamental issues about the relationships between social organization and natural resources and even encoded complex theories of ecological and economic forces.

"Ever since my arrival in Louisiana, I had tried to use my time to instruct myself in all that was new to me, and apply myself toward seeking out objects, the discovery of which might be useful to society," Le Page du Pratz announces midway through the first volume of his *Histoire*. "I resolved therefore to make a voyage into the interior lands," a journey whose purpose is "pour faire des découvertes dont personne ne parloit; pour trouver aussi s'il étoit possible, des choses que personne ne recherchoit." This line, like much of the text of these four chapters from the

French original, is not found in the English translation. It might be rendered: "so as to make discoveries that no one has spoken of, and to find, if
it was possible, some things which no one has searched for" — a curious
and paradoxical statement. Le Page du Pratz does not say he is the first to
visit this area; rather he implies that he is the only person who has tried
to go there (or perhaps ever will). The genre of exploration narrative, of
course, demanded representations of places that no European had previously seen, and Le Page du Pratz was eager to oblige. He even explained
to his companions before departing "my whole design . . . we should avoid
passing through any inhabited countries, and would take our journeys
through such as were unknown and uninhabited; because I travelled in
order to discover what no one before could inform me about." Although a
few passages in the episode refer to the Mississippi River and to lead
mines such as were found along its banks, most of the journey takes place
on an unidentified prairie. His goal was not only that of the colonial explorer but of the modern wilderness vacationer — to be alone in the landscape and to acquire a unique experience of nature. On a phenomenological level, perhaps each individual's voyage is unique, and one cannot help
but "make discoveries not mentioned by others," as the 1763 translation
put it. But at the level of discourse, it may be self-defeating to try to "find
things that no one has searched for" if this implies that no one will be able
to find them again later. And to try to "discover what no one before could
inform me about" implies its logical converse — that what he informs his
readers about may not be available for them to discover. These subtly paradoxical lines deconstruct colonial exploration and promotional writing.
Today, the intersection of exploration narrative and promotional tract
produces the guidebook, a genre that promises to lead the reader/traveler
to sites of scenic, recreational, or even spiritual fulfillment. Like a guidebook author, Le Page du Pratz enticed his readers with prospects of pris-
tine wilderness. Yet just as the success of a guidebook might lead to the destruction of the wilderness experience that it promises to its readers, his
text reveals a self-contradictory cycle in the colonial promotional tracts.
Le Page du Pratz asserts in an extreme form the colonial desire to know
and exploit the land. Yet this extremity demands to be read as satire; the
text mocks its own claims to capture and convey the value of the landscape from writer to reader, from explorer to prospective emigrant, and
finally exposes what one might call the "topo-graphic fallacy," the tendency to confuse land with writing.

"Seeking out objects . . . useful to society" is Le Page du Pratz's gentle way of announcing his quest for wealth. The opening paragraph goes on to poke fun at the common European fantasy of America as a "Land of Cockayne" where lazy colonists might reap fruit without the labor of sowing it: "one sees nothing without taking the trouble to leave one's home, and one imagines that the land is obliged to anticipate all of man's needs, to present to him all the riches it possesses ready and prepared, as he would want to have them, without buying them with the price of his labor." Le Page du Pratz critiques the objectification of nature through a satiric exaggeration, announcing at the outset that "I traveled only to discover things" and in the early stages of the trip expressing frustration that "we walked for several days without finding anything which could engage my attention or was relevant to the subject of my journey," only then to express aesthetic satisfaction amid material disappointment: "the charming land that we traveled through, which might justly inspire the most gifted of landscape painters. My own imagination was delighted with the sight of the fine countryside, diversified with large and agreeable meadows and adorned with thickets planted by the hand of nature; and interspersed with gentle ridges and dales adorned with woods, which serves as a retreat for the most timorous animals." Le Page du Pratz seems to insist that bringing back descriptions or knowledge of beautiful and newly explored places is quite different from, and less significant than, bringing back *things* of value. Yet we might also read this passage ironically as suggesting that the description of a valuable thing, and the place where it is found, can be as valuable as the thing itself, at least for those who will never go there or will never possess it. And this is true not just in the genteel aesthetics of picturesque landscapes. After all, the value of reading nature writing lies not in the opportunity to follow it like a guidebook. We cannot hope to follow Thoreau's itinerary through the Maine woods, which are now owned by timber companies and controlled by strict permitting systems. Yet this fact only enhances the appeal of his narrative.

This colonial exploration narrative both invites followers and repels them. As Le Page du Pratz prepared to depart his farm near Natchez, many of his neighbors "wanted to come on the voyage," but he refused to take any other colonists with him. His text gives several reasons. For one, "they [the French] neither have the patience, nor are made for fatigue, [and] would be ever teazing me to return again." Second, he did not want to risk being assassinated by mutinous subordinates, as Robert Cavelier de La Salle had been on his expedition to find the mouth of the Mississippi River in 1687. Third, and most important: "These men no doubt imagined that my fortune would be made by means of this journey, and they would have liked to profit from what I was able to discover. . . . I didn't want any company, not wanting to share with anyone the glory of the knowledge that I would acquire and that I promised to myself from this voyage." This line speaks of glory (*gloire*) and knowledge (*connoissances*) as if to correct the accusations of profit, and Le Page insists that "they were wrong to think that way. I traveled for my instruction and for the utility of the public," a public that, of course, includes his readers.

For companions, Le Page du Pratz chooses instead ten American Indians, or "Naturels" as he calls them, natives who are "indefatiguable, robust, and tractable." He designs a technique for using their assistance to explore as much territory as possible. While seven of the "Naturels" carry his bedding and provisions, three serve as scouts, walking a league or more ahead and to either side of him and maintaining contact by smoke signals three times each day. It is inaccurate to refer to these Native Americans as "guides," because they apparently have no previous knowledge of the land, which, after all, "no one before could inform me about." The natives' local knowledge is of no use for this journey, and "they were under apprehensions of losing themselves in countries they did not know." Rather, they serve as prosthetic extensions of Le Page du Pratz's own imperial and empirical eyes; they are completely subordinated to his colonial purpose of exploration. He dispels their fears by showing them "a mariner's compass" and explaining the manner of using it, but we might dismiss this assertion of the superiority of European technology as a time-worn colonialist trope. Elsewhere in his *Histoire*, such as in the episode of Moncacht-apé, Le Page du Pratz expresses great respect for his American Indian informants' knowledge of geography and natural history. His dismissive attitude toward these "Naturels," whose tribal affiliation is never mentioned, is another clue to the satiric nature of this passage. William Cronon points out the fallacy of imagining virgin land uninhabited and unclaimed by American Indians in "The Trouble with Wilderness; or, Getting Back to the Wrong Nature," and Le Page du Pratz makes a similar point by negation, gently suggesting the fantastic status of a place unvisited by other Europeans and unknown to the natives.

Le Page du Pratz's search for valuable and useful things soon succeeds. He first finds abundant partridges and buffalo for game. After that begins a series of mineral discoveries, first Lapis Calaminaris ("The intelligent in Minearology understands what I would be at"), then gypsum. Several sixteenth- and seventeenth-century American explorers (such as Jacques Cartier in Quebec and Michael Lok, who sailed with Martin Frobisher to Baffin Island) returned to Europe with minerals they believed to be gold, only to learn that they were actually worthless rocks. Colonial Louisiana, the object in the 1720s of a company organized by the notorious financier John Law, was also subject to such speculative frenzies, and another French colonist, Jean-Baptiste Bénard de la Harpe, had returned from an exploration of the Arkansas River in 1722 with a report of curious hard stones found near a landmark he called *"le Rocher Français"* — French Rock (Bénard de la Harpe 374; Villiers de la Terrage 277). Later in his *Histoire*, Le Page du Pratz mocked claims of other explorers to have found *"un rocher d'Emeraudes"* (a rock of emeralds) (1 : 310) along the Arkansas, explaining that even though the leader of this expedition took along with him an engineer who had invented a machine for breaking off large pieces of such precious stones, he failed to bring back any emeralds as proof. On his own journey, Le Page du Pratz also finds valuable minerals that he does not bring home. He processes the gypsum into plaster while in the field, and so he has only the proof of its utility, not the mineral itself. He then finds a piece of lead sticking out of the ground like a tree trunk and gives a piece to each of his "Naturels." He finds limestone, a bulky commodity that is not worth removing from the site. Finally, he finds only "indices," or indications, of iron and gold, not the ore itself. These valuable minerals are either so much a part of the landscape that he cannot take them back to Louisiana or France or they are wealth redistributed so that he has none of his own to show.

The most interesting such mineral discovery, however, comes when his avant-garde scout shows him "a shining and sharp stone, of the length and size of one's thumb, and as square as a joiner could make a piece of wood of the same bigness." Like the stump of lead, "[s]ome of these pieces jutted out of the earth, like ends of beams, two feet and upwards in length." He strikes this crystal against a flint and finds that "it drew much more fire than with the finest steel," without leaving the slightest mark on the crystal. The crystals are desirable to the American Indians, too, yet Le Page du Pratz wishes to prevent them from carrying any away: "I feared that some Frenchman seeing the stones would persuade the Naturels, by the force of gifts, to reveal the location of this place." He is able to prevent such betrayals by telling the "Naturels" that the crystals' aesthetic interest and fire-starting utility are less important than their value in some kind of industrial process: "I dissuaded them from this design by saying to them 'What good will it do to carry all that stuff? I admit that these stones are quite pretty to look at, but they're also harder than iron or the best-tempered steel. With what would one work upon them? What use can these stones have, if they are not workable?' . . . I made them throw aside their stones as things which were not worth the trouble to carry."

The crystal will become valuable only through the application of labor and surplus value. If nothing can cut it, it is doomed to remain as a diamond in the rough. The piece he describes, however, is hardly rough; it is a perfect square, and he finds others "with six faces, even and smooth like mirrors, highly transparent, without any veins or spots." In finding the crystal, Le Page du Pratz would appear to have discovered the "thing" that he was seeking, to have objectified the landscape into a fabulously valuable natural resource. Yet if he cannot remove and exploit the resource, its value cannot be separated from the landscape in which it is found. If the crystal is destined to remain in its place in the land and in the text, its only value will be as a natural and textual marvel. Notwithstanding his arguments to the "Naturels," these remarkable crystals deconstruct the opposition between raw natural resource and finished manufactured product. He has found kernels of aesthetic perfection so adamantine that they cannot be formed into the shape one needs but must be found in the shape one wants. Unlike diamonds, which can be cut and which have both industrial and ornamental value, the value and utility of the crystals would be limited by the number, shape, and size of the available pieces, and the colonists would in effect be forced to accommodate their desires to the forms of the land. Like the mythical Noble Savage who escapes the corruption of contact with colonists, like the definition of wilderness as land untouched by humans, the crystals are destined to remain pure and unchanged, even if the published account of them arouses a strong desire for exploration, exploitation, and possession.

The rock crystal can also stand metaphorically for this entire episode of discovery within the *Histoire de la Louisiane*. Other parts of the text contain practical information about geography, American Indian relations, and trade useful to the French colonists and perhaps even more useful to the English, who obtained Louisiana just five years after the publication of his book. Eager for words about such valuable products, the translator included most of this tale of a journey where no one had gone before, even though Le Page du Pratz's enigmatic prairie was enclosed on all sides by a crystal wall of fiction and could be of no use to anyone except for the aesthetic pleasure of reading. As he persuades the "Naturels" to discard their fragments of crystal, Le Page du Pratz claims, "I threw aside all the ones that I held, with the exception of one which I concealed, without their perceiving it. . . . For my part, I carefully observed the latitude [of the place of discovery]." Yet the text doesn't disclose this latitude to its readers, nor did he bring any of the crystals back to Paris.

In Thomas More's *Utopia*, the Utopians use gold for their chamber pots and for their slaves' shackles. Their goal is to expunge the commodity fetish for the metal by associating it with vulgar actions and persons, while nonetheless maintaining a large horde of it for use in external trade. Le Page du Pratz's fabulous story of the crystals, while like *Utopia* a satire, works in a contrary manner, exposing the colonial lust for precious metals and stones by imagining a stone whose value cannot be exploited in export markets. Yet just as Utopia was widely accepted as an actual place, Le Page du Pratz's satire ran a high risk of being misread and can be interpreted as fetishizing the value of the land rather than exposing the fetish for precious minerals. After all, his narrator remains smitten with the desire for wealth: "I had reasons for concealing my journey, and stronger reasons still to suppress what I had discovered, in order to avail myself thereof afterwards." If we take him at his word, he has discovered the riches of the New World, discursively removed the natives from the land (he passed through no native villages on his journey), and yet at the same time left the land in its bountiful and undisturbed state. In the crystal, place and resource are figured as a thing that cannot or will not be removed or changed, when in fact colonists were responsible for enormous change and exploitation in Louisiana even in the eighteenth century. If Le Page du Pratz could not export and sell his crystals, he could and did sell his book, which enticed others to go dig up the West.

This less sympathetic reading gains strength from the subsequent episode in the fabulous journey of discovery. In chapter 18, Le Page du Pratz observes and describes the beaver, and his observations lead blithely and unconsciously to violence against the animal.[5] When his party first finds a beaver dam, "[w]e set up our hut within reach of this retreat, or village of beavers, but at such a distance, as that they could not observe our fire. I put my people on their guard against making any sort of noise, or firing their pieces, for fear of scaring those animals." As they go into a blind to observe the beavers at work, he forbids his native guides from carrying their guns. Yet in the blind they do not simply sit and watch but induce an observation by cutting a small trench through the dam, which the beavers come out to repair, working in a well-organized team. "Some made mortar, others carried it on their tails . . . quite to the dam, where others remained to take it, put it into the gutter, and rammed it with blows of their tails." This first experiment a success, Le Page du Pratz continues, "I wanted to kill one, but I waited until the next day, because I was planning something more than was the work of one night, and which would better satisfy my curiosity." He makes a larger breach in the dam, and he and his "Naturels" "went to conceal ourselves all round the pond, in order to kill only one, the more narrowly to examine it." He takes care not to kill "the overseer of the works" but instead a common laborer. So with no apparent sense of perverting his motives as a natural historian, Le Page du Pratz allows his urge for observation to lead him from a blind that kept the animals unaware of any human presence to killing one of the beavers and finally to breaking apart the lodge. As he puts it, puzzlingly: "I caused to undo the roof without breaking any thing."

The observation of the beavers, like the discovery of the crystal and other minerals, insists rhetorically that it inflicts no damage on the land or its inhabitants yet enacts the violence of colonial acquisition. While elsewhere in his *Histoire* Le Page du Pratz speculates on the best means for maintaining French control of Louisiana and in one episode ruthlessly puts down a slave rebellion, in the encounter with the beavers he dons the cap of disinterested scientific inquiry that Mary Louise Pratt, in *Imperial Eyes: Travel Writing and Transculturation*, has termed the "anti-conquest," "a utopian image of a European bourgeois subject simultaneously innocent and imperial, asserting a harmless hegemonic vision that installs no apparatus of domination" (33–34). In both episodes, Le Page du Pratz disingenuously shifts the agency from his own exploration and exploitation to the land's voluntary revealing of itself. The beavers come out of the lodge and engage in the instinctual behavior of dam repair, while he merely stands by and observes.

Contemporary environmental thought attacks the notion, often attributed to Judeo-Christian religion, that the natural world was made by God for the service of humans. Le Page du Pratz seems to carry this principle even farther by making the landscape the agent of its own exploitation.

When he finds a mountain of limestone that he believes would be a fine source of lime, he writes: "I doubt that one will come to look for lime in this place, unless it is for the construction of houses in this vicinity, for this mountain will not fail to attract people someday, by the violent passion they will have to dig in its bowels." And upon finding lead ore, he exclaims: "I was ravished with admiration, on seeing this wonderful production, and the power of the soil of this province, constraining, as it were, the minerals to disclose themselves." The language of these lines recalls Annette Kolodny's thesis in *The Lay of the Land* about the tension in colonial writing between the trope of the land as mother smothering the infantilized settler with green riches and the trope of the passive virgin land that the male explorer ravishes (11, 55). Le Page du Pratz escapes even this tension, however, for he does not represent this plains landscape as Raleigh did Guiana in the famous lines: "a country that hath yet her maydenhead, never sackt, turned, nor wrought . . . her treasures having never yet beene opened, nor her originalls wasted, consumed, nor abused" (120). The plains are largely void of vegetable bounty but yield up minerals so willingly that no conscious aggression is needed and no "abuse" implied.

Like Raleigh, though, Le Page du Pratz does have a pastoral sensibility. At the end of the episode, he no longer stresses the things he has discovered, since he has not brought back any, but instead the (anti)-social value of the lonely lands he has visited. From instrumental exploitation of minerals he shifts to romantic appreciation of the landscape. After all, the adamantine crystals are permanently fixed in the landscape. This tale resembles accounts of El Dorado and the Northwest Passage in its narcotic vision of easy wealth yet differs because whereas those goals remained the same despite (or because of) many separate explorers' unsuccessful attempts, the wonders of Le Page du Pratz's plains are his alone: "I was strongly impressed with the beauties of the countries I had seen. I could have wished to end my days in those charming solitudes, at a distance from the tumultuous hurry of the world, far from the pinching gripe of avarice and deceit. . . . It is there one lives exempt from the assaults of censure, detraction, and calumny . . . we may agreeably contemplate the wonders of nature, and examine them all at our leisure."

He claims that he must keep his discoveries secret "so as to be able to profit from them in the future" but that his misfortunes in society have prevented his escaping to this land and therefore prevent his divulging its location. He wants to hide it so he won't have to share its riches, yet if the true payoff is only a chance to "agreeably contemplate the wonders of na-ture," perhaps the reader has already shared in this wealth by reading the text about it. In these concluding lines of his fabulous journey, Le Page du Pratz drops another hint that the whole episode is a tall tale by emphasiz-ing not his discovery of that which he might trade in colonial society but the discovery of an escape from that society. This paradox is no different from that induced by many classics of exploratory nature writing, such as John Muir's *My First Summer in the Sierra*, the success of which reveals American society's desire to escape from itself, even as such escapes be-come less feasible. The desire for wealth that nearly all colonists shared entailed a separation from European society and a discovery of secret riches. This frontier myth was antithetical to, yet sustained by, the goals of shared knowledge that motivated the publication of colonial promotional texts such as Le Page du Pratz's *Histoire de la Louisiane*. The histories of colonial financial scandals, such as John Law's, attest to the interdepen-dence of colonial greed and the representations of American lands.

Thus this fabulous journey of discovery tells us more about nature writ-ing than at first appears. The written description or visual representation of a natural landscape frequently is worth more than the place itself. The beauty of such reified postcard scenes as Yosemite Valley, Niagara Falls, and Delicate Arch has been exposed to millions — and used to sell mil-lions of dollars' worth of products and thereby attract so many visitors as to largely spoil the sublimity of the wilderness scene that the images promise. Le Page du Pratz set out consciously to do what others did un-wittingly: to portray an American wilderness so seductively rich that many would seek to possess it, only to learn that they could not take it home with them, that its value lay entirely in its representations. His crystals can be read as an object lesson in the commodification of landscape. And if his encounter with the beavers shows bad faith, it is little different in this from modern film and television, which represents animal life in natural habitats as if the film crew were not there disturbing that life and habitat.

Le Page du Pratz's fabulous journey plays upon a confusion between the exploitation of commodities and of knowledge, between lands and the written representation of landscapes. Colonialism sought to acquire prod-ucts such as beaver pelts and buffalo hides, but it also capitalized on writ-ten representations that offered proof of knowledge and experience in the New World. Colonial theorists (and I wish to distinguish these from post-colonial theorists) have described the separation of discourses as an instrument of colonial power, and Edward Said also stresses the division of labor among orientalists into different discourses. We should not leave these lessons behind when we turn to reading American nature writing. As ecocritics, our own desires for wilderness and its representations are bound up in similar paradoxes: the desire both to attract and exclude larger society from the places we treasure, the ambivalent ennobling and appropriating of Native Americans' claims to the land, and the conflict between protection and exploitation of the land that tourism entails. Le Page du Pratz confounds and combines these genres or discourses, playing with readers who would confuse imaginary voyage for history and take the promise of wealth for wealth itself.

NOTES

1. There are at least two notable exceptions. Alexander MacKenzie's *Journal of a Voyage to the Pacific*, the exploration narrative of the first European to cross North America, first appeared in 1801. *David Thompson's Narrative, 1784–1812* is an even more fascinating work by a Hudson's Bay Company surveyor who was the first Euro-American to descend the Columbia River from its source to the Pacific. It was not published until the twentieth century, however.

2. This edition is the only complete translation of the French original.

3. The original is *Histoire de la Louisiane, contenant la Découverte du ce vaste pays, sa Description géographique, un Voyage dans les Terres, l'Histoire Naturelle; les Mœurs, Coutûmes & Religion des Naturels, avec leurs Origines; deux Voyages dans le Nord du nouveau Mexique, dont un jusqu'à la Mer du Sud; ornée de deux Cartes & de 40 Planches en Taille douce*, 3 vols. (Paris: De Bure, Veuve Delaguette, et Lambert, 1758). The English translation is available in a facsimile reprint, *The History of Louisiana*, ed. Joseph Treagle (Baton Rouge: Louisiana State University Press, 1975). The French original is extremely rare, although a microform copy is included in the Western Americana series based on the collection at Yale. The episode I examine here is in vol. 1, 213–264, of the original. In the translation, the corresponding section is on 133–150, yet like much of the translation it is abridged and excludes many of the most interesting passages. I have translated these missing passages myself and combined them with the 1763 English translation into a continuous English text, available on my Web page at *http://darkwing.uoregon.edu/~gsayre/LePageduPratz.pdf*. Henceforth, I will quote from this complete translation, and since the Web version greatly expands the published translation, I will not cite page numbers.

4. I wish to observe a distinction between "travel narrative" and "exploration narrative." In the former, the places traveled to are already known to the writer through literary or popular sources, and the negotiation between these precon-

ceptions and the narrator's experience constitutes one of the key tropes of the genre. "Exploration narrative" records efforts to find and describe places previously unknown and carries preconceptions that are more vague and mythical. Le Page du Pratz here is writing of exploration.

5. For more on the beaver in colonial writing, see my *"Les Sauvages Américains": Representations of Native Americans in French and English Colonial Literature* (218–247).

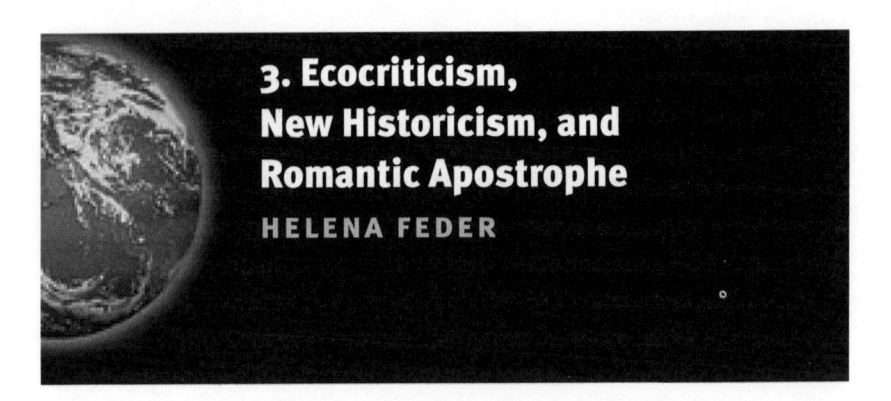

3. Ecocriticism, New Historicism, and Romantic Apostrophe

HELENA FEDER

*A genuinely ecological approach does not work to attain a
mentally envisioned future, but strives to enter, ever more
deeply, into the sensorial present. It strives to become ever
more awake to other lives, the other forms of sentience and
sensibility that surround us in the open field of the present
moment. For the other animals and the gathering clouds do
not exist in linear time. We meet them only when the thrust
of historical time begins to open outward, when we walk out
of our heads into the cycling life of the land around us. . . .
To return to our senses is to renew our bond with this wider
life, to feel the soil beneath the pavement, to sense — even
when indoors — the moon's gaze upon the roof.*
—*David Abram,* The Spell of the Sensuous

*Apostrophe is different in that it makes its point by troping
not on the meaning of a word but on the circuit or situation
of communication itself. . . . In these terms the function of
apostrophe would be to make the objects of the universe
potentially responsive forces: forces which can be asked to
act or refrain from acting, or even to continue behaving as
they usually behave. The apostrophizing poet identifies his
universe as a world of sentient forces.*
—*Jonathan Culler,* The Pursuit of Signs

These epigraphs aptly set the stage for a sort of critical
work that is too infrequently pursued by ecocritics: the close examination
of a poetic device in the context of both our current ecological crisis and recent critical theories. Just as other forms of criticism are rightly censured

for ignoring the ecological implications of the texts they examine, ecocritics too often pursue their important tasks in a kind of critical vacuum, without the mutual enrichment derived from closer contact with current practices in literary scholarship. I intend to demonstrate the value of such an approach through a closer look at a single poetic discourse, the apostrophe.

As Culler notes in *The Pursuit of Signs*, one could read a great deal of secondary material on any highly apostrophic poem and not encounter a single mention of apostrophe itself (136). Scholarship on romantic poetry offers innumerable examples of this phenomenon, from M. H. Abrams's classic essay "Structure and Style in the Greater Romantic Lyric" to current new historicist and ecocritical work. But why has the form of apostrophe itself been so often ignored? To understand why apostrophe has been taboo for critics is to understand why it is so important. Culler suggests that apostrophe has not received close scrutiny because it is too "embarrassing" for critics to address — embarrassing because the poet uses the vocative to address inanimate objects. For many broadly "formalist" critics, apostrophe is thus disconcerting because it seems to enable pathetic fallacy. Similarly, the widely accepted proscription against anthropomorphizing nature has likely kept ecocritics from taking apostrophe seriously, since direct addresses to nonhuman nature seem likely to lead to the imposition of human traits and expectations. Yet this common neglect of apostrophe obscures more important correspondences between ecocriticism and other forms of criticism, especially the strain of "politicized" new historicism that intersects with the interests and analytic frame of cultural materialism. In the pages that follow, I hope to demonstrate that a serious study of the implications of apostrophe as a form highlights at least one of these important areas of agreement. Apostrophe, I argue, literally addresses contexts in a manner that is consistent with the aims of both new historicist and ecocritical thought.

It is common in contemporary nature writing to assert that our current ecological crisis is a result of human alienation from nature; as a species, the argument goes, we have become so distanced from an intimate relation with nonhuman nature that most of us feel only a vague sense of loss at our profound disconnection from what might be the very essence of our selves. Although we normally think of this as a contemporary, ecocritical claim, in actuality it has at least one major precedent in literary culture, the rhetorical mode of apostrophe — a discourse that recognizes alienation from nature and formalizes the attempt to restore our connectedness with it. Apostrophe, particularly in a romantic context, is more than merely a poetic device; it is nothing less than a practice of awareness that emphasizes the processes of human perception, the interconnectedness of all things, and the subjecthood of Earth and its inhabitants. It is a practice intended to call our attention to the poet's interaction and connection with the natural world and the understanding that interconnectedness is in itself a form of reciprocity. For the apostrophic poet, calling out to the west wind, for example, isn't the same thing as calling out to a human friend across a field or in the next room; apostrophe doesn't anticipate a human signification as a response from the nonhuman world. Inherent in any invocation of the natural world is a recognition that reciprocity is embedded in the very interconnectedness of all things, in an awareness of the sensitivity and multiplicity of those intricate connections.

RECENT CRITICAL HISTORY

In contrast to my claim of congruency for new historicism and ecocriticism in romantic studies, much recent critical debate has portrayed the two approaches as mutually exclusive. In *Romantic Ecology*, Jonathan Bate succinctly recounts recent critical work on romanticism and contextualizes ecocritical work on romantic poetry, including his own. Bate argues that the 1980s "witnessed something of a return to history, a move away from ahistorical formalisms, among practitioners of literary criticism," citing the broadly Marxist historicism of Jerome McGann's *The Romantic Ideology* as an attempt to overthrow the apoliticism of the Yale School:

> The purpose which Jerome McGann wished to make Wordsworth serve in the historical circumstances of the early 1980s was the politicization of Romantic studies in the United States. . . . He accordingly redescribed Romanticism as ideology: the "Romantic Ideology" displaces and idealizes, it privileges imagination at the expense of history, it covers up social conditions as it quests for transcendence. . . . McGann has had tremendous success in getting what he wanted, and now it looks as if everyone is constructing Romanticism ideologically. Through a model of historical progression, what began as an attempt to overthrow a hegemonic regime has itself become hegemonic. A new challenge is needed, or another Bourbon Restoration will be upon us before we know it. (5–6)

As Karl Kroeber argues in *Ecological Literary Criticism*, Bate's call for a "new challenge" to the hegemony of new historicism reflects an "oppositionalism" characteristic of Cold War criticism. Like Bate, Kroeber acknowledges frankly that new historicism's politicization of romantic studies paved the way for other political critiques, like ecocriticism. Nevertheless, Kroeber and Bate never quite succeed in extricating themselves from the mind-set of antagonism and oppositionalism, wishing to depose rather than supplement or form a coalition with the current critical regime, to "move from red to green" (Bate, *Romantic Ecology*, 8). As Bate asserts in "Living with the Weather," "Cold War criticism is dying, Global Warming criticism is about to be born" (436).

Clearly, ecocritics ought to weigh carefully what is to be gained and what is to be lost before simply celebrating the move from red to green in romantic studies. How much genuine agreement, how many useful emphases, how many instructive practices will need to be suppressed in order to "depose" new historicism? Even at a casual glance, there seems to be a considerable area of coherence between new historicist and ecocritical thought. Kroeber himself emphasizes that any ecological approach must necessarily be materialistic (9). And it is Bate who reminds us that new historicists "taught us that poems are not free-floating aesthetic objects, that, like all texts, they have a social materiality that carries freight" (*Romantic Ecology* 42). The ecocritical recognition that poems have an actual materiality, whether they are composed of mined graphite and wood-pulp paper or composed of electrical impulses traveling through billions of miles of plastic and metal lines, is not a counterpoint but a natural extension of new historicist thought. Perhaps even more important, ecocriticism's recognition of the ways in which class impacts nature and our experience of nature owes much to new historicism's emphasis on production, labor, and the distribution of resources. Similarly, ecocriticism's deep concern with the effects of capitalism and globalization relies on the analytic frame of political economy. Finally, new historicism's insistence that every text is in complicated ways a participant in a variety of material contexts (conditions of production, social relations, and so on — including, crucially, the relations that underlie the rise and fall of critical modes, their access to publication outlets, and reception) is simply extended in scope by what is probably the central thesis of most ecocriticism — the interconnectedness of all things on Earth (poems, people, factories, and forests). It is the broadest and truest of contexts; it includes the history of our species and its relationship to the ecosphere.

This leads to the crux of why apostrophe has been so long ignored. Formalism abhors the way in which apostrophe foregrounds interconnectedness and context. New historicism might reasonably accept attention to environment as a kind of "context," but the idea of the subjecthood of nonhuman nature promoted by apostrophe is too radical. Nevertheless, romantic ecocritics have also largely ignored the apostrophe, perhaps because their professional commitment to "overthrow" the anthropocentrism of new historicism makes apostrophe look dangerously anthropomorphic. Of course, what new historicists and ecocritics such as Bate and Kroeber fail to realize is that, ultimately, they share a common goal: change. Real change, ecological and social, has not been accomplished by overthrowing critical regimes, hegemonic or otherwise. Our ecological crisis, a result of alienation from our own senses and from nonhuman nature, may only begin to be solved by radical ideas and radical changes in thinking, the first being the recognition of the subjecthood (and therefore rights) of human and nonhuman nature. This idea, proposed famously by Aldo Leopold's "Land Ethic," has a literary heritage in the apostrophe that is worth recovering.

O APOSTROPHE!

"To the River Duddon," one of Wordsworth's less frequently anthologized poems, was composed between October 1804 and March 1806 and originally published in 1807. In *William Wordsworth: A Critical Edition of the Major Works*, editor Stephen Gill notes that the Duddon, which empties into the sea "south-west of the Lake District, was the subject of W[ordsworth]'s sonnet sequence 'The River Duddon' (1820), in which ['To the River Duddon'] became XIV. W[ordsworth] was particularly fond of the river and recommended it to his readers as early as 1793 in footnote 1.171 of 'An Evening Walk'" (715).

TO THE RIVER DUDDON

O mountain Stream! the Shepherd and his Cot
Are privileged Inmates of deep solitude:
Nor would the nicest Anchorite exclude

A Field or two of brighter green, or Plot
Of tillage-ground, that seemeth like a spot
Of stationary sunshine: thou hast viewed
These only, Duddon! with their paths renewed
By fits and starts, yet this contents thee not.
Thee hath some awful Spirit impelled to leave,
Utterly to desert, the haunts of men,
Though simple thy Companions were and few;
And through this wilderness a passage cleave
Attended but by thy own Voice, save when
The Clouds and Fowls of the air thy way pursue. (306)

The initial apostrophe invokes the Duddon to praise the river for its fortune; it exists in, and is part of, the natural beauty and splendor enjoyed
by only a few: the shepherd(s), his cot, the anchorite(s), and, presumably,
the poet himself. Yet in the eighth line the poem shifts; some "awful Spirit"
impels the river to meander beyond the spots of stationary sunshine and
into the wilderness where only other wild things are. It seems that the
poet wishes to follow but feels he cannot. The joy and connectedness of
the first seven lines are tempered by the poet's belief that, somehow, he
and the river have become alienated from one another. Outside of the typical pastoral landscape of shepherds and spots of greenery, the poet and
river go their separate ways.

"The River Duddon" is in many ways an exemplary romantic apostrophic poem. Although it expresses a strong feeling of alienation from
the natural world, the poem's initial apostrophe makes an assumption of
humanity's fundamental connectedness with, and place in the context of,
the natural world. Alienation from the natural world is alienation from
one's self; the "awful Spirit" cited as the force causing the Duddon to flow
into the wilderness may be the poet himself. In a sense, the entire address
to the river is the poet's attempt to rectify the situation, to reencounter his
sense of connection with the natural world.

As Gill mentions in *William Wordsworth*, the Duddon is a real element
of the English landscape. In "Structure and Style in the Greater Romantic
Lyric," M. H. Abrams writes that poems written about real, specific places,
or "loco-descriptive" poems, are poems "in which the title named a geographical location, and which combined a description of that scene with
the thoughts that the scene suggested" (208). However, the apostrophic

loco-descriptive poem does more than simply combine description and inspiration; the apostrophic poem addresses the place itself. As noted earlier, Culler writes that conspicuously few critics discuss apostrophe when writing about apostrophic poems; he cites Abrams's essay as one of the many classic texts that systematically avoids mention of "apostrophe, though it is a feature of most of the poems mentioned" (136). Even more perceptively, Culler recognizes that critics (himself included) have unusually hostile and/or condescending attitudes toward apostrophe. Embedded in his critique is the kernel of the problem itself; he writes: "one might be justified in taking apostrophe as the figure of all that is most radical, embarrassing, pretentious, and mystificatory in the lyric, even seeking to identify apostrophe with lyric itself" (137).

"The River Duddon" is part of a long series of sonnets addressed to an actual river. In light of this fact, why isn't it plausible that the poet is at once addressing nonhuman nature and humans as well? Of course, rivers and spots of greenery are not great readers of romantic poetry; however, the poem originated from real, intense involvement with the natural world and is an expression of interconnectedness with it. Wordsworth wrote of the occasion of the poem's inspiration: "I communed with all that I saw as something not apart from, but inherent in, my own immaterial nature" (quoted in M. H. Abrams 224). As Culler has it: "The apostrophizing poet identifies his universe as a world of sentient forces . . . when they address natural objects they formally will that these particular objects function as subjects. . . . The vocative of apostrophe is an approach to the event because its animate presuppositions are deeply embedded, asserted more forcefully because they are not what the sentence asserts. . . . The vocative posits a relationship between two subjects" (139–141).

INTERCONNECTEDNESS

Of all the romantic poets, Coleridge was the most holistic thinker, acutely aware of the interconnectedness of human and nonhuman nature as well as of material and intellectual worlds. M. H. Abrams writes:

[Of Bowles's sonnets and their central structural trope, Coleridge wrote] "moral Sentiments, Affection, or Feelings, are deduced from, and associated with, the scenery of Nature" . . . Coleridge was an integral thinker for whom questions of poetic structure were inseparable from general philosophical issues, and he at once went on to interpret this device as the correlate of a mode of perception which unites the mind to its physical environment. Such compositions he said, "create a sweet and indissoluble union between the intellectual and the material world." . . . In the course of his survey of the dominant philosophy of the preceding age, it becomes clear that Coleridge found intolerable two of its main features, common both to philosophers in the school of Descartes and in the school of Locke. The first was its dualism, the absolute separation between mind and the material universe, which replaced a providential, vital, and companionable world by a world of particles in purposeless movement. The second was the method of reasoning underlying this dualism, that pervasive elementarism which takes as its starting point the irreducible element or part and conceives all wholes to be a combination of discrete parts, whether material atoms or mental "ideas." (217)

Coleridge cites Bowles's style as the model for his early work, poems composed around 1795 and published in 1796–1797, which would include the first incarnation of works such as "The Eolian Harp" and "To the Nightingale" (M. H. Abrams 216). Although neither apostrophic poem is loco-descriptive, both recognize the subjecthood of nonhuman nature. In the case of "To the Nightingale," the poet-narrator addresses an actual animal instead of a particular landscape.

TO THE NIGHTINGALE
Sister of the love-lorn Poets, Philomel!
How many Bards in city garret pent,
While at their window they with downward eye
Mark the faint lamp-beam on the kennell'd mud,
And listen to the drowsy cry of Watchmen
(Those hoarse unfeather'd Nightingales of Time!),
How many wretched Bards address *thy* name,
And hers, the full-orb'd Queen that shines above.
But I *do* hear thee, and the high bough mark,
Within whose mild moon-mellow'd foliage hid
Though warblest sad thy pity-pleading strains.

O! I have listen'd, till my working soul,
Waked by those strains to thousand phantasies,
Absorb'd hath ceas'd to listen! Therefore oft,
I hymn thy name: and with a proud delight
Oft will I tell thee, Minstrel of the Moon!
"Most musical, most melancholy" Bird!
That all thy soft diversities of tone,
Tho' sweeter far than the delicious airs
That vibrate from a white-arm'd Lady's harp,
What time the languishment of lonely love
Melts in her eye, and heaves her breast of snow,
Are not so sweet as is the voice of her,
My Sara — best beloved of human kind!
When breathing the pure soul of tenderness,
She thrills me with the Husband's promis'd name! (93).

Much has been made of this poem's participation in the romantic poets' effort to revive English poetry to the former greatness of Milton and Shakespeare; the reference to *Paradise Lost* in line 2 and to "Il Penseroso" in line 17 remind us of this. Yet these allusions are not central to the poem; what does seem to be central is the concept that Coleridge recognized in Bowles's poetry: the "indissoluble union between the intellectual and material world." The poem begins with an invocation of Philomel (the mythical figure whose tongue was cut out and was later turned into a nightingale by the gods to ease her suffering) who, as an intermediary between human and nonhuman nature, symbolizes our interconnectedness with the natural world. As in Wordsworth's poem, the poet is himself a central figure in the text; his ability to hear the song of the nightingale is the subject of the poem itself: "I *do* hear thee, and the high bough mark." The poet marks not Philomel but an actual nightingale perched on a high branch. In a reverie, the poet ceases to listen to the actual birdsong and, realizing this, makes a conscious effort to reconnect with the natural world that makes his "thousand phantasies" possible: the poet "hymns" the nightingale's name, recognizing the bird's subjecthood and the importance of the natural world for his own creative processes and the processes of poets past, including Milton and the author(s) of Philomel. The poet imagines these past poets interacting with the natural world from the windows of their garrets, which overlook city lamps and the light they shed on "kennell'd mud." That the poets are imagined to have heard the nightingale's song not in some pastoral landscape but in the city emphasizes that humanity's fundamental interconnectedness with the natural world does not stop at the city walls. Green grass grows between pavement cracks; nightingales sing from city trees.

The ease with which "To the Nightingale" moves through and in between the human and the "natural" demonstrates Coleridge's holistic perspective as well as his desire to avoid dualism, as noted by M. H. Abrams. This widely admired excerpt from "The Eolian Harp," composed at Clevedon, Somersetshire (from the 1828 variation on the Sibylline Leaves 1817 version), expresses the inseparability of poetic style and personal philosophy, and of material and intellectual worlds:

> O! the one Life within us and abroad,
> Which meets all motion and becomes its soul,
> A light in sound, a sound-like power in light,
> Rhythm in all thought, and joyance every where —
> Methinks, it should have been impossible
> Not to love all things in a world so fill'd;
>
> . . . .
>
> And what if all of animated nature
> Be but organic Harps diversely fram'd,
> That tremble into thought, as o'er them sweeps
> Plastic and vast, one intellectual breeze,
> At once the Soul of each, and God of all? (101–102)

The "one Life," the lone apostrophic "O!" invoking all of human and nonhuman nature, is what Coleridge found impossible to separate into "a world of particles in purposeless movement," into the artificial categories of "intellectual" and "material" — "a combination of discrete parts." Bate also recognizes the green message inherent in "The Eolian Harp," writing, "'Romantic ecology' . . . proclaims that there is 'one life' within us and abroad, that the earth is a single vast ecosystem which we destabilize at our peril" (40). Yet this emphasis on interconnection, which Bate reads entirely from the explicit content of the poem, is equally inherent in its form, signaled by the apostrophic "O!" At the level of form, Coleridge understood the importance of the interconnectedness of all things, for us and for Earth. "Hymn to the Earth" formalizes this tribute to the "one Life" in the form of the goddess Earth: "Earth! thou mother of numberless children . . . / Hail! O Goddess, thrice hail! Blest be thou! and, blessing, / I hymn thee! . . . Fill the pause of my harp, or sustain it with musical murmurs. / Into my being thou murmurest joy, and tenderest sadness / Shedd'st thou, like dew, on my heart" (327–328).

The recognition — and accomplishment — of this connection through apostrophic form is consistent with another philosophical project of romanticism. As M. H. Abrams has it:

> the central enterprise common to many post-Kantian German philosophers and poets, as well as to Coleridge and Wordsworth, was to join together the "subject" and "object" that modern intellection had put asunder, and thus to revivify a dead nature, restore its concreteness, significance, and human values, and re-domiciliate man in a world which had become alien to him. . . . In the *Biographia Literaria*, when Coleridge came to lay down his own metaphysical system, he based it on the premise designed to overcome both the elementarism in the method and the dualism . . . of his eighteenth century predecessors . . . his theory of knowledge, he says, is "the coincidence of an object with a subject," or "of the thought with the thing," in a synthesis, or "coalescence," in which elements lose their separate identities. In the reconciling and the recurrence of this contradiction exists the process and mystery of production and life. (218–219)

In the apostrophe, Coleridge's connecting project also exhibits affinities with recent phenomenological approaches to nature, such as David Abram's ecocritical treatise, *The Spell of the Sensuous*. Abram discusses Merleau-Ponty's philosophy of perception as philosophy "on the way to ecology" in a manner that highlights the continuing, contemporary value of the apostrophe:

> Merleau-Ponty writes of the perceived things as entities, of sensible qualities as powers, and of the sensible itself as a field of animate presences, in order to underscore their active, dynamic contribution to perceptual experience. To describe the animate life of particular things is simply the most precise and parsimonious way to articulate the things as we spontaneously experience them, prior to all our conceptualizations and definitions. . . . By linguistically defining the surrounding

world as a determinate set of objects, we cut our conscious, speaki. selves off from the spontaneous life of our sensing bodies. . . . Prior to all our verbal reflections, at the level of our spontaneous, sensorial engagement with the world around us, we are all animists. (56–57)

Merleau-Ponty's conceptualization of the participatory nature of perception is not so different from Coleridge's "coalescence" of "subject" and "object." Abram asserts that to describe the animate life of things, to assume the animate life of things linguistically, might actually be the highest form of realism in describing our interactions and interconnectedness with the natural world.

It is in this light that the commonplace notion that apostrophe is a form of pathetic fallacy must be reconsidered. In *Pathetic Fallacy in the Nineteenth Century*, Josephine Miles articulates the significance of this now much-contested notion, arguing that "the attribution of feeling to things . . . is more than a device mentioned in rhetoric books; it is a way of seeing the world and expressing that view" (1). As Kroeber has it, "the Romantics . . . believed that humankind belonged in, could and should be at home within, the world of natural processes" (quoted in Garrard 463). Apostrophe's connection to the pathetic fallacy is their common assumption of interconnectedness. It is through the assumption of reciprocity that the "fallacy" attributes "human" qualities to the "inanimate" and/or natural world. Apostrophe expresses the poet's own strong feeling, invoking the nonhuman subject to listen to the poet's lyric moment. Culler writes: "if one puts into a poem thou shepherd boy, ye blessed creatures, ye birds, they are immediately associated with what might be called a timeless present. . . . Apostrophe resists narrative because its now is not a moment in a temporal sequence but a now of discourse, of writing" (149, 152). In that timeless moment of discourse with nature, the human speaker is "implaced" within nature: the "differentiation of 'space' and 'time' was impossible," Culler asserts, "as long as large portions of the community still experienced the surrounding terrain as animate and alive, as long as material (spatial) phenomena were still perceived by many as having their own inherent spontaneity and (temporal) dynamism" (199).

For Abram, space and time are more than just another dualism; their separation marked a fundamental change in how we perceive and interact with the natural world. Abram argues that the conceptual split between space and time is reflected in the many ways in which we have closed ourselves off from our senses; to perceive fully is to experience space-time, to be in and of the world.

> When I allow the past and the future to dissolve, imaginatively, into the immediacy of the present moment, then the "present" itself expands to become an enveloping field of presence. And this presence, vibrant and alive, spontaneously assumes the shape and contour of the enveloping sensorial landscape, as though this were its native shape! It is this remarkable fit between temporal concept (the "present") and spatial percept (the enveloping presence of the land) that accounts, I believe, for the relatively stale and solid nature of this experience, and prompts me to wonder whether "time" and "space" are really as distinct as I was taught to believe. There is no aspect of this realm that is strictly temporal — for it is composed of spatial things that have density and weight, and is spatially extended around me on all sides, from the near trees to the distant clouds. And yet there is no aspect, either, that is strictly spatial or static — for every perceivable being, from the stones to the breeze to my car in the distance, seems to vibrate with life and sensation. In this open present, I am unable to isolate space from time, or vice-versa. I am immersed in the world. (204)

The way in which we perceive space-time and the dynamic interconnections of life within it is important for any ecology or any approach to living that hopes to restore balance in the world. Apostrophe demands that we, as readers, allow ourselves to be enveloped in an ever-present moment, a space of the poem that, through strong feeling and the conviction of the subjecthood of the invoked, emphasizes the poet's linguistic and physical connection with the subject of the poem. As James McKusick writes: "Coleridge's . . . conception of language as a living thing, as an integral organic system . . . represents a metaphorical extension of the cyclical view of natural processes that was expressed in the notion of the economy of nature. For Coleridge, the historical development of language is deeply conditioned by its relation to the natural environment" (391).

POETIC SYMPATHY

Shelley also explored the problem of alienation from nature and the dynamics of interconnection with it. As Jennifer Lokash notes in "Shel-

ley's Organic Sympathy," this "ecological imagination" can be seen clearly
in Shelley's poetic theory, as well as in his poetic practice. With minor differences, Shelley scholars and ecocritics Lokash, Kroeber, and Ralph Pite
all view Shelley as radically ecological; regardless of whether one claims
him as a deep ecologist or as a social ecologist, Shelley's commitment to
the idea of interconnectedness and the power of poetic sympathy remains
a centerpiece of recent ecological criticism. The highly apostrophic "Ode
to the West Wind" (the 1820 version), often used to demonstrate Shelley's
green tendencies, serves as good example of his "ecological imagination."
The first and fifth parts of the poem read:

I.

O wild West Wind, thou breath of Autumn's being,
Thou, from whose unseen presence the leaves dead
Are driven, like ghosts from an enchanter fleeing,

Yellow, and black, and pale, and hectic red,
Pestilence-stricken multitudes: O Thou,
Who chariotest to their dark wintry bed

The winged seeds, where they lie cold and low,
Each like a corpse within its grave, until
Thine azure sister of the Spring shall blow

Her clarion o'er the dreaming earth, and fill
(Driving sweet buds like flocks to feed in air)
With living hues and odours plain and hill:

Wild Spirit, which art moving everywhere;
Destroyer and Preserver; hear, O hear!

V.

Make me thy lyre, even as the forest is:
What if my leaves are falling like its own!
The tumult of thy mighty harmonies

Will take from both a deep, autumnal tone,
Sweet though in sadness. Be thou, Spirit fierce,
My spirit! Be thou me, impetuous one!

Drive my dead thoughts over the universe
Like withered leaves to quicken a new birth!
And, by the incantation of this verse,

Scatter, as from an unextinguished hearth
Ashes and sparks, my words among mankind!
Be through my lips to unawakened Earth

The trumpet of a prophecy! O Wind,
If Winter comes, can Spring be far behind? (221, 223)

The first part of the poem shows us what the west wind is: destroyer and preserver, bringing pestilence and death as well as the seeds of spring's eternal renewal. The all-encompassing spatial physicality of the wind is the cyclical nature of time, of existence. Shelley's poet reveres the west wind because it is and is not; it is the perfect intersection of intellectual and material worlds. Perhaps the most useful way to think of interconnectedness is in terms of wind and air; it is omnipresent, invisible, and essential to one's life and the life of the land (Abram 228). Similarly, in part 5 the poet connects the invisibility of the wind to the invisibility of the life force (arguably interconnectedness itself) that sustains us physically and intellectually. The poet asks the wind to carry his thoughts as it carries dead leaves and invokes the wind to scatter the poet's words, this very apostrophic poem to the wind itself, over the earth and throughout humankind.

In the lines "Be through my lips to unawakened Earth / The trumpet of a prophecy! O Wind," the poem expresses and enacts the interconnectedness of humans and the natural world and places upon itself the responsibility of conveying this idea to the rest of the world. In her essay "Apostrophe, Animation, and Abortion," Barbara Johnson characterizes "Ode to the West Wind" as "the ultimate apostrophic poem," making connections between apostrophe and animation explicit (632). But Johnson conveys a disappointingly conventional view of what or who is being animated or called to animation in (or by) this poem; she even refers to apostrophe as "a form of ventriloquism . . . turning silence into mute responsiveness" (632). However, Johnson's essay does something significantly unusual; it asserts that apostrophe and other rhetorical devices are political and can be used politically, even though "the political dimensions of the scholarly study of rhetoric have gone largely unexplored by literary critics" (630). And so one might ask: what did Shelley hope to accomplish with his apostrophic poetry? One might argue that he hoped to sow the seeds of nothing less than social and ecological justice. Shelley was a faithful disciple of the romantic idea that poetry can, and does, change the world.

One of Shelley's most poignant claims for the way poetry will help to "grow" society describes poetry as nature. "Poetry," he says, is "the root and blossom of all other systems of thought: it is that from which all spring, and that which adorns all; and that which, if blighted, denies the fruit and seed, and withholds from the barren world the nourishment and the succession of the scions of the tree of life" (Lokash 183).

Yet in order to write and to read poetry that will help us grow, we need "sympathetic imagination." Shelley's poetic sympathy allows him to commune with a sparrow on his windowsill and to apostrophize to the west wind. Our alienation, as a species, from the natural world is due, in large part, to the "scarcity of sympathetic and imaginative activity — what [Shelley] calls the poetic faculty — and the consequence is a dangerously subjective inability to imagine ourselves as part of something greater than our own minds. . . . According to Shelley, release from our circumscribed existence will come only with an infusion of imagination initiated by poetry, which prompts the kind of sympathetic activity required to break down the barriers between self and world" (Lokash 178).

As Pite argues, Shelley's poetry tries to exemplify "an extension of sympathy that reaches so far and becomes so constant that the self loses any desire to differentiate between itself and the world" (362). The very nature of apostrophe, of that seemingly atemporal but thoroughly present moment of high emotion, is a call for our sympathy as readers; apostrophe allows us to experience the poet's sympathy through immediacy and emotion. This is why the poet is always a central figure of the apostrophic poem and why the poet of Shelley's poem asks the west wind to carry his message across the "unawakened Earth." Privileging the power of neither nature itself nor of his poem, Shelley invokes both to participate in waking us to our own sensual, sympathetic experience of the natural world.

It is in this sense that apostrophe functions as an anti-anthropomorphic device, for as philosopher Edmund Husserl discerned, associative empathy enables us to escape solipsism. We escape through Shelley's poetic sympathy, through the poet's synchronicity of senses and rhythms, through reciprocity, through the recognition of interconnectedness. In the words of Gary Snyder, ecology is "a problem of love, not the humanistic love of the West — but a love that extends to the animals, rocks, dirt, all of it. Without this love we can end . . . with an uninhabitable place" (*The Real Work* 4). In concert with the social concerns of other forms of criticism, ecocritics are called by the apostrophic form to love by living in an interconnected way with the planet Earth and each other, by abandoning economic globalization and class hierarchy as well as patriarchy and racism, by encouraging the ethical participation of sustainable communities in their bioregions, by understanding that there is really no "deep" difference between social justice and ecological justice, between ecological and human rights. Apostrophe makes these connections explicit; apostrophe allows us the poet's sympathetic imagination, the poet's empathy with and love of the world, in an ever-present moment of invocation. In "Essay on Love," Shelley sums it up best:

> What is Love? . . . It is that powerful attraction towards all that we conceive or fear or hope beyond ourselves when we find within our own thoughts the chasm of an insufficient void and seek to awaken in all things that are, a community with what we experience within ourselves. . . . This is Love. This is the bond and the sanction which connects not only man with man, but with everything which exists. . . . Hence in solitude, or in that deserted state when we are surrounded by human beings and yet they sympathize not with us, we love the flowers, the grass and the waters and the sky. In the motion of the very leaves of spring in the blue air there is then found a secret correspondence with our heart. There is eloquence in the tongueless wind and a melody in the flowing brooks and the rustling of the reeds beside them which by their inconceivable relation to something within the soul, awaken the spirits to a dance of breathless rapture, and bring tears of mysterious tenderness to the eyes. . . . So soon as this want or power is dead, man becomes the living sepulchre of himself, and what yet survives is the mere husk of what once he was. (473–474)

4. In Search of Left Ecology's Usable Past
The Jungle, Social Change, and the Class Character of Environmental Impairment

STEVEN ROSENDALE

When it comes to genius, to beauty, dignity, and true power of mind, I cannot see that there is any chance for them to survive in the insane hurly-burly of metropolitan life. If I wanted qualities such as these in human beings, I would surely transfer them to a different environment. And maybe that is what Providence was planning for me to understand and to do in the world. At any rate, it is what I am trying to do, and is my final reaction to the great metropolis of Mammon.

—*Upton Sinclair,* American Outpost

As the immigrant Jurgis Rudkus and his family peer out of their train windows on their journey to Chicago in the second chapter of Upton Sinclair's *The Jungle*, the landscape undergoes a remarkable transformation. An hour before they reach the city, the Rudkuses get their first inkling of the possible nature of that change, becoming dimly aware of "perplexing changes in the atmosphere." The air around them is increasingly polluted by an "elemental odor, raw and crude . . . rich, almost rancid, sensual, and strong" (20). Although they are divided in their feelings about this odor, other elements of the environment clearly dismay the immigrants as the train carries them nearer to Chicago. For mile after mile, they witness an increasingly dense "desolate procession" of "ugly and dirty little wooden buildings," all the same, punctuated only by the occasional "filthy creek" or "great factory . . . darkening the air and making filthy the earth beneath." Gradually, as Jurgis's group stares out at the view speeding by their train, its natural elements appear increasingly drained of vigor and beauty. Colors are bleached from the visible landscape. Everything in sight becomes "dingier": the grass seems to "grow less green," the fields become "parched and yellow," the landscape progressively more "hideous and bare."

When the group detrains at their new home, Packingtown, the transformation of the landscape is apparently complete. There remains, it seems, no vestige of real greenery, no trace of unaltered, nonhuman nature. In its place, industry has remade the entire environment in its own image. The "elemental" atmosphere that first signaled the approach to the stockyards, for example, turns out to be a product of the rendering-house smokestacks, which simulate a variety of other natural forces as well. They manufacture the region's weather signs — the "vast clouds" that dominate the sky. Alternatively, their smoke is described as an oily "river" and as a "self-impelled" geological force, since it appears to have come from "the center of the world . . . where the fires of the ages still smoulder." Even the soil upon which the houses of the district sit is a by-product of manufacture: it is "made land," the original soil having been excavated and turned to brick, and the hole from the excavation refilled "by using it as a dumping-ground for the city's garbage" (20). As evening falls on the immigrants' first day in Chicago, the only relic of the natural outside that is left is the remote sun, and it is ignored as the immigrant couple survey the horizon: "Jurgis and Ona were not thinking of the sunset . . . their backs were turned to it, and all their thoughts were on Packingtown, which they could see so plainly in the distance. The line of buildings stood clearcut and black against the sky; here and there out of the mass rose the great chimneys, with the river of smoke streaming away to the end of the world" (24).

Metonymically extending "to the end of the world," the Packingtown environment has supplanted not a few particular features of nature but nature itself. Throughout the novel, Jurgis, his wife, Ona, and the narrator will continue to refer to Packingtown as a "wilderness," a "wild," "unsettled country," and the like. Soon after the immigrants' arrival in Chicago, a sound seeps into their frame of awareness, and the procession of similes the narrator provides for it suggests that the by-products of industry have encompassed the entire environment to the farthest horizon: "it was like the murmuring of bees in the spring, the whisperings of the forest . . . the rumblings of a world in motion." The same point is driven home by the narrator's comment that the narrow roads between the houses "resembled streets less than they did a miniature topographical map of a continent," with no pavements but rather miniature "mountains and valleys and rivers, gullies and ditches," with oceanic "great hollows full of stinking green water" (21).

The Rudkus family has, of course, entered the jungle, an encompassing simulacrum of nature to which Sinclair referred in an early version of the novel as the "wilderness of civilization."[1] Although Packingtown initially holds out the promise of a good life for the immigrants (on his first night in Packingtown the factories strike the optimistic Jurgis as a sublime "vision of power"), this hope is quickly gainsaid by the obviously noxious features of the industrial environment itself, a place that increasingly appears bewildering and uninhabitable to the immigrants. Some emphasis upon the crowding and monotony of the urban landscape might be expected in any tale of country folk moving to the city, but Sinclair devotes a full fifteen paragraphs to his initial description of the locale, commencing a critical view of the industrial simulation of nature that is sustained throughout the novel.

Surely one of American literature's great treatments of the environmental consequences of industrial production, *The Jungle* has nevertheless never been taken seriously as a novel with important environmental implications, a failing that this essay seeks to correct. The lack of ecocritical attention to *The Jungle* (and indeed, to the larger Left literary tradition in the United States) can be traced to several sources, the most important of which is a mistaken tendency among ecocritics to confuse the complex and necessary project of developing eco-conscious critical values with a simplistic rejection of "interhuman" concerns like urban social life and class politics. For some ecocritics, the critical focus on such interhuman concerns has simply failed to provide an environmentally acceptable set of critical values, offering instead just another version of what Glen A. Love has called literary studies' "narrowly anthropocentric view of what is consequential in life" (229). "We must break through our preoccupation," Love writes, "with mediating between only human issues, the belief that, as Warwick Fox puts it, 'all will become ecologically well with the world if we just put this or that interhuman concern first'" (227).

The anthropocentrism-busting emphasis in ecocriticism has carried with it a corresponding rejection of traditional notions of politics, including the class critiques of capitalism that so interested the Left in the twentieth century. In the face of global environmental degradation, Theodore Roszak contends, both capitalist and socialist economies resolve into a global and univocally malignant economic "style" that renders even the most basic issues of social justice moot: "We have an economic style whose dynamism is too great, too fast, too reckless for the ecological systems that must absorb its impact. It makes no difference to those systems if the oil spills, the pesticides, the radioactive wastes, the industrial toxins they must cleanse are socialist or capitalist in origin; the ecological damage is not mitigated in the least if it is perpetrated by a 'good society' that shares its wealth fairly and provides the finest welfare programs for its citizens" (33).

Roszak's point is, of course, well taken. Both of the contemporary major modes of economic organization have produced environmental damage on a massive scale, and that damage carries no marker of its political origin. In theory and in history itself, both capitalism and socialism have been driven by a commitment to unlimited production, a similar faith in the power of technology to improve human life, and a virtually identical tendency to hide the environmental costs of production.

The prominence of such ideas in the emerging ecocritical canon explains ecocriticism's failure to examine the environmental implications of Left texts like *The Jungle*. For Sinclair's text is, of course, intensely focused upon interhuman concerns. In contradistinction to the wide array of wilderness-oriented texts already firmly ensconced in the ecocritical canon, *The Jungle* is set in landscapes entirely remade by human industry and agriculture. Despite the novel's extended ruminations on the victimage of stock animals (Sinclair was a vegetarian at the time of the novel's publication), this sympathy is ultimately an anthropomorphism meant to symbolize and accentuate the emphasis on human misery. Indeed, the major political effect of the novel — the passage of federal food purity laws — had nothing to do with the treatment of animals or any other part of nonhuman nature. In fact, the entire novel appears to be focused upon "narrowly anthropocentric" issues: class struggle, the possibility of individual and family success within a complex and predetermined economic structure, and the effect of ward corruption and national politics upon working-class life. Despite Sinclair's obvious interest in describing the environmental consequences of production, environmentally minded readers are likely to object even to Sinclair's central metaphor — the jungle — which often uncritically seems to reinforce an antipathy toward nature itself. The narrative, for instance, unquestioningly describes Jurgis's exploiting economic superiors as "wild-beast powers of nature" and "ravening wolves that tear and rend and destroy" (167, 301).

Nevertheless, there are compelling reasons for reexamining novels like *The Jungle* for their ecocritical potential. A growing body of ecocritical thought has begun to suggest that the simple dichotomy of "interhuman" and "environmental" concerns that has grounded ecocriticism's general failure to address literatures of class and of urban life may itself be part of our environmental problem. As Wendell Berry argued more than two decades ago in *The Unsettling of America*, even the central concept of "environment" suppresses the possibility of a mutualistic relation that might otherwise guide our lived relationship with nonhuman nature: "Once we see our place, our part of the world, as *surrounding* us, we have already made a profound division between it and ourselves. We have given up the understanding — dropped it out of our language and so out of our thought — that we and our country create one another, depend on one another, are literally part of one another . . . and so cannot possibly flourish alone; that, therefore, our culture must be our response to our place, our culture and our place are images of each other" (22).

In a similar vein, Michael Pollan has persuasively argued in "The Idea of a Garden" that the notion of "wilderness" upon which much environmental activism is grounded must now be recognized as a concept with increasingly limited utility, precisely because it rigidly divides nature from human culture and economy: "Essentially, we have divided our country in two, between the kingdom of wilderness, which rules about 8 percent, and the kingdom of the market, which rules the rest. . . . Useful as [the wilderness idea] has been in helping us protect the sacred 8 percent, it nevertheless has failed to prevent us from doing a great deal of damage to the remaining 92 percent. The old idea may have taught us how to worship nature, but it didn't tell us how to live with her. It told us more than we needed to know about virginity and rape, and almost nothing about marriage" (425).

This kind of suspicion regarding environmentalism's reliance on the foundational dichotomy of nature and human culture suggests the need to return to Roszak's notion of the supersession of social justice issues by environmental ones ("ecological damage is not mitigated in the least if it is perpetrated by a 'good society'") with a new and more critical eye. We might, of course, reverse Roszak's formulation, observing that the traditional class-oriented, interhuman concerns that occupy Left novels like *The Jungle* are themselves not "mitigated in the least" if that oppression is perpetrated by a society that has redressed ecological disaster and developed sustainable modes of production. But the deeper point is the absurdity of conceptualizing "environmental" and "interhuman" concerns in isolation from each other, as Berry's proposition that our place and our culture mirror one another suggests.

A number of political theorists have begun an effort to frankly reassess the environmental legacy and potential of the Left in order to move beyond red-green dichotomies and style a politics that addresses human and environmental exploitation in the "kingdom of the market" that comprises the bulk of the American landscape. As Kate Soper has argued: "just as socialism can only hope to remain a radical and benign pressure for social change by assuming an ecological dimension, so the ecological concern will remain largely ineffective (and certainly incapable of reversing the current trends in the manner required) if it is not associated in a very integral way with many traditional socialist demands, such as assaulting the global stranglehold of multinational capital" (82). Integrating environmental concerns and Left-materialist political theory will surely entail a radical revision of some of the most basic assumptions that the Left has cherished. The Left, for example, will need to rethink its production-based notion of social "progress." Whereas Marxism has traditionally regarded the technological basis of production (even under capitalism) as neutral, it must now revise its model of the transition to socialism to account for the necessity of transforming (rather than simply remanaging) the technological basis of production itself.

Concurrent with these efforts to rewrite Left politics in green is an effort to recover lost theoretical precedents for the necessary changes. The last few years have seen a burgeoning of scholarship reconsidering the underemphasized ecological potential of key concepts in Marxism: alienation, the critical theory of production, the notion of natural limits, and so on (see Benton). This effort at theoretical recovery and revision strives to make areas of conceptual consonance between Left and green thought more visible. Both traditions might, for example, find common ground in their shared rejection of the preeminence of money profits over other values and in their common objection to the hiding of environmental and human costs that accompany the production of commodities.

Although "Left ecology" may be thought to have a recoverable theoretical past, there has been very little work done to discover whether a red-green synthesis might possess a cultural past that may prove valuable for contemporary environmentalism. William Empson linked the radical novels of proletarian experience and revolt produced in the first four decades of the twentieth century to the pastoral tradition, but his observation was never developed by subsequent critics. This critical lacuna is curious, for environment often emerges as a rather obvious controlling figure in a surprising number of American radical novels, which frequently compress their critiques of the social milieu into images of place: *The Jungle, Industrial Valley, Daughter of Earth, Parched Earth, Land of Plenty, USA, From the Kingdom of Necessity,* and so on. More than just an emphasis on "setting," these titles point to the American literary Left's curiously strong interest in the idea of nature and in the environmental consequences of industrial production under capitalism.

The full potential of an ecocritical approach to the Left tradition in American literature is too large a subject for this essay, but an analysis of Sinclair's *The Jungle* might serve as a token of the contributions Left literatures can make to ecocriticism and vice versa. If *The Jungle* is narrowly anthropocentric, it is also a text profoundly concerned with the relation of nature and human life: how the immigrant experience in industrial cities recapitulated and gave the lie to dominant ideologies about American pioneering, how economic classes experience the environmental damages consequent to production, how natural forces express themselves in class society, and finally, how the notion of uncorrupted nature itself might be reclaimed as a liberatory idea in a class society.

The main contribution of Sinclair's novel — its articulation of class and environmental concerns — was strikingly manifest in his intellectual development, as it was in the careers of a number of writers on the American Left.[2] Most Sinclair biographies stress the alternation of Sinclair's childhood care between his impoverished parents and a set of wealthy relatives as a formative influence on his intense interest in social class (for example, Dell 16–32). Although it is less frequently noticed, Sinclair's class experience was also closely linked to a pattern of alternation between urban and relatively natural settings. Through his adolescence, Sinclair's family depended on the graciousness of a wealthy aunt who ensconced the family in a Virginia country retreat and in a rustic Adirondack camp; when his father could get a few months' work in New York, Sinclair would return to the bedbugs and economic uncertainty suffered by "the tribe of city nomads, a product of the new age" (Sinclair, *American Outpost*, 22).

Thus alternation of geographical environments became associated with an acute awareness of class difference, with the country and mountain existence striking him mainly as an arena of fulfillment and leisure, while urban life figured as an arena of struggle and poverty. His account of city life is full of dangerous episodes (Sinclair reports, "I was able to reckon up fourteen times that I had missed death by a hair's breadth") that obviously shaped the young boy. The city life presented a vision of harsh natural selection for Sinclair, turning out hundreds of thousands of children onto the street "to develop their bodies and their wits," for "in a rough general way, those who get caught by street-cars and motor-cars and trucks are those who are not quite so quick in their escape-reactions" (24). Usually, such emphases on natural selection support a monistic materialism in which the city life is depicted as equally subject to natural law as the wild, but for Sinclair the class connotations of the urban and the wild preserve an inverted dualism: life in nature, for Sinclair, paradoxically seemed to *escape* the harshest applications of natural law that obtained in the city.

Later in his adolescence, this identification of poverty and the urban, privilege and the rural or wild, was incorporated into Sinclair's career as a writer as well. The despised work at which Sinclair began his career at the age of sixteen — cranking out potboilers and jokes for a meager living while at City College — was expressly an aspect of urban life for the young writer, while major turning points in his development of a more "serious" literary career were associated with nature, the rural, or the wild. One Christmas holiday at his rich uncle's home, Sinclair set out to read his uncle's entire library of unopened leatherbound "classics" in the frenzied course of two weeks. As would become typical of his thought in later years, Sinclair described his appropriation of the literary value of the books by recourse to the environmental metaphor: "Some poet said to a rich man," Sinclair writes, "'You own the land and I own the landscape.' To my kind uncle I said: 'You own the books and I own the literature'" (75).

The aesthetic claim to literature and landscape alike are merged in Sinclair's recollection of his conversion to the literary career. Following his reading frenzy, the young writer had a rapturous hallucination in an open park, wherein he received his literary calling. The sublime experience was repeated, Sinclair reports, many times, often "associated with music and poetry, but still more frequently with natural beauty": winter nights in Central Park, a summer night in the Adirondacks, twilight in the "far wilds of Ontario." The strangeness of the experience drove Sinclair, as it were, deeper into the woods, since, as he admits, "I wanted to be free to behave like a lunatic, and yet not have anybody think me one." After an embarrassing episode when a young girl came upon him while in his rapture, he "became a haunter of mountain-tops and of deep forests, the only safe places" (78).

When he felt ready to forsake potboilers for his first "serious" novel, a romance called *Springtime and Harvest*, Sinclair found it necessary to wait until spring was "far enough advanced so [he] could go to the country." "My one desire," he writes, "was to be alone; far away, somewhere in a forest, where the winds of ecstasy might sweep through my spirit." Building a rude cabin on the shore of an isolated lake, the author lived a summer in this "Fairy Glen" a life after the pattern of Thoreau at Walden, observing the "daily miracle" of sunrise and feeling a special kinship with "the great winds that lashed the forest trees" (91). The retreat would serve to solace him again in the throes of his first, unsuccessful marriage, but the more general association of urban environments with want (and hack writing), and of natural settings with material and spiritual fulfillment (as well as "literature"), persisted.[3]

For Sinclair, then, environment and class were inextricably linked, an association that continued to characterize his thought as he shifted from romantic idealist to "proletarian writer" during the writing of *The Jungle*.[4] In an inversion of his usual practice, Sinclair suspended his dislike of city poverty and voluntarily immersed himself for seven weeks in the brutal world of Chicago's meatpacking district, taking meals at a nearby settlement house and moving about the harrowing slaughtering lines disguised in ragged clothes and carrying a lunch pail to gather his facts. The central metaphor Sinclair developed for the staggeringly horrific proletarian district he had observed — the jungle, or "wilderness of civilization" — represented both an outgrowth and a development of his experience with class difference and its correspondence with the contrast of natural and citified environments.

Although nearly all the criticism of *The Jungle* understands its title metaphor as part of the novel's "naturalism," it would be a mistake to assume that Sinclair's jungle metaphor describes a universally deterministic condition. In fact, nothing could be further from the truth, for the jungle, whether embodied in Packingtown itself or, later in the novel, in the agri-

cultural countryside through which Jurgis tramps, is a specifically proletarian wilderness. Sinclair is at pains throughout the text to demonstrate
that the industrial environment, which appears to Jurgis as a terrifying
wilderness, is not experienced universally but only by members of a particular class under a particular economic regime. While begging for food
during a period of unemployment, for example, Jurgis is befriended by the
drunken son of a capitalist family. The young man, whom Jurgis learns to
call "Master Freddie," gives Jurgis $100, and Jurgis quickly finds himself
invited to supper at the family mansion. The house, just a short distance
from Packingtown, astounds Jurgis with its display of riches and presents
a stunning contrast to the scenes of environmental degradation that surround the novel's laboring characters. While the Rudkuses live (and die)
amid the filthy streams and "made land," the wealth they create while laboring in the stockyards allows Master Freddie a private reserve on the
lakefront. When he arrives at the address with his drunken host, Jurgis
can only perceive the vast estate, which takes up a city block, as an element of nature itself — an "enormous granite pile." Inside, the decor also
recalls a privileged relation with nature, as Jurgis walks through gleaming
stone halls. "From the walls strange shapes loomed out . . . wonderful and
mysterious-looking in the half-light, purple and red and golden, like sunset glimmers in a shadowy forest," Sinclair writes: apparently the "nature" in which Freddie lives has none of the threatening overtones of Jurgis's jungle (234–235).

Although this idea is hardly presented in sophisticated terms in *The
Jungle*, the novel does provide a strong literary illustration of one of the
Left's strongest critiques of environmentalism's claim to social neutrality.
As Hans Enzensberger argues in "A Critique of Political Ecology," envi-
ronmental impairment has long had a class character. In a description that
uncannily recalls Sinclair's portrait of Packingtown, he writes:

> Industrialization made whole towns and areas of the countryside un-
> inhabitable as long as 150 years ago. The environmental conditions at
> places of work, that is to say, in the English factories and pits, were —
> as innumerable documents demonstrate — dangerous to life. There
> was infernal noise. The air people breathed was polluted with explo-
> sive and poisonous gases, as well as with carcinogenic matter and par-
> ticles that were highly contaminated with bacteria. The smell was
> unimaginable. In the labor process contagious poisons of all kinds

were used. The workers' diet was bad. Food was adulterated. Safety measures were non-existent or were ignored. The overcrowding in the working-class quarters was notorious. (24)

Despite the apparent nature of these environmental problems, Enzensberger notes, "it occurred to no one to draw pessimistic conclusions about the future of industrialization from these facts." Not even the emergence of environmentalism in the twentieth century would adequately address this class experience of environmental damage. Environmentalism itself, he contends, is a class concern that emerged in part because of the rising cost of isolating oneself from increasingly universal environmental decline. "The ecological movement," Enzensberger asserts, "has only come into being since the districts that the bourgeoisie inhabit have been exposed to those environmental burdens that industrialization brings with it" (25). If Enzensberger's assessment of environmentalism's unacknowledged class character is even partially right, as I think it is, attention to texts like *The Jungle* might begin to provide a necessary class dimension to the project of environmental criticism.

The failure to address the specifically class character of the jungle world has led to a second error in the critical consensus about the novel that an ecocritical perspective can correct — the astoundingly uniform disparagement of the novel as an aesthetic flop that fails to execute consistently the naturalistic implications of its environmental emphasis. For virtually all critics who have written about *The Jungle*, the novel's major structural flaw surfaces in its division into three fairly distinct sections marked off by changes in the story's settings: the initial naturalistic account of the Rudkus family's destruction by economic forces within Packingtown itself, an episode in which Jurgis leaves Packingtown for a summer on the tramp, and the final chapters, in which Jurgis returns to Packingtown, undergoes a sudden conversion to socialism, and is present during a number of lengthy declamations about the Cooperative Commonwealth. Although critics have uniformly praised the uncompromising depiction of the Rudkuses' grinding existence among the Packingtown proletariat, they have also with very few exceptions disparaged the supposed disruption of the story's organic development by the later sections. Walter Fuller Taylor's treatment of *The Jungle* in *Literary History of the United States* praises the "cumulative power" developed by Sinclair's lurid description of the jungle world, which "little in Zola or Dostoevski surpasses," but also complains that the "fierce partisanship" of the novel's later chapters "estops it from being the fine naturalistic novel implied by some of its philosophical premises" (997). Harvey Swados asserts that "*The Jungle* must renew its hold on the imaginations of an entirely new generation of readers," but nevertheless Swados concedes that "the more we examine a work like *The Jungle,* the more difficult it is to defend its specifically literary merits." "No one could deny that structurally it is a broken-backed book," he continues, "with most of the intensity concentrated in the first two-thirds, which are concerned with the struggle of the immigrants to sustain themselves in Packingtown, and most of the propaganda concentrated in the last third, after the dissolution of Jurgis Rudkus's family and during his conversion to socialism." A critical perspective attuned to the ecological resonance of Sinclair's novel, however, can suggest a thoroughly different view, contesting the remarkably consistent critical consensus about the novel's structural flaws on three major points.

As the discussion above has indicated, Sinclair's fusion of class and environmental concerns ought to seriously challenge the assumptions about Sinclair's commitment to universal determinism that clearly underlie the critique of the novel's supposed structural flaws. Environmental ruin and bestial struggle are the rule in Packingtown, but there are those who live outside the determined landscape — a fact that logically allows the possibility of individual or class ascendance or escape from the jungle.

Moreover, although critics have seen Sinclair's intense interest in environmental description as simply an indication of determinism, the novel also quite evidently manifests a deep interest in the significance of the original nature that the industrial simulation has replaced. Although, as we have seen, the initial description of Packingtown suggests that the industrial perversion has entirely supplanted nature, in fact Sinclair peppers his narration with observations about recalcitrant scraps of nature that have resisted incorporation into the industrial simulation. For example, Sinclair's narrator pauses during the notorious hog-butchering passage long enough to note an exception to the dingy brown weeds (mixtures of pollution and organic life, Sinclair indicates) that otherwise appear to be the only plant life in the district ("of other verdure there is none," he remarks in the serial version of the novel, "for nothing will grow in the smoke" [Sinclair, *Lost Edition,* 39]). "In front of Brown's General Office building," Sinclair notes, "there grows a tiny plot of grass, and this, you may learn, is the only bit of green thing in Packingtown" (38). Comparing the little lawn to the anguished protests of the slaughtered hogs (and, by extension, to the protests of the exploited workers), Sinclair's narrator partially displaces the deterministic implications of his environment with what is essentially an issue of space: "in what can resistance be embodied?" or, in the environmental idiom of the novel, "what basis — literally, what ground — is there for opposition to destructive capitalism?" As Sinclair will eventually suggest, the answer to this question is that resistance — and renewal — must be embodied in a class-conscious proletariat but also in the environment itself. Redress for the proletariat and the environment go hand-in-hand, and the process of Jurgis's conscious move toward socialism begins, appropriately enough, away from Packingtown. While spending a season on the tramp, Jurgis begins to experience a less adulterated nature as a source of potential restoration. In an extended pastoral idyll that is usually understood as introducing the initial structural flaw in the novel, Jurgis enjoys the pleasures of summer as the land itself provides food, cleanliness, open space, rest, and even recreation. In a poignant episode, he bathes in a small spring, and as the accumulated grime of his industrial labors begins to wash away, he splashes about "like a very boy in his glee." Nature itself, that is, affords Jurgis a material and an aesthetic experience that the industrial simulation of nature cannot. In addition to restoring Jurgis's humanity, the countryside affords him enough respite that he can evaluate his Packingtown experience with some clarity and begin to imagine a better life: as Jurgis argues with a farmer about hiring practices, the reader is aware that his experience of the countryside has begun his progress toward class consciousness. A positive "nature" and improvement of the lot of the proletariat are intimately linked in Sinclair's narrative.

This association between the restorative powers of nature and working-class ascendancy comes to fruition in the novel's closing chapters, a fact that should substantially alter the entrenched critique of the novel's supposed structural problems. Of course, the respite the countryside provides is seasonal, and Jurgis eventually is forced to return to Packingtown, where he is again subject to the degenerative forces of the industrial environment. After suffering a number of setbacks, Jurgis's body, once the guarantor of his employability, deteriorates. Just as all signs seem to point to his destruction, he happens upon an orator whose words effect Jurgis's conversion to socialism. The speaker's case against capitalism uses the customary environmental idiom of *The Jungle*, criticizing capitalism as a perverse simulation of nature. Of the capitalist class itself, he rages: "Their life is a contest among themselves for supremacy in ostentation and recklessness, the toil and anguish of the nations, the sweat and tears and blood of the human race! It is all theirs — it comes to them; just as all the springs pour into streamlets, and the streamlets into rivers, and the rivers into the ocean — so, automatically and inevitably, all the wealth of society comes to them. . . . The whole of society is in their grip, the whole labor of the world lies at their mercy — and like fierce wolves they rend and destroy, like ravening vultures they devour and tear!" (301).

"Images of nature" ecocritics are likely to be offended by this characterization of wolves, but it would be well to remember that the image occurs in the context of a critique of the *simulation* of nature in Packingtown, in which "nature" is entirely reduced to the predatory behavior of the capitalist. Jurgis's conversion comes immediately, and following on the positive connotations of nature developed in the tramping episodes, his reaction to the speaker is described as an encounter with a wilderness more genuine than the jungle with which he is so familiar: it occurs to him that seeing the speaker is "like coming suddenly upon some wild sight of nature — a mountain forest lashed by a tempest, a ship tossed about upon a stormy sea" (296). The episode and the chapters that follow are a favorite target of naturalist critics, who charge that they introduce a radical disjunction from the stylistic and philosophical elements that comprise the early sections of the text. Granville Hicks placed *The Jungle* in the mainstream of his "great tradition" of democratic-spirited American literature but faulted Sinclair for committing a "sin against the art of the novel: failure to assimilate the material he so wisely accumulates" with the socialist message of the final section (*Great Tradition* 203). Walter Rideout also suggested that the powerful vision of the jungle world is wasted by this sudden turn, in the novel's final chapters, from naturalistic fiction to "another kind of statement altogether." The naturalistic description of Jurgis's victimization is far more creatively realized than is his existence as a socialist: "the reader cannot exist imaginatively in Jurgis's converted state even if willing, for Jurgis hardly exists himself. What it means to be a Socialist is given, not through the rich disorder of felt experience, but in such arbitrarily codified forms as political speeches, an essay on Party personalities, or the long conversation in monologues about the Cooperative Commonwealth which comprises most of the book's final chapter." "While the capitalist damnation, the destruction of the immigrants, has been proven almost upon the reader's pulses . . . the Socialist salvation, after its initial impact, is intellectualized" (34).

Even the most enthusiastic reader of *The Jungle* would recognize the accuracy of Rideout's description of the final chapters, which are indeed "another kind of statement altogether." But while virtually all critics have heretofore understood this abrupt shift as an aesthetic failing, a critical perspective attuned to emerging Left ecology might find something altogether more admirable in it.

The political optimism of the novel's ending, in which a crowd of socialist workers roar in exultation over positive election results, "CHICAGO WILL BE OURS!" seems (as does most of the explicit political rhetoric in the novel's final chapters) to conceive of capitalism simply as a property relationship rather than as a mode of production: the solution to the workers' problems consists in a transfer of ownership, so to speak, of the city's industries. But as Rossana Rossanda notes, capitalism "cannot simply be done away with by dispossessing private capitalists, even when this expropriation makes it possible in practice to render that part of surplus value available for other purposes than accumulation. The socialist revolution cannot be understood as a transfer of ownership leading to a more just distribution of wealth while other relationships remain alienated and reified. On the contrary, it must lead to totally revolutionized relationships between men and between men and things — that is to say, it must revolutionize the whole social production of their lives" (36).

In fact, Sinclair's environmental focus in *The Jungle* tends to teach just such a lesson: throughout the text, Sinclair has been at pains to describe the environmental consequences of capitalist industry not simply as the result of bad management or accumulation but as an integral feature of the productive process itself. Although a socialist takeover might result in a redistribution of the wealth created by production, there is no provision in the socialist theory propounded in *The Jungle*'s closing pages for a revision of the mode of production, which would ostensibly continue its devastation of the environment under new management. Thus the political optimism that follows Jurgis's conversion is more than a stylistic break in the novel: it is a conceptual contradiction of a more serious nature. If the mode of production is itself despoiling, as the bulk of the novel suggests, it is difficult to imagine how the situation of the workers will be improved through the kind of appropriation proposed by the novel's finale — without, that is, a substantial revision of the technical basis of production itself.

The passage describing Jurgis's conversion consistently mediates this tension through environmental metaphor. As Jurgis responds to the orator's vision, it seems as if his socialist life cannot occur upon the same solid ground as his wage-slavery. The narration depicts his transformation into a socialist as a series of catastrophic events that alter the landscape itself, an "unfolding of vistas before him, a breaking of the ground beneath him." The sky, too, "seemed to split" above Jurgis, as the words of the speaker impress Jurgis as a "crashing of thunder in his soul," the emotions stirred within him, as a "flood." "It was," the narrator explains, "a most wonderful experience to him — an almost supernatural experience." Like the "wild sight of nature" that the speaker recalls, the setting of Jurgis's new life must be imagined as a nature no longer devastated by production. From the natural wilderness setting of an imaginary mountaintop, Jurgis at last gains a useful perspective on the jungle in which he has been immersed: "It was like encountering an inhabitant of the fourth dimension of space, a being who was free from all one's own limitations. For four years, now, Jurgis had been wandering and blundering in the depths of a wilderness; and here, suddenly, a hand reached down and seized him, and lifted him out of it, and set him upon a mountain top, from which he could survey it all — could see the paths from which he had wandered, the morasses into which he had stumbled, the hiding places from which the beasts of prey had fallen upon him" (311).

Although the passage is meant to convey optimism about Jurgis's new condition, it also tends to undermine the note of the here-and-now effectivity of socialism upon which the text ends. To say that Sinclair must imagine Jurgis's socialism as occurring in nature is also to recognize Sinclair's inability to imagine a fulfilling life for his protagonist within the industrial landscape that the socialists propose to expropriate. The novel has so successfully given the picture of the city wilderness that the transition to socialism can't be imagined convincingly except in figural terms that apocalyptically erase the environmental consequences of the productive mode the socialists are about to seize.

Thus while Rideout and others have belittled the abstract, imaginative, and intellectualized nature of Sinclair's attempt to represent Jurgis's converted life, critics with an interest in the environmental implications of lit-

erary texts might usefully understand the novel's close as a logical contin-
uation of Sinclair's interest in the connections between environmental
and class politics. If, as I suggested earlier, a text like *The Jungle* can furnish
ecocriticism with a much-needed class emphasis, an ecocritical perspective can itself offer much to Left theory and criticism by discerning the way
in which Sinclair's novel embeds within an apparent formal flaw the need
for the left to recognize the non-neutrality of the technological basis of
production.

While it is doubtful that Sinclair had anything so sophisticated in mind
as the creation of a literary form uniquely capable of articulating this simple
political ecology, in fact that is just what he created. While the structural
"break" in his novel may not satisfy the accustomed aesthetic standards of
literary criticism, it does a fine job of highlighting a basic contradiction
between the technological progressivism of socialist thought and the environmental evidence about industrial production. Despite nearly a century of criticism to the contrary, neither the picture of the social world nor
the form of *The Jungle* itself is incoherent, flawed, or outworn. Rather, the
novel is ambivalent — intently focused upon both the hope of social
change and the necessity of revising production's environmental consequences. In a time when the split between environmentalism and anthropocentric social concerns is so easily accepted as an apriority of critical
thought, even Sinclair's relatively simplistic attempt to maintain a connection between the two provides a relevant literary model, a usable cultural past upon which Left ecological criticism may be built.

NOTES

1. This was Sinclair's original title for the pivotal eighteenth chapter of the se-
rial novel published in the *Appeal to Reason*, which is conveniently available in *The
Lost First Edition of Upton Sinclair's* The Jungle, ed. Gene DeGruson (Atlanta: St.
Luke's, 1988). Unless noted, all references to *The Jungle* are from the standard
Doubleday edition of 1906.

2. In addition to Sinclair, an unusual proportion of writers on the American Left
pursued their political-literary agendas while maintaining an interest in nature
writing and the outdoors. Robert Cantwell wrote the 1934 strike novel *The Land of
Plenty* — one of the central texts of the American proletarian tradition — while
also writing feature stories for outdoors magazines. Cantwell went on to write a
fine biography of naturalist Alexander Wilson. Noted Marxist critic Granville
Hicks, who edited the Communist journal *New Masses* from 1934 to 1938, was also
interested in the political possibilities of rural, regional life and economy, subjects

he explored in *Small Town*. Hicks later wrote a utopian novel, *The First to Awaken*, which featured productively restrained, regionally planned, environmentally sustainable economies. The figure with whom most environmental thinkers are likely to be familiar is Left sociologist Scott Nearing, who wrote a number of radical novels and socialist treatises but who is primarily known for his long-term sustainable living experiment, detailed in the back-to-nature bible *The Good Life*.

3. Sinclair's *The Journal of Arthur Stirling*, a fictional suicide diary of a misunderstood and neglected literary genius, was written on the Raquette River in the Adirondacks. Another work, *Prince Hagan*, explored the wilderness-literature association more directly, casting the poet-protagonist as a Thoreauvian hero who retreats to the rustic discomforts of life in the woods for spiritual and artistic rejuvenation.

4. Although this term is usually associated with the Communist and fellow-traveling writers of the 1930s, it was a term Sinclair used to refer to himself.

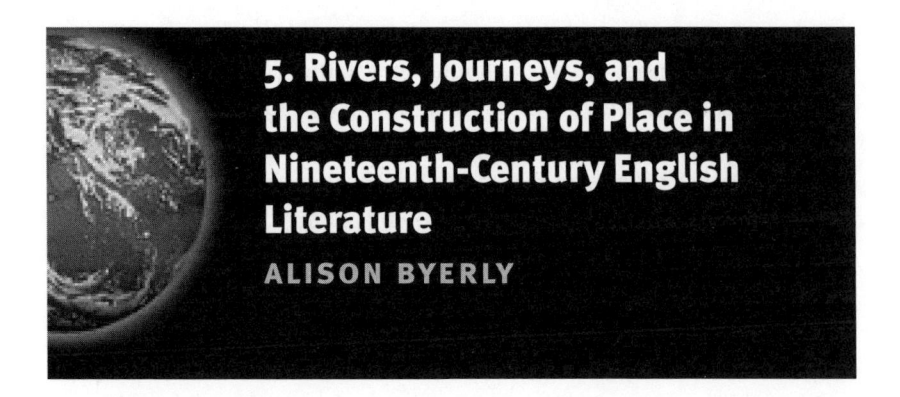

5. Rivers, Journeys, and the Construction of Place in Nineteenth-Century English Literature

ALISON BYERLY

Why do so many of the best Disney World attractions feature boats? There could be many reasons. On a hot summer day, when you have been standing in line for a long time, the splash of a flume ride can be very refreshing. A boat is a welcome variation on simple roller-coaster cars. But there are a number of rides in which the physical aspects of the ride itself — its speed, for example — are not, as with "Space Mountain," say, part of the thrill. These rides are instead essentially scenic: they move you past a series of tableaux. The pleasure comes less from physical movement than from the act of viewing. "Jungle Cruise," "20,000 Leagues Under the Sea," "Pirates of the Caribbean"— these attractions all put viewers in boats to transport them through the scenery and past the animated displays.

The designers of these rides figured out what the Victorians had already discovered a hundred years earlier: that when you want a scene to be not just realistic but illusory, you need to convey a sense of movement in connection with it. Either the scene should move, or the viewer should move in relation to it. The hyperreality of Disney attractions comes from their combination of carefully crafted, moving figures with a careful orchestration of the viewer's own gradual immersion in the scene. In each of the rides mentioned above, the water is not incidental but an integral part of the setting. They aren't just amusement-park rides that happen to occur in boats: they are representations of boat rides in which the viewer watches events that occur along the shore. In this sense, they are the logical extension of entertainment trends begun 180 years earlier, when Victorian audiences packed theaters to watch moving panoramas unfold before their eyes.

When George Eliot, in *Adam Bede* (1850), described Arthur Donni-thorne's shallow inner life through reference to the "panorama of Arthur's thoughts," she was drawing on an image with considerable popular currency. Her readers would have understood the scenic and theatrical nature of Arthur's sense of the world through Eliot's evocation of the contemporary craze for panoramas, enormous moving pictures that depicted places or journeys. The popularity of panoramas among people of all classes surged in the years 1845–1850, and interest in the form was sustained by Albert Smith's immensely popular entertainments, all of which were closely modeled on his initial hit "The Ascent of Mont Blanc" (1852). Smith and his many imitators presented monologues describing arduous journeys, with enormous scenic scrolls supplementing their travel narratives. Smith in particular was praised for his uncanny ability to magically transport his audiences to the scenes he described.

In this essay, I will trace the rise of scenic entertainments and connect them to a parallel development in literature of the period: a focus on descriptions of specific, real places that give primacy to the place itself rather than to thematic issues connected to the narratives in which scenic setpieces are embedded. Paradoxically, the hunger for "armchair travel," for vicarious or simulated travel experiences, seemed to intensify as actual travel became more accessible and expedient. The fact that many people participated in the rise of tourism by taking their "tours" in homes and theaters suggests that, even as the British empire expanded and British travelers covered the globe, some British citizens preferred to enjoy their newfound knowledge of other places in a highly mediated form.

The most popular subjects of panoramas were river journeys that provided a sense of access into foreign lands by allowing the viewer to "travel" down the Nile, the Rhine, or the Mississippi. The river journey became a powerful metaphor for the movement of British culture abroad. Rivers, after all, frequently mark political boundaries; the traveler has equal access to either side but moves inexorably toward a goal that is predetermined. The British fascination with this mode of travel reflects a deepening anxiety about the authority of British culture. It reflects what Mary Louise Pratt has called the "anti-conquest," the "strategies of representation whereby European bourgeois subjects seek to secure their innocence in the same moment as they assert European hegemony" (7).

By examining the representation of particular rivers and journeys in several nineteenth-century novels, I hope to show that rivers became an especially popular subject of representation in Victorian literature because they encapsulate conflicting notions about place and representation of place. They are both "place" and movement, both static scene and mode of travel. For this reason, rivers provide an ideal locus for an examination of what it means to attempt to capture in literature the sense of a place and convey through words on a page the sense of traveling to unknown worlds.

PANORAMAS

It is difficult to overstate the popularity of scenic panoramas in mid-nineteenth-century London and in many ways equally difficult to explain that phenomenon. In the 1840s and 1850s, there were often dozens of panorama-type scenic exhibitions in London at any one time. There were several exhibition spaces devoted exclusively to panoramas, most notably the Panorama in the Strand, which opened in 1802 and lasted until 1831, and the Panorama in Leicester Square operated by John and Robert Burford from 1823 to 1861. These spaces were designed to exhibit 360-degree scenes which the spectator viewed from a central point and also walked around to examine closely.

The alternative format for panorama viewing was more closely linked to theatrical productions. Panoramas painted on linear canvas that could be unrolled slowly while viewed from a stationary seat were also extremely popular and were usually presented in conjunction with music, commentary, or some combination of the two. Albert Smith's "Ascent of Mont Blanc" and his second major monologue program, "Journey on the Overland Mail," were typical of this genre, in which a traveler-showman provided a description of his journey to the sights being viewed behind him. A review of one such display, reprinted in "An Illustrated Description of the Diorama of the Ganges" (1850), compared it to Smith's performances, stating that "the mode of exhibition adopted is the same as that of the overland journey, the canvas being in continual motion, and seen through a circular opening. . . . In other like exhibitions, we have particular spots selected; but here we have the whole length of the view as it would really be seen if passing up the river" (John Johnson Collection of

Printed Ephemera [JJ Coll]). These displays seem generally to have aimed for a close to real-time pace of presentation that allowed the viewer to visually travel the landscape along with the lecturer.

The presence of a lecturer as a kind of tour guide was an indispensable component of the most successful panoramas. The authenticity of the representation seemed to be validated by the presence of an eyewitness who could bear testimony to the fact that the picture conveyed what it was really like. John Banvard's famous panorama of the Mississippi was able to capitalize on this sense of authenticity because it was presented by the painter, Banvard himself. Dickens said of this panorama, "It may be well to say what the panorama is *not*." He goes on to enumerate its aesthetic deficiencies before commenting:

> But it is a picture three miles long, which occupies two hours in its passage before the audience. It is a picture of one of the greatest streams in the known world, whose course it follows for upwards of three thousand miles. It is a picture irresistibly impressing the spectator with a conviction of its plain and simple truthfulness. . . . It is an easy means of travelling, night and day, without any inconvenience from climate, steamboat company, or fatigue . . . and seeing every town and settlement upon the river's banks. These three miles of canvas have been painted by one man, and there he is, present, pointing out what he deems most worthy of notice. This is history. (Oettermann 329)

The assumption that panoramas were intended to be regarded as a substitute for real travel experience is borne out by both the publicity created by panorama exhibitors and the reviewers who commented on these exhibitions. A scenic view of a Swiss waterfall incorporating "the various changes of the day" is said by an advertising handbill to produce so "enchanting" an effect that spectators "cannot help fancying themselves imperceptibly transported into the very interior of the province of Switzerland; and that they are viewing in reality, the very identical spot, on which their admiration is so intensely fixed" (JJ Coll). In other words, seeing is the next best thing to being there. The famous *Panorama of London by Night*, exhibited in the Colosseum after interest in the *Grand Panorama of London* had waned, is given this testimonial in a souvenir guide to the reopened Colosseum: "We confidently state, that it is next to impossible, that any person can lean over the balustrade for five or six minutes, and mark the fleecy clouds sailing steadily along, lighted as they come within the influence of the halo-encircled moon . . . [and] recall themselves immediately to the conviction that the scene before them is nothing but an illusion" (22).

A reviewer in *Blackwood's Magazine* struck a typically facetious note: "Panoramas are among the happiest contrivances for saving time and expense in this age of contrivances. What cost a couple of hundred pounds and half a year a century ago, now costs a shilling and a quarter of an hour" (Oettermann 113). But the absurdity of this premise is less evident in the promotional literature for these exhibits. An advertisement for "Mr. Washington Friend's Grand Tour of Five Thousand Miles in Canada and the United States of America" dryly notes that travel to Canada and the United States "is expensive, requires time, involves the chances of shipwreck . . . whereas by visiting MR. FRIEND, you are placed at once on the other side of the Atlantic by payment of One Shilling." The capacity of this kind of constructed experience to eliminate danger and overcome the boundaries of space and time is echoed in a twentieth-century description of a theme-park ride. Disney publicists describe the "Jungle Cruise" as "a favorite attraction among arm-chair travellers" because "it compacts into ten minutes the highlights, mystique, fun and excitement of an adventure that could only be duplicated through weeks on safari. Best of all, it has none of the mosquitoes, monsoons, and other misadventures of the 'not always so great' outdoors" (Wilson 161). The fact that real safaris are referred to as mere duplicates of the simulated jungle cruise suggests that the facsimile has become the standard against which the real experience can be judged (and, presumably, found wanting). Although jokes about how cheap and easy such a journey could be acknowledge the difference between a real trip and armchair travel, they also indicate that at some level viewers liked to conceive of these shows as experiences rather than exhibitions.

The guidebook for "Mr. Friend's" exhibition suggests that this mode of travel has practical applicability, too, for the "intending emigrant" to Canada or the United States, who will receive "a complete account of the principal cities, rivers, and lakes of this wonderful continent" as well as learn "the cheapest and best mode of getting there." Similar educational motives might have been expected to encourage spectators to see the "Moving Panorama of a Voyage to Australia, with descriptive lecture by Mr. Prout," advertised in a handbill of 1853 (JJ Coll). A Leicester Square panorama was even more explicit about this agenda in its advertisement: "COLONIZATION! THE EMIGRATION PANORAMA, NEW ZEALAND. If you are de-

sirous of escaping the miseries of this country, and improving your condition in life, SEE THIS PANORAMA! With Mr. Brees' information, you will be
better acquainted with the subject than those who have been to the
Colonies." Adding a further twist to the class-based appeal of this handbill, the ad continues, "To the NOBILITY & GENTRY who unfortunately cannot leave England the Panorama affords a perfect exposition of Colonial
Life" (Museum of London Collection [ML] DPA1). By presenting the prospect of emigration as a privilege denied those unfortunate enough to be
tied to England by hereditary land ownership, the exhibitors intensify the
viewer's identification of this panorama with escape from English society
and in particular its class stratification.

The implied parallel between real emigration and the imaginary journey taken by way of the panorama suggests that the marketers of these exhibitions understood the complex, even contradictory, reasons for their
appeal. They offered a mode of exploration that did not require the incon-
venience, even danger, of real travel. The correlation between this kind of
imaginative possession of a foreign place and the literal colonization of
other parts of the world is implicit in the description of a panorama of the
Rhine from 1853. This panorama presented a tour from Dover to Naples,
or Naples to Dover, alternating with each performance as the scene was
unscrolled and then reversed. The "Descriptive Book of the Tour of Europe"
that accompanied the exhibition of this "immense Moving Diorama"
makes an explicit connection between the work of the artist and the work
of European culture: "The telegraph, the rail-way, and the Steam-Boat
have been making great changes and doing their utmost to bring about a
Brotherhood of Nations; — may not also the Pencil of the Artist claim its
share of this great work; here we have the Exploration of a Continent
showing in pictorial form the energies of past ages and in the present civilized and intellectual world" (51).

The most successful panorama exhibitions tried to create an authentic
environment around the display of the panorama itself. Albert Smith was
a master at manufacturing ambience that reinforced his audience's sense
of entering a foreign land. For "The Ascent of Mont Blanc" (1852–1856),
Smith converted the Egyptian Hall into a Swiss scene that included a full-
scale chalet exterior; a pool of water surrounded by rocks and plants and
containing live fish; miscellaneous baskets, knapsacks, and other items
strewn picturesquely about the hall; and vines and creepers hanging from
the rafters. In his second season, Smith added ten Saint Bernards, which

would trot about the auditorium delivering packets of chocolate to children. A subsequent show, "Mont Blanc to China," required audiences to enter through an oriental foyer lined with souvenirs for sale, such as willow-pattern plates with Smith's picture, and replaced the chalet with a Chinese pagoda (Altick 475–477). When repair work on the dome of Saint Paul's in 1821 provided the access for an artist to make sketches he converted into a panorama of London, the 360-degree panorama was displayed in a rotunda built for the purpose that included real scaffolding constructed in front of the painting, presumably to enhance the illusion that the viewer was standing on the dome of the cathedral (141–145).

Most panoramas offered for purchase a guide to the exhibition, often written in the form of a guidebook, as if the reader were being led through a tour of the actual location. This format neatly elides the difference between being a real traveler and being the potential traveler imagined by a guidebook. In the "Illustrated Description of the Diorama of the Ganges," for example, the author offers to conduct "the stay-at-home traveller" to the places "where every enterprising traveller should go" (Altick 4). The scenes visited by the person who describes them become identical to the scenes unfolded to the viewer. "On leaving Calcutta to proceed up the country, the traveller may . . . travel by dark to Benares, a distance of 480 miles. . . . The traveller is now supposed to land from his boats . . . at sunset, to enjoy a stroll on its banks. . . . In the present instance he joins a party of pilgrims proceeding towards Benares . . ." (27). The party of pilgrims is depicted resting under a banyan tree, a scene singled out by a reviewer from *King's College Magazine* as particularly realistic: "we almost fancied we were enjoying the quiet repose of the place" (quoted in "An Illustrated Description of the Diorama of the Ganges").

Ali Behdad has suggested that the literary form of the "travelogue" was replaced in mid-nineteenth-century orientalist writing by a different form of travel writing, the "tourist guide." What distinguishes the two genres, he argues, is the "situation of the speaking subject" (39). Travelogues emphasize the role of the author-explorer, whose personal experiences provide "discursive justification and legitimization" (40). Tourist guides, on the other hand, often fail to identify their author at all, appearing instead under the aegis of an editor or publisher. When they do name an author, they provide little personal information about him or her. The "disappearance of the author" changes the text's relation to the reader. The travelogue "produces its first-person subject ('I') as the site of an act of interpretation — 'making sense' of the orient — and as someone who is author-ized to *make* meaning. The centrality and discursive authority of the first-person subject in turn imply exclusion, separating the orientalist [traveler] from the reader, whose desire for exoticism can be satisfied only as a dis-placement of or identification with the enunciative subject's desire" (41).

The tourist guide, however, "constructs the reading subject as a *poten-tial traveller* and presupposes the realization of its addressee's desire" to travel. The "discourse of tourism" manifests an "obsessive desire to in-clude, to incorporate every kind of traveller in its implied domain" (41).

The panorama descriptions quoted above seem to construct this sort of touristic relation between text and reader. Their goal is not to convey an author's unique experience to a reader who has not had, and most likely never will have, the opportunity to experience the places described. In-stead, they work on the assumption that the experience they describe is common to both author and reader. They treat the journey and the spec-tator's viewing of the journey as if they were identical processes. The reader becomes the traveler, the tourist who visits the scene. The reader thus partakes of the expertise of the "real" traveler. This may explain why so many of the advertisements for panoramas either allude to reasons why the viewer might be planning to visit the place described or maintain the polite fiction that many viewers have probably seen these sights them-selves and will be in a position to confirm their accuracy.

This particular rhetorical strategy resembles a narrative strategy com-mon to nineteenth-century novels, which may themselves have been influenced by the format of both real guidebooks and exhibition catalogs. Many novels of the period portray panoramic vistas not, as one might ex-pect, by describing a major character's response to them but by describing the typical response that might be felt by any traveler or viewer who hap-pened to stumble on the scene. While a stronger thematic point could per-haps be made by showing the scene's effect on a particular character, au-thors chose instead to present a generalized response that allows viewers to imaginatively substitute themselves for the anonymous viewer.

George Eliot's *Adam Bede*, for example, introduces an important scene by describing at length the way it appeared to "a traveller" who rides up on horseback and looks down on the town green below. He looks across at the "picture," with its undulating hills, below which "the eye rested on a more advanced line of hanging woods," beyond which "our traveller" saw a "foreground which was just as lovely" (17). While this sort of picturesque description is not new, what is noteworthy is the description's reliance on the impressions of the anonymous traveler. The scene could as easily have been described from Adam's point of view or that of any other character. But Eliot wants to evoke an objective, almost touristic response that mimics what the readers might see if they actually traveled to this spot.

Mary Louise Pratt has noted that "promontory descriptions" like the passage cited above are common in many kinds of nineteenth-century writing and in exploration literature function as ways of rendering "momentously significant, what is, especially from a narrative point of view, practically a non-event": the "discovery" of a scene that is new to the viewer but not, of course, unknown to others (202). The "act of discovery" consists of "a purely passive experience — that of seeing" (204). Eliot's inclusion of an anonymous traveler seems designed to evoke a sense of discovery in relation to a scene that would have been familiar to characters already present in the novel; the point is not simply to describe what the place is like but what the place seems like to someone discovering it for the first time. Pratt calls this sort of panoramic perspective the "monarch-of-all-I-survey" genre (201), a phrase that encapsulates the political dynamic inscribed by the relationship between viewer and scene.

Hardy's *Mayor of Casterbridge* begins with a description of what "a casual observer"(35) might have noticed about two figures walking along a country road. Rather than specifying the relationship between them, Hardy has us follow the deductions of the imaginary spectator. Again, this mechanism seems intended to distance us from the protagonists and view them as part of a scene to be visually deconstructed. Hardy begins his description of the Vale of Blackmoor in *Tess of the D'Urbervilles* by noting that it is "an engirdled and secluded region, for the most part untrodden as yet by tourist or landscape-painter," yet he goes on to present the view as it might appear to either genre of spectator:

> The traveller from the coast, who, after plodding northward for a score of miles over calcareous downs and corn-lands, suddenly reaches the verge of one of these escarpments, is surprised and delighted to behold, extended like a map beneath him, a country differing absolutely from that which he has passed through. . . . The atmosphere beneath is langorous, and is so tinged with azure that what artists call the middle dis-

tance partakes also of that hue, while the horizon beyond is the deepest ultramarine. (39)

One function of the figure of the traveler may be to add a time dimension to an otherwise static picture. By situating this scene in the context of the journey that preceded it, Hardy emphasizes the movement of the viewing figure, who pauses to look at a scene that is only one stop on his journey.

Even when Hardy is presenting the boy Jude's view of Christminster, he removes the personal perspective from the scene, emphasizing the visual qualities of a sunset landscape that transforms itself like a magic lantern show:

> Some way within the limits of the stretch of landscape, points of light like the topaz gleamed. The air increased in transparency with the lapse of minutes, till the topaz points showed themselves to be the vanes, windows, wet roof slates, and other shining spots upon the spires, domes, freestone-work, and varied outlines that were faintly revealed. It was Christminster, unquestionably; either directly seen, or miraged in the peculiar atmosphere.
>
> The spectator gazed on and on . . . the vague city became veiled in mist. Turning to the west, he saw that the sun had disappeared. The foreground of the scene had grown funereally dark, and near objects put on the hues and shapes of chimeras. (41)

Hardy is often noted for the visual, even cinematic quality of his descriptions of landscape. Natural scenes are presented from a panoramic perspective that would be impossible for a single individual to achieve under normal circumstances, as when Hardy notes that to birds soaring overhead, "Casterbridge must have appeared on this fine evening as a mosaic-work of subdued reds, browns, greys, and crystals, held together by a rectangular frame of deep green" (59). Clearly, Hardy is not attempting to place us inside the perspective of a character. Instead, he wants us to take a more global perspective.

RIVERS

Rivers were among the most popular subjects of representation for moving panoramas, for obvious reasons. While circular panoramas often represented famous cities — Paris, Rome, Pompeii, Edinburgh, Calcutta, Mi-

lan, Florence, Bombay, Cairo, and Constantinople were all popular subjects — as seen from a particular vantage point, moving panoramas generally adopted the fiction of some sort of journey, by coach, railway, or river,
to organize the perspective presented. River scenes were especially ap-
pealing, perhaps because the existence of towns along major waterways
provided more alternation between pastoral and human interest than
might be found on a typical road route. More important, the presence of
the river itself provided a sense of connection between the various scenes.
A publicity pamphlet for Burford's 1843 panorama of the Rhine praises it
for "embracing a more comprehensive coup d'oeil," as the "enchanting
views" along the banks "develop themselves and arrest the imagination in
one perpetual and ever changing chain of beauty and grandeur" (ML A2).

The Rhine, like the Mississippi, the Nile, and other large rivers, was frequently represented and was associated with a romantic, picturesque,
Grand-Touristic sense of Europe that, as we will see, contrasts sharply
with the associations generated by representations, literary and artistic,
of the Thames. Mr. Charles Marshall's Grand Tour of Europe included,
among other "imagerial visits" in this moving diorama, an "excursion
down the picturesque Rhine — and home" (JJ Coll D3). The second part
of that journey is an important one, as the return to home is what defines
the exotic otherness of the place one has visited. Marshall's tour consisted
of three canvases depicting "the three routes an English tourist would
most likely follow," as Altick notes: "the Thames to Constantinople by way
of Berlin and Budapest, Rome to Mont Blanc, and the Rhine from Bingen
to Cologne" (461). Clearly, river journeys were among the most popular
ways to organize a tour of European cities and landscape.

The Rhine initially represents a picturesque natural beauty that un-
folds itself before the educated traveler. But in later depictions, a journey
up the Rhine becomes a touristic cliché. Thackeray satirizes the English
family abroad in his novella *The Kickleburys on the Rhine*, while Trollope
asks rhetorically, "where is the man who can tell his wife and daughters
that it is quite unnecessary that they should go up the Rhine?" (102).
George Eliot's 1860 novel *The Mill on the Floss* alludes nostalgically to the
Rhine's emblematic status as the most romantic of rivers, comparing it to
the less picturesque Rhone:

Journeying down the Rhone on a summer's day, you have perhaps felt
the sunshine made dreary by those ruined villages which stud the

banks . . . telling how the swift river once rose, like an angry, destroying god, sweeping down the generations whose breath is in their nostrils, and making their dwellings a desolation. Strange contrast, you may have thought, between the effect produced on us by these dismal remnants of commonplace houses . . . and the effect produced by those ruins on the castled Rhine, which have crumbled and mellowed into such harmony with the green and rocky steeps . . . that was a day of romance! . . . That was a time of colour, when the sunlight fell on glancing steel and floating banners. Therefore it is that these Rhine castles thrill me with a sense of poetry: they belong to the grand historic life of humanity, and raise up for me the vision of an epoch. But these dead-tinted, hollow-eyed, angular skeletons of villages on the Rhone oppress me with the feeling that human life . . . is a narrow, grovelling existence, which even calamity does not elevate. (237–238)

Eliot's description characteristically mingles her own response with her readers', noting the human tendency to prefer the ideal to the real. But she goes on to compare this response to the way she imagines her readers might feel about "watching this old-fashioned family life on the banks of the Floss" (238), a phrase that conflates the stream of her narrative with the river at the center of the novel. She admits that the lives she portrays are narrow and ordinary but insists on the importance of understanding them nevertheless. Eliot's metaphoric association of a reader's journey through her book with a traveler's voyage down a famous river suggests that she recognizes that the familiar touristic perspective of the outsider encourages one to passively critique the text passing before one's eyes rather than emotionally engage it. Her goal is to overcome this distant attitude and force her readers to "feel . . . [the] sense of oppressive narrowness" (30) that shapes the lives of her characters.

Eliot may have been influenced by a passage in Ruskin's *Modern Painters* describing the valley of the Rhone with a similar emphasis on the contrast between idealism and realism. Ruskin talks about the disillusionment travelers may feel when they get closer to the picturesque scene they admire.

The traveller on his happy journey, as his foot springs from the deep turf and strikes the pebbles gaily . . . sees with a glance of delight the clusters of nut-brown cottages. . . . Here, it may well seem to him, if there be sometimes hardship, there must be at least innocence and peace, and fellowship of the human soul with nature. It is not so. . . . Enter the street of one of those villages, and you will find it foul with that gloomy foulness that is suffered only by torpor, or by anguish of soul. (312)

For these cottagers, Ruskin claims, there is "neither hope nor passion of spirit" (314). He goes on to note the irony of theatrical representations that convert such squalor into rustic charm. He might be describing Albert Smith's Alpine cottage when he writes:

Is it not strange to reflect, that hardly an evening passes in London or Paris but one of those cottages is painted for the better amusement of the fair and idle, and shaded with pasteboard pines by the scene-shifter; and that good and kind people, — poetically minded — delight themselves by imagining the happy life led by peasants who dwell by Alpine fountains. . . . If all the gold that has gone forth to paint the simulacra of the cottages, and to put new songs in the mouths of the simulacra of the peasants, had gone to brighten the existent cottages . . . it might, in the end, have turned out better so, not only for the peasants, but even for the audience. (315)

Ruskin's explicit linkage of the tourist's perspective with the theatergoer's perspective reinforces the contention that the distanced, idealized view of natural and human scenes embodied in the aesthetic of the panorama was deeply embedded in a variety of cultural discourses.

Eliot's and Ruskin's revolt against the picturesque idealization of the river as a conduit to culture is evident in the changing view of the Thames in the nineteenth century. Once, the great London river had combined beauty and commerce to form a powerful symbol of the British empire; by the mid-nineteenth century, the Thames came to stand for the pollution, deprivation, and misery of urban life. In literature as well as art, the river is symbolic of a dark undercurrent that threatens the tranquil surface of Victorian society. Dickens, for example, links the Thames with crime in *Great Expectations* and with suicide in *Our Mutual Friend*. In *David Copperfield*, an extended description of the filth and debris in the Thames ends with the prostitute Martha standing by "the polluted stream," looking "as if she were a part of the refuse it had cast out, and left to corruption and decay" (680). Dickens conveys the horror of urban poverty by emphasizing the inescapability of its products: what the culture attempts to dispose of will always float to the surface again.

Its critical role in the development of British trade and industry made the Thames a powerful symbol of British wealth and political power. The river had long occupied a privileged place in British poetry, where it developed a set of metaphoric and mythic associations that made it a rich subject for a variety of poets, including Spenser, Pope, Gray, Thomson, and Peacock. In the early nineteenth century, it also became a staple of British landscape painting, generating some of the best-known works of Turner, Constable, and lesser painters. Andrew Hemingway has shown that "the economic and social functions of waterways, and the sheer volume of discourses about them . . . made rivers a crucial pictorial theme" (291). In addition to depicting the river's natural beauty, some works also represented the leisure and economic activities that took place along its banks.

If one turns from landscape painting to genre painting, the Thames plays an important cultural role in representations of life in London. Paintings like G. F. Watts's *Found Drowned* and Luke Fildes's *Found Dead on the Embankment* reflect a more sinister side of the Thames, in which it becomes the repository of the human detritus of urban life. Martin Meisel has noted that in the paintings, literature, and theater of the period, there is a recurrent iconographic image involving "the concatenation of the stone arch, the river, the night, and the fallen woman contemplating or committing suicide" (138). In these representations, the Thames becomes a sewer in which people dispose of themselves or others.

This image of the Thames was undoubtedly influenced by controversies about pollution of the river that began in the 1820s and peaked in the 1850s and 1860s. The increased availability of indoor plumbing in and around London in the early to middle part of the century contributed to a dramatic increase in the amount of waste flowing into the river, and the cholera epidemics of the 1840s and 1850s intensified public sanitation concerns. The duke of Newcastle warned in 1857 that "the river . . . was like a vast sewer, and unless something was done before long to purify it, it would engender some frightful plague" (Luckin 17). A member of the Parliament claimed that "the noblest of rivers . . . had been turned into a cesspool" (Luckin 18). Because the worst of the pollution derived from towns upriver, beyond the jurisdiction of metropolitan authorities, the controversy became a test of how large-scale environmental problems could be handled. Bill Luckin's analysis of reports and press commentary on the issue throughout the century reveals a "movement from a sense of impending calamity to a conviction that river pollution was manageable" (29). But the image of the Thames was forever changed. No longer a shining symbol of British commerce and culture, it became a mirror of public health, reflecting generalized concerns about pollution and disease that were raised by industrial development throughout the nineteenth century.

In Dickens's novels, the Thames also becomes a mirror of psychic health, functioning at times as a scene of pleasant recreation and at others as a living embodiment of an uneasy conscience. In *Great Expectations*, Pip, protecting the convict who has been his benefactor, uses the river in an attempt to help the criminal escape. Pip notes that while his friend Herbert took comfort from the knowledge that the river "was flowing, with everything it bore, toward Clara," his beloved, he himself "thought with dread that it was flowing towards Magwitch, and that any black mark on its surface might be his pursuers, going swiftly, silently, and surely, to take him" (381). The inescapable movement of the river makes it emblematic of the workings of an inevitable fate.

In *Our Mutual Friend*, the river provides a horrifying livelihood for Lizzie Hexam's father, who retrieves drowned corpses for what he can scavenge from their bodies. The novel begins by describing the boat used for the purpose, which was "allied to the bottom of the river rather than the surface, by reason of the slime and ooze with which it was covered, and its sodden state" (1). The boat takes on the characteristics of a corpse itself, as if it might sink at any time. The sense of defilement that Lizzie feels as a result of her participation in this grim work amazes her father, who, noting her reluctance to sit near a corpse in the boat, reproaches her, "As if it wasn't your living! As if it wasn't meat and drink to you!" (1). His attitude encapsulates the dual nature of the activity: on the one hand, it depends on the danger and despair of urban life, which ensure that there will always be victims to be retrieved; on the other hand, it is a living, an economic activity that to him is no different from the other livelihoods pursued on the river. He represents the furthest extreme of capitalist enterprise, an entrepreneur who feeds on the waste discarded by the system.

For better or worse, however, the Thames *was* England — more particularly, was London — and continued to be a source of pride to the English. An 1849 guidebook, *The Tour of the Thames; or, the Sights and Songs of the King of Rivers*, describes it as "broad, bright, and beautiful" and begins its account by suggesting that touring the Thames was preferable to touring abroad:

Never was there such a summer on this side of the Tropics. . . . London a vast cauldron — the few people left in its habitable parts resembling stewed fish. . . .

At length, in a pause of the conversation, someone asked where somebody else was going, for the dog-days . . . every Englishman of the party had been everywhere already — Cairo, Constantinople, Calcutta, Cape Horn. . . . There was not a corner of the world, where they had not drunk tea, smoked cigars, anathematized the country, the climate, the constitution.

At last an . . . old personage, with a nondescript visage . . . asked, Had any one at table seen the Thames?

I determined to *see* the Thames. (3, 5)

Since we can assume the anonymous author had certainly seen at least parts of the river before, his emphasis suggests that he is drawing a contrast between the pseudo-travel experiences of his companions, who have gone abroad but taken their home with them, and his own effort to understand something about his home by seeing it with new eyes, essentially becoming a tourist in his own backyard. The ordinary old gentleman who raises the question seems to represent the British heritage they have all ignored. The fact that these Londoners are "stewing" in a cauldron of fish suggests that they are more a part of this world than they realize, and the remedy for these dog days may be to swim upstream.

In an essay describing an evening spent with the Thames police, Dickens makes a similar comparison between England and more exciting destinations. "You'll have seen a good many rivers, too, I dare say?" a companion asks, and he responds: "Truly . . . when I come to think of it, not a few. From the Niagara, downward to the mountain rivers of Italy, which are like the national spirit — very tame, or chafing suddenly and bursting bounds. . . . The Moselle, and the Rhine, and the Rhone; and the Seine, and the Saone; and the St. Lawrence, Mississippi, and Ohio; and the Tiber, the Po, and the Arno" (*Dickens' Dictionary* 527).

Dickens's clichéd catalog is as ridiculous as the assumption that traveling down each river could give him special insight into the "national spirit" of each country. Yet that is precisely how these river journeys were regarded: as a form of travel that provided a window on a land the traveler would pass through but not touch. Like the panoramas that imitated them, rivers provided an illusion of access to a moving landscape that always stayed on the other side of the window.

Not only does real travel now far surpass Victorian possibilities, the technology of "virtual travel" has expanded as well. Videotaped excursions (such as *America by Rail* and *3-D Safari*) promise a vicarious experience of places both familiar and exotic. Web sites for popular tourist destinations feature interactive representations that allow one to "walk" down a canyon ledge in Zion National Park or access real-time camera views of the ski slopes at Sugarloaf, Maine. At a time when such technology is growing exponentially, it is important to consider how the availability of what Baudrillard calls the "ironic simulacrum" affects our understanding of the world. It seems possible that the creation of such vivid illusions could ultimately diminish, rather than enhance, the value of the places they represent.

The Victorians enjoyed experimenting with the idea of art so realistic it could move beyond the realm of picture and become a kind of world. The classic narrative strategies of nineteenth-century fiction show the same "world-making" impulse, to use Nelson Goodman's term. Just as novelists were including direct addresses to their readers in an attempt to pull them into the text, artists and performers were trying to create an all-encompassing illusion for the audience to enter. But once there, the spectators were encouraged to remain passive. Travelers on a boat, like "travelers" at a panorama, would feel the world passing around them, and the movement itself would reinforce the sense that this was a direct encounter with reality. But in fact these were highly mediated encounters, in which the spectator was free at any time to exit the holodeck and return to duty. In creating these kinds of virtual travel experiences, the Victorians initiated the idea of the "vacation," an activity that is conceived of as precisely that: a vacating or emptying out of one's familiar life and the assumption of an entirely different one. The emphasis is less on what you discover than on what you have left behind. You are expected to admire not the scene before you but the success with which it carries you away.

In this respect, the Colosseum that provided a "Grand Tour of Europe" was not very different from the Magic Kingdom that takes you to Main Street, U.S.A. Leicester Square, home of the Burfords' Panorama and several competitors, was once the center of the panorama craze. Today, it features enormous IMAX theaters. One could say that entertainment has changed very little in the last 150 years; only the technology has advanced. The Victorians would have been astounded at the idea of sending a man to the moon; they might have been even more excited, however, at the prospect of going to Disney World.

PART TWO

Expanding the Subject in Ecocriticism

6. Locating the Uranium Mine

Place, Multiethnicity, and Environmental Justice in Leslie Marmon Silko's *Ceremony*

JAMES TARTER

*He had been so close to it, caught up in it for so long that its
simplicity struck deep inside his chest: Trinity Site, where
they exploded the first atomic bomb, was only three hundred
miles to the southeast, at White Sands. And the top-secret
laboratories where the bomb had been created were deep in
the Jemez Mountains, on land the Government took from
Cochiti Pueblo: Los Alamos, only a hundred miles northeast
of him now, still surrounded by high electric fences and the
ponderosa pine and tawny sandrock of the Jemez mountain
canyon where the shrine of the twin mountain lions had
always been. There was no end to it; it knew no boundaries;
and he had arrived at the point of convergence where the fate
of all living things, and even the earth, had been laid. From
the jungles of his dreaming he recognized why the Japanese
voices had merged with Laguna voices, with Josiah's voice
and Rocky's voice; the lines of cultures and worlds were
drawn in flat dark lines on fine light sand, converging in the
middle of witchery's final ceremonial sand painting. From
that time on, human beings were one clan again, united by
the fate the destroyers planned for all of them, for all living
things; united by a circle of death that devoured people in
cities twelve thousand miles away, victims who had never
known these mesas, who had never seen the delicate colors of
the rocks which boiled up their slaughter.*

*He walked to the mine shaft slowly, and the feeling
became overwhelming: the pattern of the ceremony was
completed there. He knelt and found an ore rock. The gray*

> stone was streaked with powdery yellow uranium, bright and
> alive as pollen; veins of sooty black formed lines with the
> yellow, making mountain ranges and rivers across the stone.
> But they had taken these beautiful rocks from deep within
> earth and they had laid them in a monstrous design,
> realizing destruction on a scale only they could have
> dreamed. He cried the relief he felt at finally seeing the
> pattern, the way all the stories fit together — the old stories,
> the war stories, their stories — to become the story that was
> still being told.
> — Leslie Marmon Silko, Ceremony

This remarkable turning point in Leslie Marmon Silko's 1977 novel *Ceremony* is my focus in this essay. Although it has been clear for more than half the novel that Tayo, the protagonist, has been participating in a specifically Laguna Pueblo healing ceremony, only in this recognition scene near the end of the book is the ceremony coming near to completion — now that he is standing amid the radioactive tailings of an abandoned uranium mine on the edge of the reservation. This mine is a figure for the biggest open-pit uranium mine in North America, the now-abandoned Jackpile-Paguate mine on the Laguna Pueblo reservation in New Mexico. And as Tayo sees in this passage, the mine is also a crucial component of larger systems. The scene at the mine connects Tayo with a Laguna-specific sense of place, but that sense quickly expands to include a multiethnic dimension that in turn provides the ground for the articulation of a demand for environmental justice.[1]

My purpose in this essay is to argue that *Ceremony* provides a model of a sophisticated, simultaneous attention to environmental and multiethnic issues that needs to come to the fore in contemporary ecocriticism. Instead of isolating the issues of place, ethnicity, and justice, Silko's novel consistently constructs environmental justice as emerging from responsibility to places as sites of culture. For Silko, a commitment to place, or as she puts it, a "belonging with" place (117), provides a way at least to articulate, manage, and negotiate — but not exactly overcome — cultural differences such as race and ethnicity. Although Silko is intensely interested in examining the "radioactive colonization" of native people in North America, her novel avoids a narrow parochialism by depicting specific places as grounds for intercultural relationality. Only when Tayo regains his sense of place

— through the Laguna stories — is he able to properly envision his connections with others. More than an abstract, theoretical commentary on place and its dialectical relationship with multiethnicity and environmental justice coalitions could ever do, *Ceremony* shows how stories function to interrelate people and place, how places function as forms for multiethnic relationships, and how commitment to place becomes an exigency that demands environmental justice.

"THE COMMUNICATION DEVICE": STORIES AND PLACE IN *CEREMONY*

The stories and the land are about the same thing; perhaps we can best characterize this relation by saying that the stories are the communication device of the land and the people.
—*Paula Gunn Allen,*
    "The Feminine Landscape of Leslie Marmon Silko's *Ceremony*"

At the outset of *Ceremony*, Tayo is an alienated, shell-shocked Laguna Pueblo veteran who has never truly been integrated into the community (he is of mixed blood and was considered illegitimate) and who has been badly traumatized by his participation in World War II's bloody Pacific theater. In order to regain his mental and physical health, he learns after he returns to Laguna that he must go through a healing ceremony, a process that forms the plot of the novel and which ultimately does succeed in curing him. To simplify, the ceremony functions to relocate and reintegrate him within the Laguna Pueblo community. The ceremony, which shows repeatedly that the Laguna community does not only include human beings, involves a set of steps that carefully develop his relationships with many of the nonhuman members of the community. It is rich with specific references to Laguna culture and its symbolic meanings, many of which are associated with specific plants, animals, and places in the landscape of the Laguna Pueblo reservation in New Mexico.[2]

In this respect, there is a crucial difference between Silko's sense of place and a Western environmentalist's likely understanding of the land. For Silko, the community of the land is not an abstract concept (as it is, for example, in Leopold's concept of "the land"), nor is it simply conceived of as a backdrop for human or other action (the "environment").[3] It is a *particular* place, the land in and around Laguna, with detailed relationships between actors in the community within a specific bioregion that has its own unique geophysical features. It is a whole culture that includes history and the largely ahistorical, essentialized concept that Westerners call nature or the environment.

To develop such complexity takes time; it requires history and long-term tenure on the land.[4] Laguna culture has developed intricate meanings tied to specific plants, animals, and geographical features like water holes, knobs of rock, or *Tse'pi'na*, Mount Taylor, the Old Woman in Clouds, around which Tayo's quest revolves. Not long after Tayo returns to Laguna at the beginning of the novel, the medicine man Ku'oosh comes to see him. At first Tayo struggles to understand what the old man is talking about. But then, in this passage, something changes:

> Ku'oosh . . . spoke softly, using the old dialect full of sentences that were involuted with explanations of their own origins, as if nothing the old man said were his own but all had been said before and he was only there to repeat it. Tayo had to strain to catch the meaning, dense with place names he had never heard. His language was childish, interspersed with English words, and he could feel shame tightening in his throat; but then he heard the old man describe the cave, a deep lava cave northeast of Laguna where bats flew out on summer evenings. He pushed himself up against the pillows and felt the iron bed frame against his back. He knew this cave. (34–35)

The lost, deracinated Tayo finds a way to begin to understand Ku'oosh through a common experience with this one place. Mention of the cave touches off a series of memories of its snakes, bats, and crickets and of Tayo's childhood play there with his brother. At last he can understand Ku'oosh: "He nodded to the old man because he knew this place. People said back in the old days they took the scalps and threw them down there. Tayo knew what the old man had come for" (35). Tayo's personal history with this particular place begins to reconnect him with Laguna culture, but it also begins to connect him, perhaps uncomfortably, with an extensive history invoked by the reference to the "old days" of scalping in the Indian wars. As Silko asserts in her book of essays, *Yellow Woman and a Beauty of the Spirit*:

> location, or place, nearly always plays a central role in the Pueblo oral narratives. Indeed, stories are most frequently recalled as people are

passing by a specific geographical feature or the exact location where a story took place. The precise date of the incident often is less important than the place or location of the happening. "Long, long ago," "a long time ago," "not too long ago," and "recently" are usually how stories are classified in terms of time. But the places where the stories occur are precisely located, and prominent geographical details recalled, even if the landscape is well known to listeners, often because the turning point in the narrative involved a peculiarity of the special quality of a rock or tree or plant found only at the place. (33)

In *Ceremony*, the first conversation Tayo has with the Navajo medicine man Betonie emphasizes the importance of a similarly historical relationship to the place where he lives:

"People ask me why I live here," [Betonie] said, in good English. . . . "They keep us on the north side of the railroad tracks, next to the river and their dump. Where none of them want to live." He laughed. "They don't understand. We know these hills, and we are comfortable here." There was something about the way the old man said the word "comfortable." It had a different meaning — not the comfort of big houses or rich food or even clean streets, but the comfort of *belonging with* the land, and the peace of being with these hills. (117, emphasis added)

Betonie is teaching Tayo about a sense of belonging *with* that is far different from property ownership and more sophisticated than the familiar reversal of property ownership (as in the popular bumper sticker quoting Chief Seattle, "The land does not belong to the people / the people belong to the land"). The difference is in the use of *with*: it is a "mutual appropriation," as N. Scott Momaday has it, a belonging *with* that involves a co-equal relationality between person and place. Such a "comfortable" relationship, Betonie implies here, takes a long time to develop; as he implies later (just as Silko often does in her essays and interviews), it takes not just years but many generations. The general reason place or landscape in Silko's text works this way is because, as Silko has said, "The landscape sits in the center of Pueblo belief and identity. Any narratives about the Pueblo people necessarily give a great deal of attention and detail to all aspects of a landscape" (*Yellow Woman* 43).

This precise, detailed kind of long-term relationship to particular places — not an innate but a historical relationship to the land — is crucial in all of the important recognition scenes in *Ceremony*. The intricacy of this relation between people and place emerges even more clearly in the following example from the novel, in which the mediating factor, the connection between people and place, is stories.

> The spider came out first. . . . He remembered stories about her. She alone had known how to outsmart the malicious mountain Ka't'sina who imprisoned the rain clouds in the northwest room of his magical house. . . . The frogs came out from their sleeping places. . . . Josiah said they could stay buried in the dry sand for many years, waiting for the rain to come again. Dragonflies came and hovered over the pool. . . . There were stories about the dragonflies, too. He turned. Everywhere he looked, he saw a world made of stories, the long ago, time immemorial stories, as old Grandma called them. It was a world alive, always changing and moving; and if you knew where to look, you could see it, sometimes almost imperceptible, like the motion of the stars across the sky. (94–95)

Tayo's memory of this event is a turning point in his reconstruction of his Laguna identity because he recognizes that his identity only comes from being part of that community or culture and that other living things in that place are also a part of the culture — they all have their stories. Only by knowing their stories can one see that they are all alive, that one is actively engaged with them. His relationship with them must be formed in explicitly cultural terms: it is a matter of knowing their stories, too, and periodically visiting them and giving them care, attention, and respect. He learns to be part of the community, in short, and that community — that culture — includes many more forms of life than the human alone. As Paula Gunn Allen (Laguna Pueblo) states, "the stories are the communication device of the land and the people" (120).

Because *Ceremony* presents a thoroughgoing, detailed narrative of the process of healthy identity formation through interrelation with a radically historied, multipopulated place, it differs in important ways from the bildungsroman. Although the process for Tayo is one of ego development, the community in which his identity is implaced is connected to place itself in a radical way that makes the concepts of "identity," "place," and "community" indistinguishable.

Thus, if Silko's novel is an "environmental" one, it is only so in a specific, critical sense that troubles the implicit distinction between human and nonhuman realms that the very term "environment" betokens, for its paradigm of place is intrinsically intersocial, historical, and cultural (mediated by stories). In Silko's work, the nonhuman is not simply connected to the human culture — which would still be a Western nature/culture dualism — it is utterly cultural, born of a long tenure at a particular place.

FROM PLACE TO MULTIETHNIC COALITION

These features of the concept of place at stake in *Ceremony* have been noted by other scholars and critics. But it is important to push the analysis of Silko's notion of place a bit farther and examine not only the specifically Laguna context for place we have just seen but also an even more implication-laden multicultural context for place that emerges in the novel, a linkage that eventually culminates at the uranium mine.

This multicultural context is established through Silko's assertion of a categorical distinction that takes priority over cultural and ethnic difference — a distinction between "destroyers" on the one hand and "humans" on the other. Betonie describes the destroyers to Tayo in a long incantation that includes this passage:

Then they grow away from the earth
then they grow away from the sun
then they grow away from the plants and animals.
They see no life
When they look
they see only objects.
The world is a dead thing for them
the trees and rivers are not alive
the mountains and stones are not alive.
The deer and bear are objects
They see no life.
They fear
They fear the world.
They destroy what they fear.
They fear themselves . . .
They will kill the things they fear
all the animals

the people will starve . . .
They will take this world from ocean to ocean
they will turn on each other
they will destroy each other. (135–137)

The passage refers specifically to Pueblo witchcraft, but more important, it portrays destroyer psychology as built around the idea of inanimate place: in this passage, all the living things the destroyers kill are shown to be things they consider to be already dead, including both living things and things like rocks and rivers that Westerners do not consider alive. From the destroyers' point of view, all these entities are lifeless, dead objects, "resources" to control, exploit, and destroy. Despite the specific reference to Pueblo witchcraft in this passage, it will quickly become clear that the epithet "destroyer" applies as well to components of other cultures as well.

The figure of the destroyer is placed in opposition to a Laguna definition of human beings, a notion that has been defined earlier in the novel by Ku'oosh in terms that characteristically emphasize the role of storytelling: "It took a long time to explain the fragility and intricacy because no word exists alone, and the reason for choosing each word had to be explained with a story about why it must be said this certain way. That was the responsibility that went with being human, old Ku'oosh said, the story behind each word must be told so there could be no mistake in the meaning of what had been said; and this demanded great patience and love" (35–36).

This definition is not *only* racial or ethnic, although it is ethnic, in terms of the specifically Laguna stories. Ku'oosh is talking about responsibility to the place, to the whole local community, which is "the responsibility that [goes] with being human." Silko's twin concepts of "destroyers" and "humans," however, work to indicate a criterion for alliance between those who choose to remain or become human beings — the patience and love that allow for a proper story, a proper relation to place and all that place entails. This is precisely the responsibility Tayo begins to take once he learns to see the world as alive, for as we have seen, he can only see the world as alive once he sees it as a world made of stories.

For Silko, this is an explicitly antiracist and anticulturalist conception (that is, it is not specific to race or culture). Indians can be destroyers, too; as old Betonie says, "You don't write off all the white people, just like you don't trust all the Indians" (128). A little later Betonie elaborates this idea further: "'That is the trickery of the witchcraft,' he said. 'They want us to believe that all evil resides with white people. Then we will look no further to see what is really happening. They want us to separate ourselves from white people, to be ignorant and helpless as we watch our own destruction. But white people are only the tools that the witchery manipulates'" (132).

Destroyers are clearly destructive to the environment, which in Pueblo terms means that they destroy culture and community, the possibility of relationship in and with place: "they work to see how much can be lost, how much can be forgotten," Betonie says. "They destroy the feeling people have for one another" (229). Thus, in addition to reinforcing the concept of community and place at stake in *Ceremony*, Silko's human/destroyer distinction also points toward a transethnic definition of humanity, suggesting the possibility of a multiethnic coalition around a common vision of living place.

ENVIRONMENTAL JUSTICE AT THE JACKPILE-PAGUATE URANIUM MINE

Silko's narrative of Tayo's return to health, his increasing consciousness of the destroyers, and his reconnection with place climaxes with his epiphany at the mine with which my discussion began. At the mine, the novel's sense of place is most radically historicized and politicized as Tayo's traditional, place-based ceremony is inserted into a particular, contemporary historical context that calls for action.

As Silko has asserted in *Yellow Woman and a Beauty of the Spirit*, "by its very ugliness and by the violence it does to the land, the Jackpile Mine insures that, from now on, it too will be included in the vast body of narratives that makes up the history of the Laguna people and the Pueblo landscape" (44). Stories — and hence notions of place — change. They are not reified, ahistorical entities, and the particular changes that have taken place at Laguna since the mine opened have been drastic.

Some history, diffused in *Ceremony*, is useful to condense here. The Jackpile-Paguate uranium mine began operations at Paguate on the Laguna Pueblo reservation in 1952. At that time, the Anaconda Copper Company, a subsidiary of the Atlantic-Richfield Corporation (now ARCO), was issued a lease by the Bureau of Indian Affairs to 7,500 acres of Laguna Pueblo land. The operation was comprised of a huge open-pit uranium mine, at 2,800 acres the largest of its kind in the United States, and an adjoining milling operation, which ran night and day for thirty years until 1982. In the passage quoted at the start of this essay, Tayo has a vision of sweeping interconnections between the mine and what was going on beyond Laguna land, both on native land in the region and overseas, and concludes about this vision: "he was not crazy; he had never been crazy. He had only seen and heard the world as it was: no boundaries, only transitions through all distances and time" (245–246).

In this climactic passage, Tayo envisions the "converging" of all the different "lines of cultures." He sees that very different and physically far-flung cultures have in common the fate the destroyers have realized (or planned) for them. Such a vision is a major turning point in the novel, for it locates Tayo's newly reconstructed Laguna Pueblo identity and community within a contemporary system of uranium mining and nuclear technology. Tayo sees here that his people and the Japanese have been caught in the global web of destruction of their communities and cultures, a web of destruction that includes much more than just the people involved; it involves their entire communities in the broadest environmental sense. Now the two communities, as Tayo sees, are "united in a circle of death." This vision repudiates any essentialist congruency that unites Native American and Japanese people because they are ancient kin somehow still more in touch with nature than Euro-Americans. Instead, both the Pueblo and the Japanese appear to Tayo as caught up in a larger story: the story in "the witchery's final ceremonial sand painting," which is not only engraved in the rocks around Tayo but also inscribed throughout New Mexico and throughout the world of the Atomic Age. As Tayo realizes, "From that time on, human beings were one clan again, united by the fate the destroyers planned for all of them, for all living things."

At the mine, Tayo makes a connection between his project of reintegrating into that particular place and finds that the project entails seeing relationships with others outside the reservation: he sees how "all the stories fit together." He sees relationships between different cultures in a way that has respect for basic differences, for the specificity of other cultures, but at the same time this passage also suggests all kinds of relationships with other groups of people: citizens of New Mexico, Laguna miners and those Laguna residents living downstream from the mine, the corporation and military people involved in the mine operation, and even past citizens of Hiroshima, where a bomb made from Jackpile uranium exploded in 1945. In defiance of any expectation that Laguna culture will be placed in the context of U.S. history or global capitalism, however, all of these stories are subsumed within the Laguna story, the "story that is still being told." In a paradox of great magnitude, Tayo's culturally specific emplacement — his Laguna sense of place — is what enables relationality to many other people and stories: Tayo's vision of precise, politicized lines of interconnection ("transitions" rather than a simplistic collapse of all distinctions) can only come as he reaches a "belonging with" his own particular place.

"RADIOACTIVE COLONIZATION" AND ENVIRONMENTAL JUSTICE IN *CEREMONY*

In the sequence at the uranium mine, the "story" Tayo envisions is not simply about relationality itself. Rather, the particular relationships Tayo imagines are actually potential lines of alliance against the "radioactive colonization" that has been practiced globally as well as locally. The passage carefully ticks off particular real places in the region that are part of the system of integrated environmental and cultural colonization Tayo has begun to recognize, including Trinity Site at White Sands, Los Alamos, and Cebolleta (where the adjoining mill operation is located, including a 50-acre tailing pond and a 350-foot-tall pile of radioactive tailings). The mine area itself at Paguate is, of course, a primary example of place devastation, where radioactive tailings drain radioactive water into local springs and aquifers.[5]

According to Ward Churchill, as a result of this situation, the Lagunas' only substantial source of surface water, the Rio Paguate, has been seriously contaminated (according to two Environmental Protection Agency reports) by radium-226 and other heavy metals, while the Government Accounting Office revealed that all of the groundwater into which the Laguna Pueblo wells are tapped was also highly irradiated (Churchill 273). The fact that such an environmentally devastating policy was carried out in many forms in the Four Corners area — mainly on native land — led the U.S. government to designate the entire Four Corners region as a "National Sacrifice Area" in 1974. Since indigenous societies are land linked or place based, the "sacrifice" of this particular region implies a government policy that involves the sacrifice of the native peoples and cultures who live there.

As the United Church of Christ study *Toxic Wastes and Race in the United States* suggests, such a situation would not have occurred in a middle-class white neighborhood. According to this report, people of color suffer a "disproportionate risk" to their health, their communities, and their environments. *Toxic Wastes and Race* defines this situation as environmental racism, which is "racial discrimination in environmental policy-making and the enforcement of regulations and laws, the deliberate targeting of people of color communities for toxic waste facilities, the official sanctioning of the life-threatening presence of poisons and pollutants in our communities, and the history of excluding people of color from positions of leadership in the environmental movement" (quoted in Di Chiro, 304). Environmental degradation, as Robert Bullard has argued, is experienced differently by certain ethnic, racial, and class groups. "Toxic time bombs are not randomly scattered across the landscape," he asserts, and he goes on to report on a considerable body of evidence from studies that find race

> to be the single most important factor (i.e. more important than income, home ownership rate, and property values) in the location of abandoned toxic waste sites. . . . Native American reservations, from New York to California, have become prime targets for risky technologies [such as uranium mining]. Native American nations are quasi-sovereign and do not fall under state jurisdiction. Similarly, reservations are "lands the feds forgot," and their inhabitants "must contend with some of America's worst pollution." Few reservations have infrastructures to handle the risky technologies that are being proposed for their communities, and more than 100 waste disposal facilities have been proposed for Native American lands. (*Unequal Protection* 16–17)

Because of such historical patterns in U.S. and corporate policies, these issues are common native environmental justice issues in other regions of the United States.[6]

These issues have not, unfortunately, been very visible in contemporary ecocriticism nor in its preoccupation with wilderness ethics and a narrow canon of Western nature writing. Silko's depiction of a triangular relationship established between place, multiethnicity, and environmental justice, therefore, might provide a much needed initial step toward integrating these vital concerns into ecocritical debate. As Gary Snyder has argued in *A Place in Space*, "a non-nationalistic idea of community, in which commitment to pure place is paramount, cannot be ethnic or racist. Here is perhaps the most delicious turn that comes out of thinking about politics from the standpoint of place: anyone of any race, language, religion, or origin is welcome, as long as they live well on the land" (234).

In terms of this larger process, Silko's text warns us to be "inclusive of everything," historically and culturally speaking, at the same time as we are, as Wendell Berry has it, "digging in" to particular places. If a primary ecocritical goal is "living well on the land" and if that hope includes interethnic cooperation and justice, Silko's book instructs us that we don't have to completely invent the grounds for such a movement — there are cultural bases with long-term tenure on the land. This last comment is not a point about appropriating native cultures but rather about taking seriously writers like Silko who invite their non-Indian audiences to listen, learn, and work together on a coequal, nondeficit basis where our stories can begin, in part and in certain limited ways, to "converge."

NOTES

1. Since the landmark United Church of Christ study, the term "environmental racism" has become increasingly well known, generally as the unequal protection or even systematic targeting of people of color for environmental hazards. The concept has become a rallying point for many movements and multiethnic coalitions that have become known as environmental justice groups; the term clearly distinguishes these kinds of groups and coalitions from mainstream environmentalism. Environmental justice groups and networks have organized on a multicultural basis in order to draw public attention to connections between environmental issues and social justice issues such as race, class, and gender. Perhaps the most effective and well known coalition is the Southwest Network for Economic and Environmental Justice (SNEEJ). For more information, see Bullard (*Environmental Racism, Unequal Protection*); Bullard and Johnson; Hofrichter; Bryant; and Alston.

All around the country, native people have been effectively calling attention to native environmental justice issues. On native issues of environmental racism and environmental justice, the best sources are Churchill and LaDuke; Churchill; LaDuke; Grinde; Austin and Schill; Hall; and Weaver. The one article on *Ceremony* that seems to address the issue is Zamir's "Literature in a 'National Sacrifice Area.'" Zamir cites a portion of the passage at the uranium mine and offers a bit of the information that is gathered about the situation there by Churchill and LaDuke, but

Zamir's argument generally fails to address these issues in the context of environmental racism, contending instead that Silko's novel subverts itself by depending on the Arthurian grail myth.

2. For examples, see Allen; Swan; Silko (*Yellow Woman*); and Nelson (*Place and Visitation*).

3. Place is a broader term than environment, as the latter is usually understood (and as ecocritics have unintentionally reinforced) to mean "nature." In contrast to environment, place always has more emphasis on *sense* of place, as Lawrence Buell says, which emphasizes the human interaction with the nonhuman: "place being by definition perceived or felt space, space humanized, rather than the material world taken on its own terms" (253).

4. Understanding anything about this complexity also takes time and a level of scholarly commitment from readers that likely exceeds the effort needed to understand other kinds of place literatures, and the non-Laguna reader must depend on Laguna writers, ethnographers, and studies by Native American scholars familiar with the culture, such as Swan and Allen.

5. "Altogether more than 500 million gallons of radioactive water have been discharged. This water, already radioactive from contact with uranium ore underground, is pumped over the 260-acre tailings pile. . . . From the tailings pond, this radioactive water either sinks back into the aquifer, evaporates, or seeps out of the tailings pond into the arroyos and drainage channels of the tiny Rio Mequino stream that is fed by a natural spring near the tailings dam" (Churchill 272).

6. See Hall; Austin and Schill; LaDuke; Churchill; Grinde; and Weaver.

7. Landscape in Drag
The Paradox of Feminine Space in Susan Warner's *The Wide, Wide World*

ANDREA BLAIR

Since the 1970s, the feminization of space has piqued the interest of geographers, feminists, and ecocritics alike. The essentializing link between women and the environment has become either a union to esteem — as some early ecofeminists affirmed — or to vilify. Recently, the ecocritical treatment of gender and the environment has been dominated by thinkers who rigorously condemn any determinist bind between women and the natural world. These writers have sought to sever the discursive equation of land and the feminine, viewing this equation as one that reduces women and nature to biological functions and fosters infantile, masculinist relations that are harmful to women and land alike. By equating women with the natural world, they reason, women are diminished to biological impulses and unalterable gender codings. Conversely, by gendering landscape female, the same arguments used to subjugate and control women are used to subjugate and control nature. Land is seen as the inviting concubine, waiting to be despoiled; as the chaste virgin, needing protection from rape; or as the all-forgiving, long-suffering Mother Earth, who patiently tolerates abuse from her human children. Nina Baym has argued that the supposedly universal, psychological basis for the feminization of landscape actually hides a masculine bias, for in her view, female writers are not likely "to cast themselves as virgin land. . . . If women portray themselves as brides or mothers, it will not be in terms of the mythic landscape" (136). For ecofeminist thinkers like Annette Kolodny, who was one of the first critics to examine the gendered landscape, navigating the social results of the feminization of land is a virtually impossible project for women. The metaphor land-as-woman is seen as a patriarchal construct developed by the "male metaphors" of "erotic mastery or infantile repression" (*Land Before Her* 8).

In striving to minimize any biological parallelism between women and nature, critics have ignored more complex examples of the feminization of landscape in literature. Accepting and dismissing categorically the metaphor of land-as-woman as masculinist are both dubious practices. Obviously, a median between the wholesale equation of women to the environment and the rejection of any connection must be possible. This essay intends to explore and define such a middle ground, widening the debate and opening up further possibilities of exploration.

This purpose is especially important given the current situation of ecocriticism. These are clearly important issues, freighted with far-reaching implications for any critic interested in the representation of nature, but few ecocritics actively engage in the theoretical work that might assist us in thinking through the relationship of gender, representation, and landscape. Semiotics, performativity theory, and feminist geography all have potential contributions to make toward a new understanding of landscape representation in which feminized space need not be embraced or rejected invariably as a masculinist construct.

In the first section of this essay, I will examine these three theoretical sources. First, I will offer a brief reading of Julia Kristeva's theory of semiotics and the hermeneutics of the maternal body in an effort to understand more fully the impulse to define landscape as feminine and its psychological effects. Second, I will outline Judith Butler's work on cross-dressing and performativity theory, which implies that "feminine space" might be as manipulable as any other body spatiality. Lastly, I will attempt to construct a compromise position between these conflicting theories by looking at Gillian Rose's concept of paradoxical space. After laying a middle ground for exploring gendered landscape representation, I will test this approach by applying it to Susan Warner's 1850 novel, *The Wide, Wide World*.

I

Julia Kristeva's work in semiotics is particularly useful in developing a vocabulary to discuss spatiality issues and to explore the psychological and linguistic reasons we gender landscape. She describes the semiotic state as being presymbolic — that is, experienced before the acquisition of language.[1] It is closely affiliated with the unconscious and "expresses itself as the organization of instinctual drives through the resources of rhythm, intonation, gesture, and melody" (Burke and Gallop 111). In this prelinguistic state, the infant experiences a feeling of oneness with space — the infant's body and mother's body and everything the infant perceives are all interfused as a singular experience. Kristeva labels this primal space the semiotic *chora* — a space "without interior or exterior" (Oliver 36). This earlier state is pre–Law of the Father, pre–sexual difference, prepatriarchal, and it remains "a constant and subversive threat to the symbolic order of things" (Smith 16).

Kristeva argues, however, that the semiotic state is challenged when the infant acquires language (the symbolic). With language, the infant experiences a fracturing of the self and of spatial unity as the *chora* is replaced by the symbols of the Law of the Father. In contrast to the undifferentiated space-concept of the *chora*, the advent of the linguistic state introduces differentiation, in which the subject begins to perceive distinctions between self and surroundings and between self and others. The semiotic is supplanted, but it is not eliminated: "Because the subject is always *both* semiotic *and* symbolic, no signifying system he produces can be either 'exclusively' semiotic or 'exclusively' symbolic, and is instead necessarily marked by an indebtedness to both" (Kristeva 24). Kristeva advocates a balance between the two, encouraging a reexperiencing of the often forgotten semiotic. This can be done in numerous ways but particularly through art, poetry, love, and word play.

Kristeva's work on psychoanalysis can help us understand the desire to gender landscape. She asserts that the infant's first "place name" represents the mother and that initially "every space is the place of the mother" (Oliver 36). Leonard Lutwack forwards a similar thesis: "Harboring the child within her body, woman herself is a place, an enduring place, from the child's point of view" (82). He notes that Erich Neumann's Freudian model "'Woman = body = vessel = world' [is] an archetypal chain which depends on the infant's experience of the mother's body as his first environment" (82). The infant's first landscape is the maternal body, and all space, according to Kristeva's postulation, is initially enveloped in the semiotic *chora*. Following this logic, the persistent use of the land-as-woman metaphor is thus a reflection of the subject's desire to reexperience the semiotic. The subject tries to replicate the semiotic oneness of space by projecting these desires onto the landscape, gendering it female. This gendering results in the subject experiencing feelings of harmony and contentment — and possession of landscape.

Kristeva's theories are not without problems, and Butler points out one of the most serious: "If the symbolic is structured by the Law of the Father, then the feminist resistance to the symbolic unwittingly *protects* the father's law by relegating feminine resistance to the less enduring and less efficacious domain of the imaginary [semiotics]" (*Bodies* 106). Butler's criticism highlights the intrinsic contradiction within Kristeva's work: How can language, tyrannized by patriarchy, ever be used to express the inexpressible, the semiotic? In addition, Kristeva's metaphors reduce the world to innate gender binaries, with the masculine (the "bad") always assuming the dominant role over the feminine (the "good"). In her critique of ecofeminism, Caroline New warns of the problems of this type of essentialism, noting that the "enemy of women and nature is not men but dichotomized gendered subjectivity itself" (190). Despite these intrinsic problems, the vocabulary Kristeva develops is useful in naming and describing various paradigms assigned to space and, when incorporated alongside Butler's and Rose's theories, in defining a dialogical middle ground.

Butler, in many ways the philosophical opposite of Kristeva, adds another stratum to the debate. Butler's performativity theories offer the chance to escape the bind of Kristeva's biologism, which reduces psychological impulses to gender binaries, and the chance to create alternate reiterations in formulating landscape representation. If it is to be accepted that gender/sex/sexuality are all learned (as opposed to strictly biologically determined), as Butler argues, then surely the same can be said about how we perceive and represent landscape. Butler's emphasis on social constructivism might plausibly open a space for optimism in the ecocritical sphere: since our representations of landscape have been socially constructed, then certainly we can learn new ways to imagine them.

Defining herself against psychoanalytic theory, Butler argues that gender, sex, and sexuality are all socially constructed and produced or, in her word, "performed." By a "forced reiteration of norms" (*Bodies* 94), we become gendered, sexed, and sexualized subjects, backing up what Adrienne Rich terms "compulsory heterosexuality." This performance "is not a singular 'act' or event, but a ritualized production, a ritual reiterated under and through constraint, under and through the force of prohibition and taboo" (95).

Ruptures in the reiterative performance occur when the subject "fail[s] to repeat loyally" cultural performatives: "It is this constitutive failure of the performative, this slippage between discursive command and its appropriated effect, which provides the linguistic occasion and index for a consequential disobedience" (124, 122). This failure to repeat loyally can occur in the drag performance. Drag, Butler notes in *Gender Trouble*, "fully subverts the distinction between inner and outer psychic space and effectively mocks both the expressive model of gender and the notion of a true gender identity. . . . *In imitating gender, drag implicitly reveals the imitative structure of gender itself — as well as its contingency*" (137).

Butler, interested in body spatialities, does not project her theories onto the larger landscape, though the extension here is logical. As Henri Lefebvre notes, the subject's understanding of "its own body determines its relationship to other bodies, to nature, and to space" (204). Just as we project reiterated norms onto ourselves and others, we also project them onto space, sexualizing and gendering landscape. And as we can "fail to repeat loyally" cultural performatives, we can fail in the repetition of landscape representation, creating representations that contest the status quo.

But by professing such a strict social constructivist rhetoric, Butler creates another predicament: she downplays biological differences between the sexes. The materiality of the body is reduced to the sum of an elaborate social code. In addition, performativity theories never get behind the "smoke and mirrors" of gender representation; is there any foundation — either psychological or biological — behind the elaborate masquerades? Applied to the issue of landscape representation, Butler's absolute social constructivism seems troubling as well, as it appears to negate the consequence of nature's materiality. Since both scientific ecology and political environmentalism take so seriously the materiality of nature itself, valorizing the natural tendencies of ecosystems as a primary measure of environmental health, the suggestion that landscape ought to be thought of as infinitely malleable through discourse is likely — and rightly so — to strike many ecocritics as severely problematic.

Perhaps, however, a compromise between strict biologism and strict social constructivism can be made, in which we can embrace the potential subversiveness of social construction but still maintain the idea that this construction rests on some confederation of psychological and corporeal reality. In both gender and landscape studies, this dialogical strategy expands now-limited interpretive possibilities, creating a space where contrary theories can coexist, challenging and modifying each other.

The theoretical basis for the compromise between these views that I wish to propose may be found in Gillian Rose's notion of "paradoxical space," articulated in *Feminism and Geography*. Influenced by Lacanian theory, she sees space as currently constructed by masculinist paradigms. Landscape "implies a specific way of looking," a "visual ideology" that privileges the masculinist gaze (193, 194). Rose writes that in popular and academic discourses, landscape — as the passive, objectified Other that awaits the gaze for signification — plays the role of the feminine. She proposes that alternative readings of a space "beyond patriarchy" must be attempted (154). Unlike Butler, however, Rose does not dismiss the potential for difference in particular spatialities; she turns to paradoxical space as an alternative. She defines paradoxical space as that "which straddles the spaces of representation and unrepresentability" and "simultaneously grounds and denies identity." In this space, the very descriptions that have been used to subjugate a group can be claimed and subverted, allowing for the "possibility of radical difference" (154). But recognition of difference is, ideally, not one of segregation into binaries. Rather, it allows for a space where multiple differences and dialogics exist in relation to and harmony with each other. In paradoxical space, marginalized groups can find a unified sense of power by first claiming an identity assigned by dominant culture and then rejecting the position of Other. The term "queer," I argue, is an example of such a space. Once a slur used to malign and objectify, "queer" has been appropriated and subverted by the gay and lesbian communities, becoming a rallying call for social and political activism. "Queer" occupies an ironic, or paradoxical, space both inside and outside cultural norms, Same and Other at once.

A similar strategy might usefully be considered by writers and ecocritics as they continue to probe the implications of how the environment itself is represented. That is, the very descriptions used to subjugate women and nature can be reappropriated, creating a paradoxical space in which alternative reiterations of gender norms are possible for both female bodies and material nature itself. Traditionally restricted by their biological functions, women can seize these paradigms by applying them to a particular landscape and then claiming this space as their own. Paradoxically, the reclaimed metaphor land-as-woman, so often used to control and dominate women and the natural environment, offers a space where an alternative feminine identity can be attempted. By creating their own landscape fantasies, women can create new ways to imagine themselves and the natural environment.

This practice of subversive landscape gendering is analogous to Butler's drag theory. Texts (whether by writers or visual artists) that undermine traditional landscape representations by failing to repeat loyally accepted cultural norms in effect create a landscape-in-drag. In such a representation, landscape performs the feminine, but there is always the possibility of a failure of the performative that challenges the structure of gendered representation. Thus landscape that is gendered feminine but is constructed as active rather than passive, as dialogical rather than monological, as subversive rather than hegemonic, and as the site of feminine rather than masculine fantasies, might disrupt restrictive gender codings for women and environments alike.

II

Susan Warner's 1850 *The Wide, Wide World* may seem an unlikely text to examine when imagining new approaches to landscape representation because the novel occupies a site of contestation and dispute even when landscape is left out of the debate. At first glance, the novel appears to conform to restrictive patriarchal paradigms. The novel details the psychological traumas and dilemmas of Ellen Montgomery, a young girl who is left an orphan early in the novel. Ellen is tyrannized constantly — by cruel children, by her aunt (Miss Fortune Emerson), by a shopkeeper with sadistic tendencies, and particularly by male father figures, who dictate her every move, decreeing what she must think and read, where she may go, what she must do, when she may speak. The male characters do so in order to teach Ellen her proper role; she must learn to submit to them as she would to Christ. Her mother's advice in the opening scene foretells the novel's theme: "though we *must* sorrow, we must not rebel" (12). Ellen's humility is brought to the test as she is moved from one tyrannical male household to another: first, from her indifferent biological father's, who tears her dying mother away from her in a move to England; then to her "brother" John Humphreys's house, whom she loves but who nevertheless seeks to regulate her every thought, molding her into a proper Christian; then to her sadistic Uncle Lindsay's home in Scotland; and finally back to John's home, as his perfectly controlled wife.

Given the novel's overall message of female submission to patriarchal norms, it would seem that descriptions of landscape back up the novel's predominant theme. The mountain, which is described in feminine terms, would be constructed by the masculinist gaze, to use Rose's theory. As "visual ideology" backing up hegemonic norms, it would alternately be depicted as the passive, all-loving mother, the seductive virgin, or the horrifying Medusa.[2] The land-as-woman metaphor would "have only dangerous consequences," as Kolodny concludes in *The Lay of the Land* (158). In sum, the feminized mountain would be nothing more than a fetishized object dependent on the gaze for signification: no subversion of cultural norms would be possible.

But despite its overall message, there are times when the novel's "ideology of duty, humility, and submission to circumstance" (Tompkins, "Afterword," 585) seems to escape Warner. Ellen certainly performs an agonizing ritualized repetition of humiliation — to the point where the novel's sadomasochistic bent can't be denied. But through this ritual, as Jane Tompkins notes, "'submission' is transformed into 'self-command,' and the extinction of the self into the assumption of a god-like authority" (*Sensational* 168). By becoming godly, Ellen, "the dutiful woman[,] merges her own authority with God's" and gains an associated power through the highest authority (163). Hovet and Hovet declare that Ellen masters Emersonian "transparency" by learning the demands of the gaze and "masquerading" these expectations. According to Emerson, "human consciousness can render the material world 'transparent' or turn 'the world to glass' in order to discern a higher spiritual reality" (Hovet and Hovet 335). Ellen learns to negate her identity so that a higher power — the image of Christ — is seen *through her* by "the masculine rhetoric of vision" (335). But this transparency, write the Hovets, can be performative and subversive: "[B]y understanding the expectations of the male gaze, the woman can gain some control of the feminine image by presenting herself as a replica of transparency, thereby providing a mask behind which a space can be established for self-development" (342).[3]

The novel is full of paradoxes, of "gaps and fissures" in the sediment of "reiterative or ritual practice," to use Butler's terminology (*Bodies* 10). And nowhere are these fissures more evident than in Warner's portrayal of the feminized landscape. The mountain is not without its storms, and Ellen and Alice Humphreys (John's sister) are once caught in a blizzard while descending it. But throughout the novel, the mountain is a symbol of maternal comfort and female strength, where the novel's women characters gather to find inspiration and respite from submission to patriarchal demands. Ellen is constantly escaping to the mountain, especially when the injustices of coerced conformity become too great. The mountain is given explicitly feminine qualities: it comforts the motherless child, Ellen, by seeming to bridge the distance between her and her mother; it is the physical location of the figurative mother, Alice; and it is the home of the independent, autonomous mountain woman, Mrs. Vawse, and her disruptive, rebellious granddaughter, Nancy. Although John Humphreys and his father also live at the Humphreys home (located halfway up the mountain), only the women are shown appreciating the views and turning to the mountain for maternal comfort. The city and isolated roads prove dangerous to Ellen, but the mountain is a landscape of comfort and protection, and it is the only space where she is allowed to roam at will, unhampered by domestic duties and controlling patriarchal figures.

Ellen first encounters this wild landscape when running away from her aunt. She has just discovered that Miss Fortune has opened a letter addressed to Ellen from her invalid mother. In outrage over this assault on her privacy, Ellen escapes to the mountain. Resting on a rock, "[h]er eye sought those distant hills,— how very far off they were! and yet all that wide tract of country was but a little piece of what lay between her and her mother. Her eye sought those hills,— but her mind overpassed them and went far beyond, over many such a tract, till it reached the loved one at last" (Warner 148).

Warner uses the phrase "her eye sought those [distant] hills" twice in this paragraph, underscoring the importance of the mountain view to Ellen. The landscape momentarily closes the distance between Ellen and her mother. The mountain panorama, rather than remaining the passive Other, becomes a scene of activity — one of movement and fluidity. In this wild space, the distance between mother and daughter is bridged, and Ellen feels a momentary consolation. But peace escapes her: "I cannot reach her!— she cannot reach me!" she cries. Seeking comfort, "she slid from her seat at first, and embracing the stone on which she had sat, she leaned her head there; but presently in her agony quitting her hold of that, she cast herself down upon the moss, lying at full length upon the cold ground, which seemed to her childish fancy the best friend she had left" (148).

Clearly, given Ellen's own position of powerlessness and the description of her association with the mountain, Kolodny's thesis of feminized space being constructed and controlled by "erotic mastery" is not apropos (though Ellen's relationship to the mountain is, at times, erotic) — nor is Rose's gaze concept applicable. Butler's performativity theory works well here: the mountain is clearly constructed as feminine. The title of this chapter, "Mother Earth Rather than Aunt Fortune," reminds the reader that Ellen turns to the mountain, rather than to her aunt, for maternal comfort. It also makes the feminine qualities of the mountain explicit and even ironic: not only is the mountain given feminine qualities, but the title makes this gendering blatantly clear. The mountain, if you will, conforms to Butler's definition of drag: *"in imitating gender, drag implicitly reveals the imitative structure of gender itself"* (137). In Warner's text, the mountain certainly imitates and parodies gender performatives. Ellen — like Alice and Mrs. Vawse — constructs the mountain as feminine, and it becomes the site of her projected fantasies. She attempts to escape from the rhetoric of dominance and subordination by projecting her frustrations, fears, and desires onto landscape. And by having the mountain perform various feminine roles, Ellen is able to experiment, however slightly, with her own gender performances.

While Butler's theory is useful in pointing out the performative nature of gendered landscape, it does little to explain why Ellen (and Alice and Mrs. Vawse) feel the need to construct landscape as feminine and, specifically, as maternal. Kristeva's terminology is useful in scrutinizing Ellen's reactions. In her grief, Ellen merges the elements of the landscape with her mother, creating a physical substitute for Kristeva's semiotic *chora* and evoking the corporeal memory of her connection to her mother. As in the semiotic state, Ellen experiences a reunification of the self with fractured spatialities. She, her mother, and the landscape all merge into one. Ellen finds no comfort in the arms of her aunt, and "Mother Earth," "the best friend she had left," becomes a surrogate for her mother and the location of the *chora*. In this landscape, Ellen can express the inexpressible: the "unspeakable destruction and unspeakable pleasure" linked with semiotics (Smith 16). She can articulate what she is not allowed to in the valley: the discontentment that the various social hierarchies declare she cannot feel. Ellen expresses her anger and loss through "[c]onvulsive weeping" and "fits of violence," crying "the last pitch of grief and passion" into the moss (Warner 149). In her anguish, Ellen becomes "mad": that is, in what Kristeva describes as the "body-to-body discourse with the mother," the "unsayable" language of madness is expressed (Burke and Gallop 112). Ellen screams out her frustrations until she is overcome with an almost sexual exhaustion: "In one of these fits of quiet . . . she lay as still as the rocks around her" (Warner 148).

The recipient of the semiotic projection changes when Ellen hears a voice of "silver sweetness" ask, "What is the matter, my child?" The voice belongs to Alice Humphreys, also motherless, a stranger who soon proves "a better friend than the cold earth had been like to prove her." Alice sits "on Ellen's stone" and embraces the young woman, who "hid her face in [Alice's] bosom" (149). The breast of the mountain seems "cold" in comparison to the flesh-and-blood Alice's, and Ellen gratefully transfers her affections. At this point the mountain is only a temporary, and not very satisfactory, succor, and Ellen turns from the mountain with disdain.

After comforting Ellen, Alice guides her farther up the mountain to where "the broken wavy outline of mountains closed in the horizon." Watching the sunset, "[b]oth exclaimed at the beauty before them." Alice cries, "How beautiful! Ellen dear, — he whose hand raised up those mountains and has painted them so gloriously is the very same One who has said, to you and to me, 'Ask and it shall be given to you'" (153). Having just mourned the separation from her mother and wailed out her frustrations of powerlessness, Ellen finds solace in Alice's words. She may be defenseless and vulnerable, but God will supply her needs; power is accessible through God. Alice's religious interpretation is unique; throughout the novel she quotes the Bible to remind Ellen of her duty of submission before patriarchal authority. The theme of empowerment ("Ask and it shall be given") is rarely broached by Alice, but surrounded by the extensive views of the mountains, where Alice herself feels free, this allusion seems appropriate.

The following day, as Ellen climbs the mountain to visit Alice, "her spirits began to rise" as she walks away from her aunt's oppressive valley farm (161). When the two enter the Humphreys home, Alice immediately directs Ellen's gaze to the view. Alice explains that she "felt half smothered to be so shut in" by the trees surrounding the house. At Alice's prompting, her brother had cut down the trees that were blocking the view. "I should grow melancholy if I had that wall of trees pressing on my vision all the time," she states (162). Feelings of enclosure and imprisonment promote psycho-physical ailments in Alice. Because she is the daughter of an exacting patriarch and sister to the domineering John Humphreys, perhaps Alice's claustrophobia is due — at least in part — to her exhaustive performance as the dutiful woman. Alice, like the other mountain woman, Mrs. Vawse, has learned to hide her earthly desires behind the veil of transparency. In return, she is allowed access to a moderate amount of power; her "good girl" status allows her to travel the countryside alone, pastor other women, and influence patriarchal figures (getting John to cut down the trees, for example). However, this performance is not without a price — a melancholia of confinement. In looking off into the distance, Alice finds serenity: "[I]t always comforts me to look off, far away, to those distant blue hills" (162).

Ellen and Alice climb the mountain one winter afternoon to visit the elderly Mrs. Vawse, who lives on the mountaintop. As they walk, the air gets colder and the wind sweeps "round the mountain-head and over them with great force" (186). Ellen asks Alice why her friend "will live in such a disagreeable place." Upon approaching the home, Ellen finds the house "did not look so uncomfortable. . . . It was perched so snugly in a niche of the hill that the little yard was completely sheltered with a high wall of rock" (187). She thinks, "It looked as if one might be happy there; it looked as if somebody *was* happy there" (190). Despite the cheerfulness of the home, Ellen states to Mrs. Vawse that she wouldn't want to reside there all alone in the cold. The widow responds patiently, "I like to be alone" (191), one of the first indications of her independent nature. Again Ellen asks why Mrs. Vawse chooses to live in the lonesome place with the wind howling about. She replies:

> I'll tell you the reason my child. It is for the love of my old home and the memory of my young days. Till I was as old as you are, and a little older, I lived among the mountains and upon them; and after that, for many a year, they were just before my eyes every day, stretching away for more than one hundred miles, and piled up one above another, fifty times as big as any you ever saw; these are only molehills to them. I loved them — oh, how I love them still! If I have one unsatisfied wish . . . it is to see my Alps again; but that will never be. Now, Miss Ellen, it is not that I fancy, when I get to the top of this hill that I am among my own mountains, but I can breathe better here than down in the plain. I

feel more free; and in the village I would not live for gold, unless that duty bade me. (192–193)

Ellen once more asks if the widow is lonesome "all alone so far from every body," to which Mrs. Vawse responds, "I am never lonely" (193). Ellen's fear of the mountain demonstrates that her relationship is one of abjection; she finds temporary maternal comfort on the mountain, but it remains Other. The young Ellen approaches landscape as an infant does the maternal body: she wants instant gratification of her needs. Once she is sated, the mountain no longer has a hold over her and she loses interest. Mrs. Vawse's relationship is more mature. She admits a semiotic attachment to mountains, which informs "the memory of my young days." She spent her youngest years living on the mountains; later, as an early teen, she moved out of the mountains, but they remained always in her vision. A spatial separation resulted, distancing Mrs. Vawse from the semiotic landscape of her early girlhood, but she retains her feelings of connection to this space. With the distant mountains before her, Mrs. Vawse finds a balance between the semiotic and the symbolic, to use Kristeva's theories, gaining the equilibrium Kristeva states is necessary for psychic health. Warner explains Mrs. Vawse's harmony in metaphors of landscape: "Those storms [of earlier passions] had all passed away; the last shadow of a cloud had departed; her evening sun was shining clear and bright toward the setting" (190). This balance makes Mrs. Vawse the "most completely happy and fulfilled person in the novel," as Jane Tompkins terms her (*Sensational* 167). Alice tells Ellen that her mentor is always "cheerful and happy, as a little girl" (Warner 195). Mrs. Vawse also experiences a great amount of freedom. Alice notes that "there is not a more independent woman breathing" (194). Alone in her mountain home, Mrs. Vawse finds spatial, spiritual, and economic freedom.

Though her relationship to the mountain illustrates Kristeva's semiotics, Mrs. Vawse is self-conscious of the roles she and the environment play. She is cognizant that the landscape of eastern New York is only a substitute for her Alps. These "molehills" will never replace the landscape that she still loves, but they are a reminder of it. The mountains are clearly performative, enacting the fantasy of her childhood landscape, and Mrs. Vawse is conscious of this performance. Additionally, Mrs. Vawse perfectly performs cultural norms, learning to imitate transparency; she is gentle, industrious, and godly. Her transparency, however, like Alice's, allows her access to a sanctioned power denied to Aunt Fortune and Mrs. Vawse's grandchild, Nancy, who refuse to ascribe to established performatives. Mrs. Vawse lives outside of the cultural constraints that rule the valley. She is allowed this independence because she performs her role so well. Her nod to "duty" illustrates this point. Mrs. Vawse notes she would not leave her mountain home unless "that duty bade me." Of course, she isn't faced with any such obligation, and her sanctioned status gives her financial independence. Her house is provided by a "good old friend of hers" (187), and she "has friends that would not permit her to earn another sixpence if they could help it" (195). Tompkins writes that the elderly woman "claims that the secret of her contentment is 'letting go of earthly things . . . for they that seek the Lord shall not want any good thing,'" but Mrs. Vawse "in fact has everything she wants" (*Sensational* 167).

As Alice and Ellen walk down the mountain toward the village below, a great snowstorm blows in. The two "ran on, holding each other's hands and strengthening themselves against the blast" (Warner 195). As they progress down the mountain, the storm gets stronger and more violent, the sky darker, and they are unsure of where they are. "Slowly and patiently, with painful care groping their way, they pushed on through the snow and the thick night" (198). Just as they are about to give up hope, they see a light: it is Mr. Van Brunt holding a lantern, coming back from the barn. He brings the "two wet and weary travellers" into the house, where they are made comfortable by his mother (201).

This storm, encountered as Alice and Ellen walk down the mountain away from the cheerful home of Mrs. Vawse, represents the undiluted semiotics and serves as a warning. If unprepared for the experience, the semiotic landscape can be frightening. Mrs. Vawse, however, tucked away in her mountain cottage with her carefully prepared provisions, understands the wildness of this place and prefers it. She tells Ellen she has no fear of snowstorms because she can always "make a good blazing fire," and she "like[s] to hear the wind whistle" (193). Unlike her two visitors, Mrs. Vawse has already learned to balance the semiotics with the symbolic, and the wilderness of the mountain has become a harmonious and supportive landscape.

Mrs. Vawse is described in metaphors of nature at peace, but her wild grandchild, Nancy, is associated with elements in uproar. Mrs. Vawse tells Alice, "She'll not come [in] if there's a promise of a storm . . . she often stays out all night" (193). Nancy first bursts into the scene on the heels of the snowstorm, which has kept Ellen housebound for days, and she continues to appear whenever Ellen suffers fits of frustration. As a "wild, unpredictable child of storm, aligned with nature and natural passions rather than with the dominant social conventions," Nancy Vawse "substitutes for Ellen unconscious nature" (Stewart 1, 7). Nancy is passionate, willful, and selfish; she tells tales, manipulates authority figures (including the cantankerous Miss Fortune), and speaks her mind. Nancy, who like Ellen and Alice is motherless, is also explicitly linked to the mountain and its storms, although this is an association she loathes. The child finds the isolation of the mountain tiresome. Interest is found in the valley below, where she can pester Ellen and flatter Miss Fortune. Veronica Stewart links Nancy to the semiotic and Ellen to the symbolic and argues that the continual contestation between the two "generates a significant subversion of authoritative power" (9). Nancy is unable to find a balance between the semiotic and the symbolic, however; like the snowstorm in which Alice and Ellen are temporarily lost, she is the semiotic at its most undiluted. Because her semiotic responses are not sanctioned, she remains ever on the margins; her access to power is extremely limited, as she refuses to conform to "transparency" ideals. A substitute for Ellen's unconscious, Nancy is most visible when Ellen herself is most defiant toward social restriction. As Ellen learns to control her temper and use transparency to her advantage, combining the semiotic with the symbolic, Nancy fades from view.

With time, following the examples set by Mrs. Vawse and Alice, Ellen learns to conceive of landscape as more than an abject Other in which to find a temporary semiotic substitute. Her evolving maturation becomes evident when she escapes to the mountain to find comfort after Alice dies of consumption — the same disease that carried off Ellen's mother soon after Ellen's first scene of grief on the mountain. The orphan slowly walks up the footpath to her favorite part of the mountain:

> She passed the place where Alice had first found her, — she remembered it well; — there was the very stone beside which they had kneeled together, and where Alice's folded hands were laid. Ellen knelt down beside it again, and for a moment laid her cheek to the cold stone while her arms embraced it, and a second time it was watered with

tears. She rose up again quickly and went on her way, toiling up the steep path beyond, till she turned to the edge of the mountain and stood on the old place where she and Alice that evening had watched the setting sun. . . . She sat down on the stone she called her own, and leaning her head on Alice's which was close by, she wept bitterly, but not very long; she was too tired and subdued for bitter weeping; she raised her head again, and wiping away her tears looked abroad over the beautiful landscape. Never more beautiful than then. (Warner 441–442)

Ellen experiences sorrow this time, not rage or "madness," and allows the performative of landscape to soothe as never before. As she rests her head on Alice's favorite stone, she watches the sun come up over the valley, bathing the village and distant lake in silver, and listens to the birds "singing like mad." Despite her grief, Ellen "loved all these things too well not to notice them even now." Like before, the consolation she receives from the landscape is temporary, halted by the realization that her flesh-and-blood comfort is gone: "*She* will look at it no more!" A Bible verse comes to mind: "Behold I create new heavens, and a new earth; and the former shall not be remembered, nor come into mind. Thy sun shall no more go down; neither shall thy moon withdraw itself: for the Lord shall be thine everlasting light, and the days of thy mourning shall be ended." Alice, she realizes, is at peace in a perfect landscape. Consoled, she does not wail out her rage and frustration as she did before but sits quietly weeping, "looking down into the brightening valley or off to the hills," envisioning her friend in the inviolate landscape of paradise (442).

As Ellen listens to the church bells of the valley toll in recognition of Alice's death, John Humphreys appears — the only time in the novel he invades the female space of the mountain. He speaks in a low tone, quoting a verse from Psalms, "I will lift up mine eyes unto the hills, from whence cometh my help!" (443) — echoing Alice's earlier note that "he whose hand raised up those mountains" will give Ellen what she needs (153). His words are a balm to Ellen, who communicates her grief best through metaphors of landscape, and she embraces John. He asks, "Shall we go home now?" ready to guide her down the mountain. In subservience, she replies, "Oh, yes — whenever you please." Before leaving the scene, John reminds Ellen, "Dear Alice is well — she is well, — and if *we* are made to suffer, we know and we love the hand that has done it, — do we not Ellie?" (443). John's remark, "*we* are made to suffer," is reminiscent of Mrs. Montgomery's counsel to her daughter early in the novel: "though we *must* sorrow, we must not rebel" (12). This command is too much for Ellen. Instead of affirming John's assertion, she covers her face with her hands, feeling "her heart would break" (443–444). Ellen's "duty" to submission requires her removal from the feminine space of the mountain. She has realized that the extreme passions of the semiotic — the "unspeakable destruction and unspeakable pleasure" (Smith 16) — have a limited potential. Imitating transparency is more productive. Mollified and subdued, Ellen is escorted hand-in-hand by John down the mountain — the last time Ellen is shown in this female-identified, female-empowered landscape. Her submission to John and patriarchal norms, it appears, is almost complete.

The novel concludes with John effectively breaking into the Lindsay home in Scotland, where Ellen is cloistered soon after the last scene on the mountain. He tells her, "I think you belong to me more than to any body," to which she eagerly agrees. After being assured that Ellen is still heeding his moral lessons (including "Read no novels" [Warner 564]), John wins permission to correspond to Ellen. The "seed so early sown in little Ellen's mind" blossoms, "and at the point of its young maturity it happily fell again into those hands that had of all been most successful in its culture." The last paragraph suggests that, after "[t]hree or four more years of Scottish discipline [that] wrought her no ill," Ellen marries John: "to her unspeakable joy, she went back to spend her life with the friends and guardians she best loved, and to be to them, still more than she had been to her Scottish relations, 'the light of the eyes'" (569).

Ended here, the text seems to suggest the complete transparency and disappearance of Ellen's will. The novel closes with Ellen becoming nothing more than a dim beacon for stifled femininity. But this is not the original ending. A final chapter, not published until the recent reissue of the novel, gives Ellen more chance for subversion. Ellen does indeed marry John, effectively taking Alice's place and becoming mistress of the mountain household where, like Alice, she enjoys a level of independence. With marriage, she receives what Virginia Woolf asserted many nineteenth-century women craved — "A room of her own and five-hundred a year" (Woolf, *Room*, 94). Ellen is given her own study (that John has decorated and stocked), complete with engravings, stationery, books, and furniture to receive guests — and her own lock and key. John promises a riding horse for her and instills a head housekeeper, freeing Ellen from domestic duties. To modern readers, these paltry rewards for Ellen's trials seem insufficient. Ellen has been taught to submit all her desires before patriarchal authority and has seemed to lose all personality. But this submission is a performative act that gives her access to a limited power. As Hovet and Hovet point out, Ellen's position as object also has a "strong subversive element" (342). By masquerading as the transparent object, Ellen gains a type of autonomy. Playing drag, Ellen *appears* to conform to expectations of female behavior and position — but she also gets what she wants: she has escaped from her sadistic uncle's household and has become mistress of her own home. Her apparent conformity is rewarded, and she is allowed a level of freedom she has never experienced before: access to her own room, her own horse — and her own money, of which John promises, "I shall never ask you how you spend it" (Warner 582).

But the novel's most potent metaphor is Ellen's return to the landscape of freedom. Living halfway up the mountain, Ellen is granted a limited independence. She does not have the level of autonomy that Mrs. Vawse does, but she does return to the semiotic landscape, where she can view the mountain from her windows and climb it at will and where the example of Mrs. Vawse, who lives at the very top of the mountain, provides an alternative femininity. Thus, although *The Wide, Wide World* appears on one level to advocate the restriction and control of women's minds and bodies, on another, a landscape of subversion is imagined. Ellen Montgomery, Alice Humphreys, and Mrs. Vawse all *appear* to submit wholeheartedly to patriarchal expectation and religious instruction, performing sanctioned gender and social roles flawlessly. Their performances allow their frequent escapes to the semiotic mountain to remain unchallenged.

Learning the performative aspect of transparency, these women "occupy both the center and the margin, the inside and the outside"— the definition of Rose's paradoxical space (155). The mountain is the physical emblem of this paradoxical space. Located on the periphery of the town, this landscape is close enough to civil and religious rule not to raise suspicion; the mountain is ringed by settlement and seems an extension of the cultivated valleys. But the wild isolation of this space allows for the development of alternative reiterations. Alone or with other women in this undeveloped environment, Warner's female characters find inspiration, rejuvenation, and freedom from overt pressures of patriarchy.

As these women enact their sanctioned gender roles, they project gender onto the landscape, sexing it female. The mountain is given nurturing qualities: its "breast" is a maternal substitute for Ellen. The mountain is also the site of unpredictable, semiotic storms — and the abode of the "child of nature," Nancy. But nature is, at times, exceptionally sympathetic, particularly in regard to the motherless child, Ellen (as well as Alice). While the mountain performs the traditional roles of the comforting mother or the terrifying Medusa conjuring up storms at will (but never, it should be noted, performing as the seductive virgin), these tropes transcend stereotype, and the mountain is constructed as an active participator in the plot. The paradoxical mountain challenges expectations of gender performatives. It acts "feminine," but it is not dependent on the masculinist gaze for signification. In fact, men are almost never seen in relation to the feminine mountain. Only once does John approach Ellen when she is in this landscape, and none of the male characters appreciates the mountain or its views as the female characters do. The first time Ellen sees the mountain, she exclaims, "How beautiful! Oh, how beautiful!" to Miss Fortune's farmhand, Mr. Van Brunt, who responds "in his slow way, 'it'll be a fine day for the field.'" Ellen again guides his eyes to the view, but "Mr. Van Brunt didn't know what to say to this" (Warner 131). The mountain landscape is constructed as an exclusively female environment, and Ellen, Alice, Nancy, and Mrs. Vawse are explicitly connected to the mountain.

In exploring the crossroads between semiotics, performativity theory, and feminist geography, a new language and set of metaphors are incorporated into the debate surrounding *The Wide, Wide World* — and into the wider debate regarding gender and the representation of landscape generally. As illustrated by this novel, the metaphor land-as-woman can be constructed as paradoxical — as land-as-drag. In Susan Warner's novel, landscape and the women associated with a particular space can undermine gender expectations by working within them. By performing and masquerading traditional roles, women can use landscape fantasies to create paradoxical spaces in which to experiment with freedom and subversion. Full opposition to gender and sex roles is rarely, if ever, possible in novels that explore these issues (just as it is rarely, if ever, possible in real space), but texts such as Susan Warner's *The Wide, Wide World* give the reader a glimpse of the possibility of an alternative reiteration — the possibility of appropriating conventional approaches to landscape and gender representation and then subverting them. The metaphor land-as-woman, so often used to control and dominate women and the natural environment alike, can offer a space where an alternative feminine identity can be attempted.

NOTES

1. For Kristeva, the semiotic is not a physical state of child development "but the memory, the inscription of this state in language." The semiotic is situated in a bodily memory (or "mnemonic traces") left over from the various "destructive and pleasurable drives" encountered before the infant experiences separation from the mother; this memory of intense pleasure and pain is "unspeakable" but can be communicated through various forms of "imaginative practice" (Smith 16–17).

2. Gillian Rose notes that the maternal landscape can threaten to emasculate men by subsuming them: as the "desired and feared Mother, both phallic and castrated," "[l]andscape can then be not the welcoming topography of nurturing mother but terrifying maternal swamps, mountains, seas, inhabited by sphinxes and gorgons" (106).

3. Hovet and Hovet write, "That Warner has Emerson's rhetoric of vision in mind in portraying the gaze is clear not only in the frequent echoes of Emerson in John's discourse, but also because, as David Leverenz has noted, one of the central characters, Aunt Fortune Emerson, might be sarcastically named after the Concord Sage because 'any woman would find it a "misfortune" to be an Emerson'" (338).

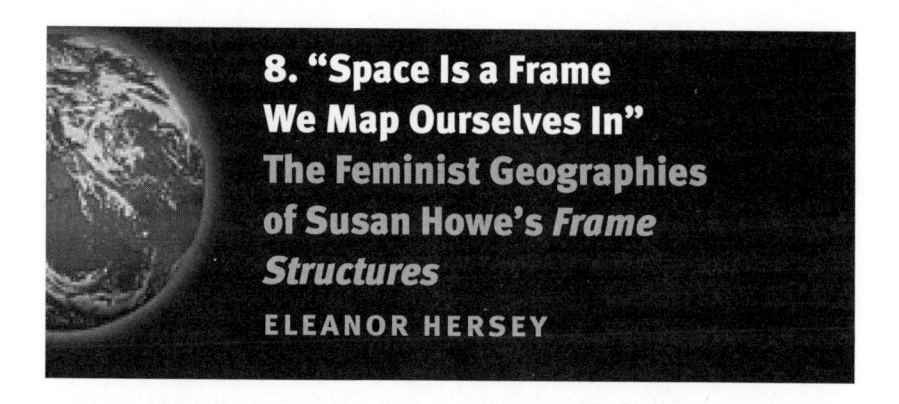

8. "Space Is a Frame We Map Ourselves In"
The Feminist Geographies of Susan Howe's *Frame Structures*

ELEANOR HERSEY

The beginning of Susan Howe's essay "Frame Structures" contains an 1812 sketch entitled "The Second Oldest View of Buffalo." Ships are anchored in the harbor, and buildings and sections of shoreline are marked with tiny white numbers, some nearly illegible as they fade into the landscape. The caption states that the sketch accompanied a report to the secretary of the navy on the capture of the *Detroit* and *Caledonia*, yet the key is missing, and the significance of the numbers is lost. On the next page, the text begins with Howe's memory of a trip to the zoo in Delaware Park on December 7, 1941, the date of the Japanese attack on Pearl Harbor: "On that Sunday in Buffalo the usually docile polar bears roved restlessly back and forth around the simulated rocks caves and waterfall designed to keep brute force fenced off even by menace of embrace" (3). The juxtaposition of these two wartime images of Buffalo, created over a century apart from contrasting perspectives, reflects the text's preoccupation with the (im)possibilites of cartographic representation in what Howe calls a "field of history." With these images, Howe introduces a central question posed by *Frame Structures*: how does one represent the historical and cultural complexity of a place that is always already divided, conquered, framed, and structured by others? Is it possible to reclaim, remark, remake, remap this place in order to reflect one's own partial perspective?

"Frame Structures," written in 1995 as the introduction to a collection of early poems published under the same title, focuses on Howe's multi-dimensional, unstable, and often paradoxical relationships to the places in which she and her family have lived. Howe's commitment to place and to situated knowledge link this prose-poetic essay to the anthologies of feminist geographical writing that appeared in the 1990s, including *Writing Women and Space: Colonial and Postcolonial Geographies* (1994), *Feminist Geographies: Explorations in Diversity and Difference* (1997), *Space, Gender, Knowledge: Feminist Readings* (1997), and *Making Worlds: Gender, Metaphor, Materiality* (1998). In a creative expression of some of the major innovations of feminist geography, Howe disrupts the colonial vision of transparent space, investigates the paradoxical spaces of the academy, and challenges the assumption that domestic space is exclusively private or feminine. These aspects of Howe's work demonstrate the value of formally innovative writing to the broader project of environmental literary criticism. Rather than making straightforward, didactic claims about the value of "the environment," Howe employs a fragmented, nonlinear style to demonstrate the subjective nature of all human experiences of the environments in which we live and work. The juxtaposed images of colonial, academic, and domestic spaces in "Frame Structures" challenge environmental literary critics to engage with feminist geographies in order to achieve a nuanced understanding of our postmodern culture.

"TRUST THE PLACE TO FORM THE VOICE": *FRAME STRUCTURES* AND FEMINIST GEOGRAPHY

Howe's interest in landscape, mapping, boundaries, margins, surveying, and architecture preceded, and in a way motivated, her career as a poet. In an interview with Lynn Keller, Howe claims that her decision to move from lists of words to composed lines was inspired by the role of archaeology, mapping, and space in the work of Charles Olson and Robert Smithson, as well as by the advice of a friend: "Before we moved out of New York I had started making environments — rooms that you could walk into and be surrounded by walls, and on those walls would be collage, using found photographs (again a kind of quotation). Then I started using words with that work. I was at the point where I was only putting words on the walls and I had surrounded myself with words that were really composed lines when a friend, the poet Ted Greenwald, came by to look at what I was doing and said to me: 'Actually you have a book on the wall. Why don't you just put it into a book?'" (6).

The movement in this passage from a specific place, New York, to the action of making environments, to the specific identity of the book, reflects the connection between the physical places in and about which Howe writes and the location of her words on the page. In the Keller interview, for example, Howe links the experience of reading "Thorow" at a twelfth-century church in southern France to the loss of space on the page in larger-press editions of her poems. The freedom to let the elements of a particular location inspire the reading disappears when the poet must "fight for every inch of space" (18). Despite the close connection in Howe's poetics between place and page, critics often discuss the latter at the expense of the former or conflate the two through the use of geographical metaphor.[1] Yet Howe challenges us to "Trust the place to form the voice" (*Birth-mark* 156), to take seriously the origins of her poetic work.

The movement in Howe's career from "putting words on the walls" to creating a geographical poetics parallels the movement in feminist geography from studying so-called women's space to challenging the epistemological foundations of the discipline. In *Space, Gender, Knowledge,* Linda McDowell and Joanne P. Sharp summarize the reasons that "space matters" to feminism:

> Spatial relations and layout, the differences between and within places, the nature and form of the built environment, images and representations of this environment and of the "natural" world, ways of writing about it, as well as our bodily place within it, are all part and parcel of the social constitution of gendered social relations and the structure and meaning of place. The spaces in which social practices occur affect the nature of those practices, who is "in place," who is "out of place" and even who is allowed to be there at all. But the spaces themselves in turn are constructed and given meaning through the social practices that define men and women as different and unequal. (2–3)

The section titles of McDowell and Sharp's book reflect some of the major debates and issues that continue to engage feminist geographers. The section title "in the beginning there were two positions" suggests the binary oppositions that much recent work has fought to destabilize: radical feminism and socialist feminism, active and passive, public and private. Although the phrase "different and unequal" in the quotation above demonstrates the continuing influence of the rhetoric of difference, *Space, Gender, Knowledge* is one of several recent anthologies of feminist geographical writing that charts the attempt to move beyond these oppositions. Another section title, "Decentering 'woman,'" suggests the influence of postcolonial and postmodern feminist theories that emphasize fluidity, hybridity, and multiplicity, while another section of the book describes the recent interest in image and discourse that links geography to the humanities and social sciences.

Howe's autobiographical project in *Frame Structures* is linked to contemporary developments in feminist geography primarily through her commitment to what Adrienne Rich calls a "politics of location" and Donna Haraway calls "situated knowledge." In "Notes toward a Politics of Location," Rich claims: "As a woman I have a country; as a woman I cannot divest myself of that country merely by condemning its government or by saying three times 'As a woman my country is the whole world'" (212). In "Situated Knowledges," Haraway also claims: "The only way to find a larger vision is to be somewhere in particular" (590). In "Geographic Metaphors in Feminist Theory," Geraldine Pratt argues that these ideas need to be reiterated yet today, when metaphors of dislocation, exile, and marginality allow many feminist scholars to evade their responsibilities to specific locales: "There seem serious reasons for reexamining the positive ethics of dwelling in place and for holding these in close tension with the rhetoric and romance of margins and mobility" (20). These theories, which have been extremely influential in the formation of an antiessentialist feminist geography, contextualize Howe's choice to open "Frame Structures" with a personal memory located in place and time: the Delaware Park zoo in Buffalo on December 7, 1941. Howe's focus on her childhood homes, Buffalo and Cambridge, reflects her interest in her own unique cultural and political development, which is not reducible to one manifestation of a universal female experience.

The complex, contradictory voice and fragmented, nonchronological style of *Frame Structures* parallel the subversions of conventional academic discourse made by many feminist geographers. Gillian Rose describes the written voice of geography as "unextravagant, unembellished, unpretentious, unexceptional. Un(re)marked" (8). In order to defy this discourse, women geographers write personal narratives of their careers (Women and Geography Study Group 23–41) and create and present epistolary exchanges (Bammer et al.). *Frame Structures* also defies conventional geographic discourse through thirteen sections of varying length that blend autobiography with familial, national, and international histories, juxtaposing prose taken from historical documents with lyrical sections that defy fixed interpretation. The pragmatic function of Howe's essay as an introduction to the poems in *Frame Structures* may be compromised by this formal complexity. Yet its form and content parallel the preoccupations of contemporary feminist geography as they have evolved alongside Howe's poetics from words on walls to an examination of the discourses of representation itself.

"WILD LANDS": COLONIAL GEOGRAPHIES

Howe's focus on colonial space and mapping in "Frame Structures" begins with a brief history of the Holland Land Company. This group of wealthy gentlemen "agreed to purchase huge undeveloped tracts, then referred to as 'wild lands,' in the central and western parts of New York and Pennsylvania" to sell to poor settlers from Germany, Scotland, and Ireland (4). Through word play and autobiographical anecdote, Howe links this vision to that of the Royal Niger Company, "a private organization established to meet the requirements of British trade along Africa's third largest river during the European 'scramble for Africa' of the 1880s" (11). Together, these companies represent a colonial vision of the "wild lands" along the Niagara and Niger Rivers as transparent spaces for European men to purchase, survey, and develop. As Alison Blunt and Gillian Rose claim in *Writing Women and Space*, "Through transparent space, all places can be mapped in terms of their relationship to Europe. Imperialist maps not only describe colonies: they also discipline them through the discursive grids of Western power/knowledge" (15).[2] Beginning with the image of Buffalo in 1812, Howe emphasizes the violence implicit in such discursive grids and demonstrates alternative ways of mapping the field of colonial history.[3]

In her discussions of the Holland Land Company, Howe disrupts the syntax of colonial discourse in order to deconstruct the myth that American land was fought for and fairly won by oppressed European settlers. Although John Adams helped to draft a Declaration of Independence based on freedom and equality, Howe notes: "His not being able to see why no one who is not an owner can be recognized by law to be a possessor" (*Frame Structures* 3). The logical gap in the rhetoric of American liberty is represented by an incomplete sentence filled with negatives, reminding us that "historical imagination gathers in the missing" (3). The subject of the sentence is negative, a gap, his "not." The verb is missing, emphasizing the arbitrary distinction between owner and possessor while compelling readers to engage actively in the reconstruction of a historical imagination rather than passively receiving information. Howe critiques the exhaustive vision of traditional European cartography: "Federalism: its breadth and all-embracing perspective. Lines represent the limits of bodies encompassed by the eye" (5). To disrupt the discursive grid represented by lines on maps of the New World, Howe draws attention to the limits imposed by bodies of water, like the Atlantic Ocean, and by the physical body and partial perspective (eye/I) of the cartographer. The double meaning of the word "encompassed," to include and to enclose, suggests the close connection between the myth of an all-inclusive, all-embracing European gaze and the historical necessity of enclosing the space of the New World within limits imposed by European power/knowledge.[4]

In the subsection of "Frame Structures" titled "Craigie Circle," Howe links the imperial geographies of the Holland Land Company to those of the Royal Niger Company, which was created to demarcate the borders of "what land was still theoretically unclaimed in the African continent" in the late nineteenth century (12). Howe takes the boundaries of the territory from an old encyclopedia: "NIGERIA. A British protectorate in West Africa occupying the lower basin of the Niger and the country between that river and Lake Chad. . . . It embraces most of the territory in the square formed by the meridians of 3° and 14° E., and the parallels of 4° and 14° N., and has an area of about 338,000 sq.m" (12). Howe's claim that "irony is saying one thing while meaning another" (11) frames this example of conventional geographical discourse, in which words like "protectorate" and "embraces" allow the ostensibly unbiased writer to represent European colonization as an intimate relationship. The encyclopedia entry for Nigeria is followed by those for Niger and Niagara, appearing side-by-side in a discursive remapping of the former British empire. Placing the weight of comparison on similarities of sound rather than on the (colonial) map of the world as we know it, Howe emphasizes the discursive foundations of colonialism and destabilizes the "divide-and-conquer" logic of the British empire.[5]

The troubled relationship between Howe's maternal grandparents, John Fitzmaurice and Susan Manning, represents the always unsettled relationships between colonial and colonized places and between male and female experiences of empire. Her descriptions of the Mannings' movement between a home in Ireland and a colonial outpost in Nigeria take both places seriously: "So there are two images. Two phases of thought many miles apart" (15). Howe describes her grandfather as "[i]rrelevant, eccentric, cross; when he did come home he drank and was bad tempered so they didn't miss him when he left again. Leaving leaving arriving arriving. Even a civilized person will kick a door whatever the policy if modernity surrounds every threshold point of contact" (12). The adjectives that Howe uses to describe her grandfather emphasize his identity as a colonizer: nonproportional, off-center, located at the intersection (cross) between cultures yet rejected by both. The mobility of both husband and wife ("Leaving leaving arriving arriving") challenges the absolute distinction between center (Britain) and margin (colonial outpost). The image of a "civilized person" kicking (in?) a door creates a compelling reversal of the project of colonization: Britain is invaded by its own colonial subject in the unsettling geographies of modernity. As a "threshold point of contact," Ireland also represents the liminal spaces of the British empire, neither home base nor colony but an intersection of the two, another example of the impossibility of representing the history of British colonization with a single grid or chronology.

In "Th'expence of Spirit in a waste of shame," Howe establishes an alternative genealogy, linking the New World to the Old through the deeds of her paternal ancestors: "Lustful and manifest in action, men in the early d'Wolf and Howe families were generally sea captains, privateers, slave traders; some involved in the China trade, others in whaling; most sailed out of Bristol, Rhode Island" (20). Howe links her family history to her academic interests through the figure of Weetamoo, "squaw-sachem" of the Wampanoags, whose dead body washed up on land that would become Weetamoe, the Howe farm:

Narrative voices of landowners map a past which is established. The person taking possession talks of the lure and loot long after the shock of first assault. Mow(e) rhymes visually with how(e) and aurally with moo. Of course there would be mowed lawns around the house because the soul is conceived to be a facsimile of the body. Fields where cows graze are closer to primordial verbal material. . . . In the nineteenth century *Weetamoe* was a working farm owned by gentleman farmers. Just think of your ears as eyes over mirrors Weetamoo.

Cinder of the lexical drift. (22)

In this passage, the logical relationships between sentences break down, destabilizing the false concept of a "past which is established" and reflecting the experience of a Native American woman who was chased through the woods for years, constantly being taken captive by and escaping from "murderous Christian soldiers" (22). Syntax based on word play and mirroring blurs the distinctions between words and animal sounds, mowed lawns and wilderness, the soul and the body, reflecting the point of contact between the gentleman's farm and the washed-up corpse. Only the "lexical drift" leaves a trace, a map made of ashes, a language fluid enough to reflect the "primordial verbal material" of the colonial encounter.

"THE ANGEL IN THE LIBRARY": ACADEMIA AS PARADOXICAL SPACE

The subsection title "The Angel in the Library" represents Howe's unsettled and unsettling relationship to the academy as a female poet-critic. As an allusion to the phrase "Angel in the House," the title recalls feminist critiques of the historical confinement of women to the home and their exclusion from the academy.[6] Yet "The Angel in the Library" extends this critique to more subtle forms of inclusion and exclusion, which can neither be mapped onto distinct places nor explained by oppositions like professional and domestic, public and private, mind and soul. While the Angel in the House is ostensibly a thing of the past, a literary stereotype crippled or killed by feminism, the Angel in the Library is a contemporary phenomenon. Howe writes in *The Birth-mark*: "I am drawn toward the disciplines of history and literary criticism but in the dawning distance a dark wall of rule supports the structure of every letter, record, transcript: every proof of authority and power. . . . I know this and go on searching for some trace of love's infolding through all the paper in all the libraries I come to" (4). In this passage and in "Frame Structures," Howe experiences academia as a paradoxical space. As Gillian Rose claims, "This space is multidimensional, shifting and contingent. It is also paradoxical, by which

I mean that spaces that would be mutually exclusive if charted on a two-dimensional map — centre and margin, inside and outside — are occupied simultaneously" (140). Howe's approach to academic space privileges contradiction ("I know this and go on searching") and infolding, an image of fluidity and enclosure represented by the page rather than the wall.

In "Craigie Circle," Howe contrasts the ways in which critic I. A. Richards, psychologist B. F. Skinner, and poet Henry Wadsworth Longfellow experienced the academic spaces of "both Cambridges," England and Massachusetts. Howe critiques the theories of Richards and Skinner by linking them metaphorically to the colonial geographies of the Holland Land Company and Royal Niger Company. Extending a metaphor from *The Birth-mark*, "I go to libraries because they are the ocean" (18), in "Craige Circle" Howe describes Richards's scathing criticism of Longfellow's poetry as an act of piracy: "The waters of the Atlantic closed over the Wreck of the Hesperus" (8). If the library is an ocean, then literary critics are its coast guard, policing the wild lands of poetry with the disciplinary grids of "deep structure." Howe also provides a fragment of (auto)biographical information about Skinner: "My sister Fanny remembers her fear of open spaces between Berkeley and Huron because somewhere close to us the Skinners' daughters were being brought up in boxes. When the boxes called air-cribs were put outside for air she thought she saw internal objects. I must have blocked them out" (10). In a perversion of the Angel in the House ideal, Skinner's daughters are infantalized, bestialized, and objectified by a confinement that extends to the Howe sisters, causing Fanny to develop a fear of open spaces and Susan to restrict her vision.

Whereas Richards and Skinner are associated with confinement, enclosure, and the attempt to discipline poetic space, Harvard professor-poet Henry Wadsworth Longfellow represents the remapping of Cambridge as an arcadian wilderness.[7] Howe associates the children's footpaths through the town with the first lines of Longfellow's *Evangeline: A Tale of Acadie*: "'This is the forest primeval. The murmuring pines and the hemlocks, / Bearded with moss, and in garments green, indistinct in the twilight'" (10). The similarity between the words "Acadie," "arcadian," and "academy" link this nineteenth-century poem to the "wilder patches" of the college town of Cambridge, where the children of professors experience a breakdown of linguistic, historical, and geographical boundaries.

Yet the lines that follow those cited by Howe suggest the poem's thematic connection to the verse-novel *The Angel in the House*:

> Ye who believe in affection that hopes, and endures, and is patient,
> Ye who believe in the beauty and strength of woman's devotion,
> List to the mournful tradition, still sung by the pines of the forest;
> List to a Tale of Love in Acadie, home of the happy. (Longfellow 57–58)

Although Howe finds Longfellow's discursive remapping of Cambridge more liberating than the models she finds in Richards and Skinner, the invocation of "woman's devotion" suggests that even arcadian wilderness is often confining for women.

In "The Angel in the Library," Howe focuses on the experience of the poet-critic in the academic library:

> What is it about *documents* that seems to require their relegation to the bedroom (a private place) as if they were bourgeois Victorian women? Honored, looked to for advice, shielded from the rabble by guardians of "tradition"/ "aesthetic taste," available only to particular researchers (husbands or bachelor machines) and caretakers (librarians cataloguers secretaries) so long as they are desirable (readable not too tattered) capable of bearing children (articles chapters books) rearing them (aiding research), they remain sheltered at home (museum collections libraries). (18)

The syntax of this passage both enacts and disrupts the separation between domestic space, coded as private and feminine, and academic space, coded as public and masculine. The use of parentheses rather than commas, periods, or semicolons creates a single, fluid sentence about bourgeois domesticity into which academic activities are inserted, reflecting the feminine reality in which academic work must be brought home rather than kept separate in the space of a study or office. Placing the rhetoric of desirability and maternity next to that of reading and research, Howe evokes and destabilizes the view of pages, texts, and materials as feminized objects for the penetration and inscription of masculine pens. The description of the library as a bedroom and of the texts as desirable, in contrast to the rhetoric of tradition and taste, also emphasizes the often erotic nature of academic work that claims to be disembodied and objective.[8]

Like Howe's description of her exclusion from Harvard's Widener Library as a teenager (*The Birth-mark* 18), an anecdote about the Sterling Library at Yale in "Frame Structures" reflects her lingering feeling of exclusion from the academy. "I was struck by a reproduction of an early American painting, 'Congress Voting Independence,' and thought I might use it on the cover of this book. . . . I found the right shelf but all issues of the periodical had been removed to the Franklin Collection Room, a place so far unknown to me" (18–19). This room turns out to be guarded from the public by a librarian who asks Howe to produce credentials, proof of her official connection to the academy. Even after passing this barrier, Howe experiences difficulty negotiating the space in which all texts are stored that "even obliquely concern Benjamin Franklin or Philadelphia I'm not sure which because so many people consider both man and city as ideal stand-ins for America's Age of Reason" (19). Howe was searching for a painting representing a major event in American history, but it is "sheltered from the public gaze" (19) in a room dedicated to men and reason.[9] Howe's inability to make out the "scheme of order" of the Franklin Room is reflected in her decision to place a photograph of David von Schlegell's *India Wharf Sculpture* on the cover of *Frame Structures*. This skeleton of beams leaning out over Boston harbor can be read as a rejection of the closed space of the academic library, a public celebration of an art of inclusiveness, exposure, and trespass in direct contrast to the Franklin Room with its inaccessible painting.

"'NICE' CHILDREN GOOD MANNERS IN ARCHITECTURE": RECONFIGURATIONS OF DOMESTIC SPACE

The narrative of *Frame Structures*, a mélange of autobiography and biography, personal and national history, consists of details taken from texts or memories: a faded blue parasol, the carved banister of a stairwell, the tiny ivory bell in the entrance of a carved pagoda. Through these details, Howe renders the domestic spaces of her childhood both familiar and unfamiliar, as they refuse to correspond to the conventional association of domestic space with the feminine. Howe's descriptions of Longfellow House on Craigie Circle and her grandfather's apartment on Louisburg Square illustrate Rose's claim: "For many feminists now, to think of the geography of difference is extremely complex. This geography can no longer simply be a mapping of social power relations onto territorial spaces: masculine and feminine onto public and private" (150–151). In Longfellow House, the boundary between public museum and private dwelling is as thin as a velvet rope; in her grandfather's apartment, the traces of a single-family dwelling mark the hallways with the complex social history of the area. Howe interrogates the connections between memory and writing through shifts in narrative position between child and adult: "Writing from perception to recollection I imagine a carved human figure at the door on each landing, semitransparent. Innocency. A pure past that returns to itself unattackable in the framework. Restoration" (26). Referring both to architecture and to memory, "Restoration" signifies the maintenance of domestic spaces within this text.

Howe begins "Craigie Circle" with a history of restorations, in which Vassall House on Tory Row becomes Craigie House on Brattle Street becomes Longfellow House on Craigie Circle, a museum run by the National Park Service. Howe's childhood visits to this house after church demonstrate its paradoxical nature:

> Later we might sit in the dining room of Longfellow House eating lunch on one side of a roped-off area while the resident poet-caretaker guided sightseers single-file along the other side of the barrier pointing out ornaments, furnishings, portraits, structural details; as if we were ghosts. If private space is the space of private writing, objects must be arranged in position (witnesses and vanishing points) not looking both ways at once. Something about nature "nice" children good manners in architecture. Space is a frame we map ourselves in. (9)

The situation is wonderfully ironic: since the restoration of Longfellow House is only half-finished, visitors are confronted with the image of Longfellow's descendants and their young visitor, Susan Howe, eating lunch in the section that is still a private residence. The symbolic barrier, like many others in "Frame Structures," fails to separate past from present, public space from private space, simulacrum from reality; it represents a "vanishing point" of these distinctions, in which museumgoers as "witnesses" must look "both ways at once." The space of "private writing" is superimposed on a space of public consumption through an obsessive attention to its ornaments, furnishings, portraits, and structural details, while the poet-caretaker represents the merging of (male) author and (female) housekeeper. Howe's comparison of herself and her family to ghosts destabilizes the possibility of nice children and good manners in architecture, suggesting that all domestic spaces are haunted by their own contradictions.

The story of the gruesome death of Fanny Appleton Longfellow provides another glimpse of the ghosts that haunt this place. As she sits in the family library melting wax to close locks of her daughters' hair in boxes, Fanny's dress catches fire, and she burns to death. The link between domestic confinement and physical danger is clear: "Envelopes and boxes are often metaphorically linked with motherly contrivance. Domesticity is in her hands" (14). When she catches fire, she is "[e]nveloped in flame" and smothered with a rug by her frantic husband. This connection is complicated, however, by the rhetoric of war: "As shadows wait on the sun so a shot soul falling shot leaves its body fathomless to draw it out. The armies are tired of their terrible mismanagement not counting the missing" (14). Echoing the phrase "Historical imagination gathers in the missing" (3), this language recalls the opening of "Frame Structures" on Pearl Harbor Day. Howe emphasizes the relationships between familial and national histories by framing a childhood trip to the zoo and Fanny Longfellow's death with American wars. The description of Fanny waking after death to a world without pain emphasizes the connection between these historical moments: "Edenic mapping of the New World Acadie. Softly softly hear the noise of distant falls of many wars and wars for national independence" (15). The juxtaposition of the American colonists' war for independence and Acadie reflects the spatial history of Longfellow House, in which George Washington "planned and commanded the siege of Boston" from the room that Henry Wadsworth Longfellow would later occupy (8). Personal and national histories form a narrative palimpsest written on this place, precluding its exclusive identification with the private, the feminine, the domestic.

In "Irish American English," Howe describes the living space of her androgynous paternal grandfather, Mark Antony DeWolfe Howe, in which the transition of a single-family home into an apartment building marks a transition in the distinction between public and private space. Although the hallway and stairway of the building are now public, the architecture of the restoration requires visitors to pass through Mark Howe's bedroom to reach his living room, trespassing into an "intimate space, normally closed to the public in genteel domestic arrangements of the 1940s" (25).

As a child, Howe became fascinated with the bed in which her grandfather was born at Weetamoe: "If a house is a stage for the theater of the family this was a stage within a stage because the mattress was so high off the ground it could have been a platform and the four mahogany bedposts had curtains though I don't think he ever pulled them shut" (25). This stage within a stage further complicates the spatial dynamics of this apartment: as a bed within a 1940s bedroom it remains a private place, yet as a stage with open curtains, accessible to every visitor, it is a public one.[10] Howe's mention of the year in which her grandfather was born, "as long ago as the same year Abraham Lincoln was assassinated" (25), breaks down the boundaries between present and past, between the history of her great-grandmother's labor and the history of the nation. The reference to "The Little Red Riding Hood," a classic tale of gender-bending and an unwritten pun on the old family name, d'Wolf, suggests that this bed occupies a space beyond essentialist notions of gender performance.

The ivory pagoda in the dining room, another place within the domestic space of the Louisburg Square apartment, links the family's colonizing past to the haunted Longfellow House. Howe imagines that it "must have been acquired in China by a predatory d'Wolf or an entrepreneurial Quincy and brought back to Bristol or Boston as loot. . . . If there is a sudden vibration in the dining room on our side of being . . . even a draft from the window is enough, all the skeletal bells shake as if the present can coexist in thin paper dress" (26). This description of the pagoda emphasizes the intersections between the d'Wolf past and the Howe present, China and America, the spaces of the dead and the living, art and architecture, map and building, representation and reality, that are all implicit in the title and project of *Frame Structures*. The enigmatic phrase "the present can coexist in thin paper dress" suggests a multiple present made up of coexistences, held in tension with one another on the page on which Howe maps these possibilities, the most paradoxical place of all.

In *The Fate of Place*, Edward S. Casey distinguishes between the Western philosophical concepts of space (universe) and place (cosmos), asserting that "the universe is mapped in physics and projected in theology: it is the transcendent geography of infinite space. The cosmos is sensed in concrete landscapes as lived, remembered, or painted: it is the immanent scene of finite place as felt by an equally finite body" (78). My reading of *Frame Structures* has focused on Howe's commitment to place, in the explicitly feminist context of the politics of location. Yet the phrase that begins the title of this essay, "Space is a frame we map ourselves in," suggests Howe's subtlety as a philosopher of place and, by extension, the relevance of postmodern writing to contemporary ecocriticism. By defining it as a frame in which we make sense of ourselves and of the world, Howe transforms space, the infinite and universal, into place, the finite and particular, reflecting the trend of contemporary thought that Casey notes at the end of his text: "space is being reassimilated into place, made part of its substance and structure" (340). Although postmodern literature is often linked to space and/or displacement, *Frame Structures* focuses on the political, economic, ecological, and emotional primacy of place for late-twentieth-century writers. Reminding us that "we map ourselves," Howe also emphasizes the active role of the reader in the identical activities of negotiating identity and representing place.

NOTES

1. George F. Butterick represents Howe's interrogations of material space as metaphors, claiming that she fights epic encounters in "her own New England of the mind" (316) and that she lives "on a frontier of the imagination, along with a family of thought in a wood of words," (319). Paul Kenneth Naylor's reading of "Thorow" in "Where Are We Now in Poetry?" reflects the tension between metaphorical and material interpretations of Howe's poetic landscape: while he insists that "she participates in the tradition of pure poetry that seeks to create a world of words," he claims that "she does not attempt to seal this world off from the real world of historical fact" (39). Hank Lazer takes Howe's commitment to the specificity of place seriously: "She resides at . . . the theological/spiritual/conceptual Nile of early America, the Connecticut River Valley (which, in light of Howe's compositional fragmentation, might be read as connect-I-cut)" (62). Bob Perelman's brief discussion of "Thorow" in *The Marginalization of Poetry* also avoids the temptation to metaphor by attending to the role of autobiography, gender, and history in the construction of landscape, as does Michael Davidson's discussion of the dynamics of the page in *Ghostlier Demarcations*.

2. In *Frame Structures*, Howe stresses that the "wild lands" that the members of the Holland Land Company saw as empty and uninscribed had been settled for years before their explorers and surveyors divided it up: "He [Joseph Ellicott] renames the village New Amsterdam although members of the Seneca nation living there under British protection since 1780, along with other traders, trappers, and farmers, already refer to the settlement as Buffalo Creek" (28). While the word "renames" emphasizes the existence of a previous name, destabilizing the colonialist notion that to name is to own, "New Amsterdam" signifies the Europeans'

attempt to discipline this space. In contrast to the local name Buffalo Creek, New Amsterdam represents the assumptions that the village is "new" (uninhabited by Europeans) and an extension of Europe/ Holland/ Amsterdam. For analyses of the role of the wilderness in Howe's poetry, see Rachel DuPlessis's discussion of Howe's work as a textual hunt in *The Pink Guitar*, Ming-Qian Ma's discussion of language and violence in "Articulating the Inarticulate," and Bob Perelman on the narrator as scout in *The Marginalization of Poetry*.

3. Howe reinforces the connection between colonization and war by interrupting her historical accounts of the Holland Land Company with autobiographical accounts of her father's absence during World War II, creating a link between the invasion of Hawaii by Japan on December 7, 1941, the date with which Howe opens "Frame Structures," and the invasion of New York by the Holland Land Company's representatives in the eighteenth century. Howe's reminder that "women and children experience war and its nightmare" (7) also links the women and children displaced by World War II to those whose deaths are not recorded in the history of the settlement of America.

4. Howe also draws attention to these limits by focusing on her role as archivist and the location of these official histories in the "wilderness" of local libraries: "Land speculators, surveyors, promoters, publicists, and primitive judges were extraordinarily free in terms of strategic flight into the wilderness. If one sticks to the letter, now where are their names indexed?" (*Frame Structures* 6). Interrupting her description of Joseph Ellicott's almost total control over the location of towns, cities, and villages in New York, Howe informs us that "I learned about him from out-of-print records and journals published by local antiquarian societies" (5). Ellicott's influence is written on every map of this territory, yet the fact that his story is out of print reflects an American investment in forgetting certain aspects of colonial history. The records of local antiquarian societies also reflect the importance of local knowledge in Howe's work, in contrast to the totalizing vision of European colonists.

5. Howe also disrupts the discourse of this entry by citing "volume XIX MUN to ODDFELLOWS of the eleventh edition of the *Encyclopaedia Britannica* . . . three years before uncontrollable modernity before the whole world goes wild" (13). This citation emphasizes the fact that the boundaries of a country are not fixed and immutable but are constantly subject to change when the world "goes wild" and boundary disputes lead to modern wars.

6. The phrase that has come to be synonymous with an idealized vision of feminine domesticity, maternity, sympathy, charm, selflessness, and purity originates in Coventry Patmore's popular verse-novel *The Angel in the House* (1854–1863). In the essay "Professions for Women," Virginia Woolf describes this figure as a phantom that haunts her to the point that "whenever I felt the shadow of her wing or the radiance of her halo upon my page, I took up the inkpot and flung it at her. . . .

Killing the Angel in the House was part of the occupation of a woman writer" (*Essays* 286). The number of literary critics who continue to incorporate this phrase into the titles of their articles suggests its relevance to contemporary feminist theory.

7. In *Frame Structures*, Howe claims that Mrs. Craigie let her room to William Wadsworth Longfellow, "the newly appointed Smith Professor of French and Spanish at Harvard College" in 1837 (7–8). However, it was Henry Wadsworth Longfellow who rented a room from Mrs. Craigie in 1837, held the position of professor of modern languages, and wrote the poems to which Howe refers in this paragraph. In a biography published in 1891, Henry's brother, Samuel Longfellow, describes the poet's paradoxical experience of the Harvard environment in detail, including his impressions of Craigie House and of the eccentric Mrs. Craigie (253–278).

8. Howe's account of her parents' study in several interviews extend this discussion of the physical spaces of the academy. Rose describes the study as a space in which the masculinist Cartesian subject has traditionally been maintained through the exclusion of others (149–150). In the *Difficulties* interview, Howe reflects on the study as paradoxical space. She describes it as "my father's Study" in connection to his office at the all-male Harvard Law School, yet she compares it to her own work space and notes that the entire family used it as a "living room" (40). Howe considers the tension between the magic represented by her mother's side of the study and the reality represented by her father's in a discussion with Robert Creeley: "It seems to me that my definition of poetry all these years later moves between those two poles" (Creeley and Howe 21). Creeley's response, "What an extraordinarily particular place" (21), suggests that the specificity of the study as appropriated, occupied, and shared by Howe and her mother and sisters constitutes a paradoxical space associated with multicultural experience and magical realism.

9. Howe's list of Franklin's allegorical aliases (*Frame Structures* 19) implies that his association exclusively with man and reason is ahistorical. While "Father Abraham," "a certain public-spirited Gentleman," and "the clean plain old Man with white Locks" clearly emphasize Franklin's masculinity, "Silence Dogood" is a female persona, a widow that the sixteen-year-old Franklin invented when he wished to submit satirical pieces anonymously to the *New-England Courant* (Clark 20–21). "Mrs. Dogood's" critique of Harvard and her belief that women should be educated (Ford 116–117, 263–264) suggest that the spatial dynamics of the Franklin Collection Room, maintained by the library to exclude unqualified scholars, fail to reflect the young Franklin's own beliefs.

10. The theater plays an important role throughout *Frame Structures* as a space linked to, yet distinct from, both academic and domestic spaces. In "Craigie Circle," Howe describes her mother's work as drama director for Radcliffe and

Harvard during the war and remembers "the heavy curtain in itself a spectacle whose task it was to open at a certain moment in connection with distancing tactics directed by my mother. Her thought over here mapping the deep area where no stage set was ever permanent actors being one character then another according to movement she blocked out" (16). Having chosen to apprentice at the Gate Theatre in Dublin rather than to attend college ("Speaking" 29), Howe suggests that her writing is a kind of theater: "Sometimes I think what I'm doing on the page is moving people around on stage" ("Interview" 13). In the context of Howe's representations of the theater as a fluid space negotiated by a woman director, her decision to describe her grandfather's bed as a "stage within a stage" is particularly significant, linking it to the performance of identity rather than to an essentialized notion of nineteenth-century domestic femininity.

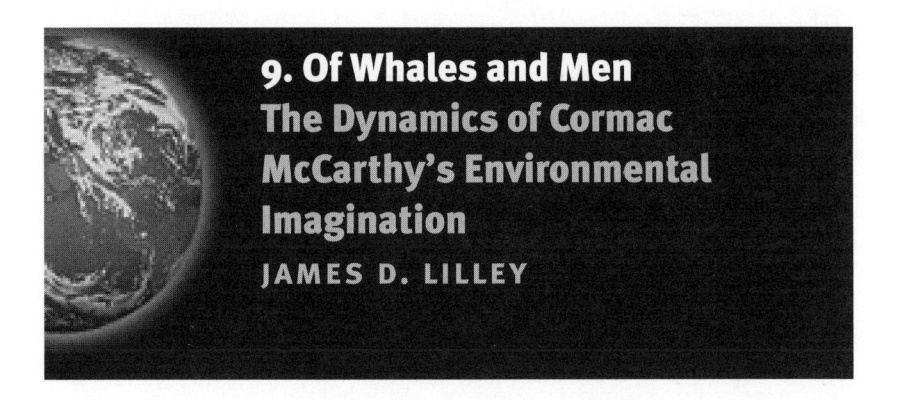

9. Of Whales and Men
The Dynamics of Cormac McCarthy's Environmental Imagination

JAMES D. LILLEY

But why do we feel so alien in this world? Isn't it in a very real sense because we are no longer here? Language is a way of containing the world. A thing named becomes that named thing. . . . We were put into a garden and we turned it into a detention center.
— *Cormac McCarthy,* Whales and Men

What is man but a mass of thawing clay.
— *Henry Thoreau,* Walden

Cormac McCarthy's *Blood Meridian* opens with a challenge directed toward a nameless, orphaned child: "Only now is the child finally divested of all he has been. His origins are become remote as is his destiny and not again in all the world's turning will there be terrains so wild and barbarous to try whether the stuff of creation may be shaped to man's will or whether his own heart is not another kind of clay" (4–5). Although we may sense something of the bildungsroman in this announcement (this "kid" is about to try his luck on the western frontier), it also speaks on a more literal, corporeal level and raises questions that lie at the heart of all McCarthy's fiction: What is the nature of the body's interaction with the environment? Do we reach out from our bodies and fashion our surroundings, or do they encroach upon, penetrate, and mold us? Are we shapers of, or shaped like, clay?

McCarthy's work brings forward the material presence of the body. Yet as anyone who examines the slippery borders of the human body will soon discover, to bring forward the body is also to bring into focus a whole host of other structures and systems that interface with the body. In McCarthy's texts, the boundaries that hold the body in its discrete, impenetrable place soon begin to distend and reconfigure themselves, transforming the site of interface — the frontier of the body — into a fluid, hybrid borderland. As Dana Phillips notes in a provocative essay on *Blood Meridian*, one of the most significant interfaces McCarthy dislocates and reconfigures is the ostensibly static relationship between the human body and its natural surroundings. In these borderlands, bodies and rocks form dynamic interrelationships rather than discrete categories: "[A]ll phenomena were bequeathed with a strange equality and no one thing nor spider nor stone nor blade of grass could put forth claim to precedence. . . . [H]ere was nothing more luminous than another and nothing more enshadowed and in the optical democracy of such landscapes all preference is made whimsical and a man and a rock become endowed with unguessed kinships" (247). Or, as Phillips succinctly puts it, "The world of nature and the world of men are parts of the same world" (447).[1]

After McCarthy completed *Blood Meridian*, he appears to have started work on a screenplay titled "Whales and Men."[2] At one point during this screenplay, Peter Gregory — "a titled Irish aristocrat" who later takes his seat in the House of Lords in order to help save the whales (12) — laments that language is incapable of mapping the terrain of the natural world:

> What gradually became apparent to me was that language was a thing corrupted by its own successes. What had begun as a system for identifying and ordering the phenomena of the world had become a system for replacing those phenomena. For replacing the world. . . . Language usurps things. That's what it does. More and more I began to understand that we were not living in the world as given. . . . More and more language seemed to me to be an aberration by which we had come to lose the world. Everything that is named is set at one remove from itself. Nomenclature is the very soul of secondhandness. We endow things with names and then carry the names away with us. But the name is not the thing and we experience nothing. (57–59)

Just as Peter Gregory insists that language is "an aberration by which we . . . come to lose the world," Lawrence Buell argues in *The Environmental Imagination* that at the heart of the nature-writing enterprise lies a frustrating and irreconcilable antagonism between the text and the natural world: "Even when it professes the contrary, art removes itself from nature. Physical texts derive from dead plants" (84). In a similar vein, Chris Fitter in *Poetry, Space, Landscape* argues that all representations of the natural world are ultimately informed and patterned by a network of cultural biases and projections: "Historical communities and individuals, intimately conditioned by social, economic and ideological forces, will project varied structures of attention onto external nature, thereby actualizing different configurations of feature and meaning. No landscape can ever thus be 'autotelic' — bearing a perennial and 'objective' appearance and significance independent of its 'reader': cultural projection by a landscape's beholder will complete its necessarily partial 'self-formulation'" (8–9).

It is, then, a precondition of all writing — nature writing included — that the presence of an embodied observer always hovers somewhere between the lines of the text. Nature writers are, according to Buell and Fitter, caught within a doubly frustrating structure of representation: their medium for expression is inherently incapable of capturing the organic essence of its subject, and the results of their enterprise cannot help but illuminate the inevitable anthropocentrism that colors our vision. However, to acknowledge the anthropocentrism of our vision — to discover that the boundaries between the embodied observer and the natural world are not as strictly delineated as some realists would have us believe — is not necessarily to reject the endeavor of nature writing. Indeed, as Buell argues, in order to appreciate the achievement of writers such as Henry Thoreau, Mary Austin, and Aldo Leopold, it may well be more appropriate to view the writer-nature relationship as a continuum rather than a discrete binary system capable of relinquishing the presence of an embodied observer: "For none of [these writers] did relinquishment mean *eradication* of the ego," Buell avers. "The aesthetics of relinquishment implied, rather, suspension of ego to the point of feeling the environment to be at least as worthy of attention as oneself and of experiencing oneself as situated among many interacting presences" (178). By applying an exacting focus on the natural world, writers like Thoreau and Austin uncover a fluid interface between the body and its surrounding environment. "What is important above all," Buell insists, "is Thoreau's vision of the coextensiveness of the human body with the inanimate earth" (170), and for Buell, these nature writers uncover and inhabit a "greatly expanded space now continuous with, impinging upon, and interwoven with their [bodies]. Cut those trees and I bleed" (178).

McCarthy's first novel, *The Orchard Keeper* (1965), opens with a typically McCarthyesque scene of violence and dismemberment; this time, however, the victim is an ancient elm tree: "The tree was down and cut to lengths, the sections spread and jumbled over the grass. . . . He took hold of the twisted wrought-iron, the mangled fragment of the fence, and shook it. It didn't shake. It's growed all through the tree, the man said. . . . The Negro was nodding his head. Yessa, he said. It most sholy has. Growed all up in that tree" (3).

In McCarthy's fiction, the natural world and the human body interact and interface with each other as fluid, coterminous, coextensive systems. As Phillips argues, it simply is not possible to delineate the human from the natural in McCarthy's landscape; from this author's "point of view," he argues, "the human does not stand out among the other beings that make up the world" (443). Even inanimate, made objects like iron fences, designed by humans to keep the natural world in abeyance, are in McCarthy's landscape consumed and embraced by the natural world. Steven Shaviro goes so far as to claim that McCarthy's vision captures "[m]inute details and impalpable qualities . . . with such precision that the prejudices of anthropocentric perceptions are disqualified. The eye no longer constitutes the axis of vision. We are given instead a kind of perception before or beyond the human. This is not a perspective *upon* the world, and not a vision that *intends* its objects: but an immanent perspective that already *is* the world, and a primordial visibility, a luminescence, that is indifferent to our acts of vision because it is always passively at work in whatever objects we may or may not happen to look at" (117).

For Phillips, McCarthy's vision is "cosmic without being metaphysical, as if [his words] had been written by a transparent eyeball that has learned how not to be Emersonian" (447). Of course, as Buell and Fitter remind us, to disqualify and relinquish our anthropocentrism completely — to unlearn the influence of Emersonian transcendentalism — may ultimately be impossible. (Indeed, the pathetic fallacy we commit when we compare a representation of the natural world to an eyeball — albeit transparent — reveals the dogged persistence, rather than the possibility for elimination, of anthropocentrism.)[3] However, it is important to examine how McCarthy renders — brings forward — the presence of the natural world in the pages of his text. What are his aesthetics of relinquishment?

Blood Meridian is a book about many things — U.S. imperialism, the myths of American individualism, the structure of violence — but it is also a novel about writing and representing nature. Set along the southwestern U.S. frontier, *Blood Meridian* is itself a novel on the border — caught between the last of McCarthy's Tennessee novels, *Suttree*, and the first installment of his "Border Trilogy," *All the Pretty Horses*. Although, as *The Orchard Keeper*'s fence-eating elm tree reminds us, McCarthy has always been a writer of the border between the human and the natural world; it seems as if the author, faced for the first time with the expansive geography and history of the West, is attempting in *Blood Meridian* to see just how far language can carry him in these immense borderlands.[4] Whereas McCarthy's earlier work, situated along the frontier where civilization meets its feral hinterlands, is more explicitly concerned with issues of community and society ("How does the body live — interface — with its community?"), *Blood Meridian*, *All the Pretty Horses*, and *The Crossing* — in the true spirit of the West — extend their interest into what Shaviro calls "open topography" (113). In this respect, then, *Blood Meridian*'s Judge Holden surfaces at a pivotal moment in McCarthy's work — at a time when the problem is not so much how to translate one's own insatiable otherness into the discourse of a hostile community but rather how to make one's mark, how to inscribe the "alien insubstantiality" of the flesh (*Outer Dark* 17), on the equally hostile desert surface of the natural world.

Judge Holden appears to have taken to heart Buell's argument that "physical texts derive from dead plants." Driven by a desire to signify the entire surface of the natural world within the pages of his ledgerbook, Holden is acutely aware of the problematics of representation. As the appropriately named character "Webster" comments, the judge is known to his company as a "draftsman," a grotesque and demonic Audubon who "tabernacle[s]" the natural world in his ledger by inscribing, then destroying, the objects of his ruthless gaze:

The judge wrote on and then he folded the ledger shut and laid it to one side. . . . Whatever exists, he said. Whatever in creation exists without my knowledge exists without my consent. . . . He nodded toward the specimens he'd collected. These anonymous creatures, he said, may seem little or nothing in the world. Yet the smallest crumb can devour us. Any smallest thing beneath yon rock out of men's knowing. Only nature can enslave man and only when the existence of each last entity is routed out and made to stand naked before him will he be properly suzerain of the earth. . . . The judge placed his hands on the ground. He looked at his inquisitor. This is my claim, he said. And yet everywhere upon it are pockets of autonomous life. Autonomous. In order for it to be mine nothing must be permitted to occur upon it save by my dispensation. . . . The freedom of the birds is an insult to me. I'd have them all in zoos. (*Blood Meridian* 199)

Judge Holden's philosophy of nature writing offers a surprising solution to the problem of anthropocentrism: if our representations of the natural world are always hindered and biased by the presence of an embodied observer, simply "tabernacle" and then destroy each "autonomous" natural object. The "pockets of . . . life" that so affront the judge can thus be rendered in "autotelic" fashion: signifier and "suzerain" stand triumphant over a natural world that can no longer inspire such varied and subjective representations. Instead of practicing an aesthetics of relinquishment, the judge destroys and reappropriates the natural in the name of the human. For Judge Holden, to know nature is to name and possess it: he is driven by a desire to reduce the mystery of the natural world to the surface of his ledgerbook, imprisoning its flora and fauna in his own encyclopedic zoo. Although Holden at times voices an ecological concern for the natural world — lecturing that "our mother the earth [is] round like an egg and contain[s] all good things within her" (130) — as master of a devouring symbolic order that consumes the environment, the limits of the judge's body soon become indistinguishable from the circumference of the natural world: he directs, confounds, and then ingests all the actors (Mexicans, Native Americans, innocent children, puppies, members of his own company) who perform in his profligate dramatic production so that the surface of his body and the pages of his ledgerbook can contain and command the entire material substance of "mother earth":[5] "There is room on the stage for one beast and one alone. All others are destined for a night that is eternal and without name. One by one they will step down into the darkness before the footlamps" (331).[6]

Critics have been quick to read Judge Holden as an eloquent spokesperson for Manifest Destiny, a character who forces us to rethink the unappetizing moral implications of expansion in the American West: "The aptly named 'judge' makes it clear," argues Thomas Pughe, "that the notion of [Western] 'progress' is just a Eurocentric obfuscation of the 'law' of the more powerful and more ruthless" (381). However, the judge's brutally precise method of representation reminds us of the environmental, as well as the moral, consequences implicit in Manifest Destiny's (and in the Enlightenment project's) vision of the natural world. Holden's obsessive program of representing, naming, and possessing the natural world leads to a disdain for the wonderful heterogeneity of life in McCarthy's landscape. In the epilogue to *Blood Meridian*, McCarthy once more highlights the interface between the human and the natural world as readers witness a man preparing the ground for fence posts that will soon be needed as property borders along the western frontier. However, like the image of the ancient elm tree in *The Orchard Keeper*, McCarthy's description of human participation in the natural world is far from impartial and detached, and the text, the landscape, of *Blood Meridian* responds by rejecting and resisting penetration and inscription: *"In the dawn there is a man progressing over the plain by means of holes which he is making in the ground. He uses an implement with two handles and he chucks it into the hole and he enkindles the stone in the hole with his steel hole by hole striking the fire out of the rock which God has put there"* (337). McCarthy's repetition of "hole" here reminds us that the progression of these fence posts, like the movement of westward expansion, the judge's dance, and his ledgerbook, involves evacuating and destroying the land. Whereas the judge's mode of vision revels in a destructive and hubristic partitioning of the natural world, McCarthy's nature writing, his environmental imagination, "makes apparent that the 'I' has no greater claims to being the main subject than the chickens, the chopped corn, the mice, the snakes and the phoebes — who are somehow interwoven with me" (Buell 179).

In "Whales and Men," Peter Gregory laments the insufficiencies of language in a way that responds to Judge Holden's philosophy of nature writing: "Language is a way of containing the world. . . . We were put into a garden and turned it into a detention center" (57). Peter and the crew of his friend's ship, the *Farfetched*, have their lives "changed forever" when they watch a group of whales swim to their slaughter — an event that leads them to question their own relationship to the environment and that eventually propels Peter into environmental activism and causes John Western, a wealthy doctor, to give up his practice in the United States and volunteer his services to a war-torn "third world country" (128). "Whales and Men" attacks the inherent destructiveness of the judge's mode of vision, his method of writing history, and his grotesque anthropocentrism and instead celebrates the heterogeneity and autonomy of the natural world:

> We occupy a small band of visible light, a small band of audible sound, a small band of shared existence. We are imprisoned by what we know. . . . It's not just that the sea is hostile to monuments. It's the other thing. The state of immediacy. That other way of being. This is where we divide. . . . [T]he case is that the whale has no need for monuments because the whale has no history. . . . Our history — which we are at such pains to preserve and which we imagine contains our freedom — is exactly what enslaves us. . . . History particularizes. . . . Everything unexpressed is still whole. What is experienced is broken down into parts it was never even made of. We have no faith in being because we have fractured it into history. And this is the way we live. In archives of our own devising. Among sketches and bones. . . . There is no book where the world is written down. The world is that book. (96)

Such environmentally conscious thoughts, entered by John into the ship's log, stand in stark contrast to the "sketches and bones" of Judge Holden's ledgerbook. Like the union of "ardenthearted" wild horses in *All the Pretty Horses*, the untranslatable immediacy of the whale community is, in "Whales and Men," juxtaposed against the "fractured" symbolic discourses of the human world.[7] "[T]he whale's world," notes the marine biologist Guy Schuler, "is not ours. . . . And that world is invisible to us. . . . It is the world. Perceived with an immediacy that is foreign to us. When we describe something we see, we translate visual images into sounds and then speak them. But the whale sees with sound in the first place. . . . It's another way of being altogether" (93–94). What whales and wolves — the subject of the second volume of McCarthy's "Border Trilogy," *The Crossing* — have in common is an inbuilt and immediate compassion for the suffering of others: whales and wolves will put their own bodies in danger in order to assist a member of their community; they take care of their dead and dying. (Indeed, in all of McCarthy's fiction we find someone or something attending to their dead. From Uncle Ather's preoccupation with a nameless skeleton in *The Orchard Keeper* to Lester Ballard's grotesque community of decaying corpses in *Child of God*, taking care of the dead is one of the most fundamental [natural?] activities in McCarthy's landscape.) And so McCarthy's communities of whales and wolves, united by an innate, extralinguistic sense of togetherness, are set against the judge's project of signification and his quest to raise the anthropocentric signifier over the outrageous, unsignifiable autonomy of the natural world.

For McCarthy, the consequences of disengaging from the natural world are far-reaching. As soon as we erect communities rooted in a "second-hand," symbolic relationship with the environment, we begin, McCarthy suggests, to lose the ground of our own existence. Here the judge is again helpful to clarify matters. For Holden, war is god because "war is at last a forcing of the unity of existence" (*Blood Meridian* 249). But existence lacks unity for the judge because it cannot be accurately and exhaustively rendered on the surface of his ledgerbook. As a result, Holden is only truly happy — *really* existing, by his definition of the term — when he is actively forcing his environment into abeyance and "secondhandness"; violence and environmental destruction become, then, signs of life rather than augurs of death: "Suppose two men at cards with nothing to wager save their lives. What more certain validation of a man's worth could there be?" (249). In Judge Holden's model of human interaction, bodies can reach out from, and become coextensive with, other bodies only through "the letting of blood" (329). However, as Elaine Scarry's work suggests, the body in pain cannot express the nature of its pain, cannot articulate its interiority, since "[p]hysical pain — unlike any other state of consciousness — has no referential content. It is not *of* or *for* anything" (5). In other words, a community of bodies in pain is no community at all: the only way that these bodies can share and participate in the world is to hear their own pain echoed in the screams of another. "Whales and Men" suggests, then, that we do not do violence to the whale in order to harvest its economic value; rather, we reach out to it in order to find our own pain, our own existence, mirrored in and validated by the structure of our natural environment: destruction and pain, as Peter Gregory comments, erase and replace the autonomous communities of the natural world and force the environment into "archives of our own devising":

> [Guy] Schuler I close upon you. You said that our claim to need the whale's products was like the inquisitor's claim to need his victim's information. The vast apparatus of the enterprise suggests something different. Because the true object of these inquiries is agony. Pain is the perfect obsession because its requirements can never be satisfied. . . . The one thing so all-consuming that it can replace the world. . . . What is it that we desire that even blood cannot satisfy and that only blood

can legitimize? What is there about our existence that is so fraudulent that only bloodshed can redeem it? What is it that we expect to hear in the screams of the suffering? . . . With these howls we hope to provoke the silence of the universe into its own betrayal. For what we require above all is a witness. Something to say that we are here. . . . What else could this man be about with his irons and thumbscrews? . . . This man who is me. What else could he be seeking except evidence for the reality of the world? That is why we cannot stop. . . . Because deep in our hearts we fear that we do not exist. . . . We lack the power to share another's pain . . . [b]ut the pain of the whale is shared by all. . . . Amplified and repeated throughout the living web of those beings until the seas themselves vibrate at a single frequency of unendurable anguish. (119–120)

Although the protagonists of "Whales and Men" openly voice their concerns for the environment, the crew of the *Farfetched* represent a minority — albeit vocal — of McCarthy's characters. The majority of McCarthy's texts engage issues of ecology and environmentalism in much more subtle ways. After all, McCarthy's environmental imagination is still subject to the paradoxes and problematics of *writing* nature, and in this respect at least, his texts cannot completely distance themselves from Judge Holden's ledgerbook. How does a McCarthy text navigate the natural world and bring forward the coextensiveness of body and environment?

The American West, with its immense, austere geography, poses a daunting challenge to those wishing to record and represent it. The work of photographers Ansel Adams and Edward Weston grew out of their responses to the geography of the West, and their methods and philosophies of representation provide an interesting analogy to McCarthy's nature writing. Adams and Weston, along with the group of photographers they worked and exhibited with, brought about a revolution in American photography in the 1930s. Although Group f/64, as it came to be known, was hardly an organized movement, it did bring together several artists with similar approaches to photography. Adams even created a manifesto for the group, nailing it to the walls of the De Young gallery in San Francisco where the group held its first meeting: "The name of this Group is derived from a diaphragm number of the photographic lens. It signifies to a large extent the qualities of clearness and definition of the photographic image which is an important element in the work of the members of this

Group. . . . The Group will show no work at any time that does not conform to its standards of pure photography. Pure photography is defined as possessing no qualities of technique, composition or idea, derivative of any other art form" (quoted in Alinder 87).

The fact that Adams felt the need for a manifesto suggests that the work of Group f/64 — at least in Adams's eyes — was always intended to be more than simply "pure" observation of the natural world; as evidenced by Adams's involvement in the Sierra Club, implicit in Group f/64's mode of vision was a politics of ecology as well as a revolutionary aesthetics of photography. In other words, their reaction to and representations of the natural world were always already part of a wider nexus of cultural concerns: to see the world as Adams saw it was to revolutionize and reorient the boundaries of our vision — to force us to rethink the structure of our relationship to the natural world. Group f/64 was, of course, greatly influenced by American modernism; as Jonathan Spaulding comments, "In the early decades of the twentieth century, photography was undergoing a shift similar to that which occurred in poetry through the influence of Ezra Pound and the imagists. Like these poets, American photographers were rejecting the excesses of nineteenth-century romanticism for a more precise realism. [Edward Weston's] often stated photographic credo, 'To see the *thing itself* is essential; the quintessence revealed direct, without the fog of impressionism,' parallels the dictum of the American poet William Carlos Williams, 'No ideas but in things'" (88).

In a very real sense then, the work of Group f/64 grew out of a crisis of representation; like Williams's poetry of things in themselves, Weston's purification of photography stemmed from a distrust of overtly stylistic representations of the natural world. In the same way that McCarthy's landscape obliterates the "fog" of the human perspective, so, too, those in Group f/64 were eager to remove any focal point or "depth" to their photography, thereby allowing the material essence of the natural world to manifest itself in the pictorial space. As a result, everything in an Adams or Weston photograph is in focus: it makes no sense to talk about foreground and background in their work, just as the "optical democracy" of McCarthy's landscape levels the distinctions between the human and the natural world. The effect of such a visual surface is, in both text and photograph, to highlight the sheer physicality, the corporeality of nature. In Spaulding's words, Adams "produced a flattening of pictorial space, which reduced the sensation of depth and emphasized the two-dimensional relationship of values in the print" (89–90); or, echoing Dana Phillips's discussion of McCarthy's cosmic yet un-Emersonian authorial vision, Jussim and Lindquist-Cock point to the transcendent perspective of an Adams photograph: "It would seem that Ralph Waldo Emerson's 'Transparent Eye-Ball' wanted transforming into a machine which would not necessarily record the presence of God, but the absolute materiality of the physical world" (45). Because such a vision eschews the refractive and distortive propensities of the human gaze, "value" in the photograph is established metonymically, rather than symbolically, along the horizontal axis of materiality: without a privileged human perspective or focus, the size, the "value," of Adams's stark mountains can be gauged only through their relationships with the other physical material of the photograph.

McCarthy's topography also provides its own means for establishing "value" and "meaning" in the text without degenerating into a traditional mytheme or symbolic trope. And whereas the judge's mode of representation engenders a disdain for the variety and autonomy of the natural world, McCarthy's exhaustive inventory of the environment betrays a sense wonder and fascination:

> When he went on again the fire seemed to recede before him. A troop of figures passed between him and the light. Then again. Wolves perhaps. He went on. It was a lone tree burning on the desert. A heraldic tree that the passing storm had left afire. The solitary pilgrim drawn up before it had traveled far to be here and he knelt in the hot sand and held his numbed hands out while all about in that circle attended companies of lesser auxiliaries routed forth into the inordinate day, small owls that crouched silently and stood from foot to foot and tarantulas and solpugas and vinegaroons and the vicious mygale spiders and beaded lizards with mouths black as a chowdog's, deadly to man, and the little desert basilisks that jet blood from their eyes and the small sandvipers like seemly gods, silent and the same, in Jeda, in Babylon. A constellation of ignited eyes that edged the ring of light all bound in a precarious truce before this torch whose brightness had set back the stars in their sockets. (*Blood Meridian* 215)

McCarthy's "heraldic tree" does not, of course, herald or signify anything; its function is not so much to provide the text with a symbolic depth as it is to supply the reader with a light source — or what Steven Shaviro would call "a primordial visibility, a luminescence" — that amplifies the zoological relationships being established along the desert floor. Without the help of the burning tree to gauge our vision of the desert, we are blind to the heterogeneity of the life that traverses its surface: the kid can only just make out "a troop of figures. . . . Wolves perhaps." But as soon as the tree provides us with a scale — and a camera flash — for our vision, we can begin to differentiate the various creatures of the desert from the depthless dark of the "inordinate day." Within this flash photograph of text, taken by our "Transparent Eye-Ball," McCarthy captures the "strange equality," the "optical democracy," of a landscape in which human being, spider, and lizard are juxtaposed and set against each other and at the same time captures this vision from a viewpoint that flattens these differences so that we are left contemplating the material, natural bond — the desire for warmth — that ultimately unites all these life forms.

We witness a similar vision in the beginning of *Outer Dark* as Culla Holme struggles to find his way back home through a disorienting, dark forest after leaving his newborn son to die:

> He followed [the creek] down, in full flight now, the trees beginning to close him in, malign and baleful shapes that reared like enormous androids provoked at the alien insubstantiality of this flesh colliding among them. . . . When he crashed into the glade among the cottonwoods he fell headlong and lay there with his cheek to the earth. And as he lay there a far crack of lightning went bluely down the sky and bequeathed him in an embryonic bird's first fissured vision of the world and transpiring instant and outrageous from dark to dark a final view of the grotto and the shapeless white plasm struggling upon the rich and incunabular moss like a lank swamp hare. He would have taken it for some boneless cognate of his heart's dread had the child not cried. It howled execration upon the dim camarine world of its nativity wail on wail while he lay there gibbering with palsied jawhasps, his hands putting back the night like some witless paraclete beleaguered with all limbo's clamor. (17–18)

Once again, McCarthy's landscape confuses and confounds, refusing to adhere to any pattern that might facilitate navigation. In the dark that engulfs Culla before the lightning flash, the distinction between animacy and inanimacy is fused so that tree becomes human and flesh becomes "alien," insubstantial bark. When finally the reader's vision is restored from above by the flash of lightning, the distinctions that can be made between Culla and his son are obliterated by their essential similarities: Culla is reborn in this "embryonic bird's first fissured vision of the world," and it is only the cry of his child that indicates a border exists between his "palsied jawhasps" and the "white plasm" of his child's own "lank" flesh. From this final transcendent perspective, both father and child are stripped of their symbolic differences and reduced to their ultimate, material kinship as motile, audible tissue.

As McCarthy brings forward the materiality of the body into an exacting focus, we begin to witness the fluidity and reciprocity of its interface with the surrounding natural environment. In a sense, Culla's "gibbering" in the above quote from *Outer Dark* seems to ask, "Where does my body end and the natural world begin?" However, since the human body is intimately involved in the natural world, Culla is also asking another question: "Where does my body end and my son's flesh begin?" Indeed, this translation of Culla's "gibbering" is given more weight by the fact that his child is a product of his incestuous relationship with his sister, Rinthy. Earlier in the novel, McCarthy explores the grotesque connectivity between father/brother, sister/mother, and son/nephew by bringing forward Rinthy's body-in-transition:

> He did think that she had died, lying there looking up with eyes that held nothing at all. Then her body convulsed and she screamed. He struggled with her, lifting her to the bed again. The head had broken through in a pumping welter of blood. He knelt in the bed with one knee, holding her. With his own hand he brought it free, the scrawny body trailing the cord in anneloid writhing down the blood-slimed covers, a beetcolored creature that looked to him like a skinned squirrel. (14)

What for Mikhail Bakhtin signals the grotesque in fiction has become for McCarthy an incontrovertible fact of life: the fusion, the fluidity, between the human subject and the natural world — "The [grotesque] object transgresses its own confines, ceases to be itself. The limits between the body and the world are erased, leading to the fusion of the one with the other" (Bakhtin 310). When Rinthy gives birth to her child, Culla translates the scene into a graphic representation of the body's transgressive powers. For Culla — who always attempts, in vain, to keep himself clean and to establish the proper, symbolic boundaries between his body and the natural world — Rinthy's body's ability to transgress itself, to multiply and shed its blood outside the boundaries of its normal limits, transforms and grotesquely inverts childbirth into a scene of bloody murder. Here the body has, quite literally, turned itself inside out, and Culla is left holding a baby that looks as if its skin, its boundary with the outside world, has been forcibly removed.

At the close of *Outer Dark*, Culla comes across a blind man "at the Lord's work." However, this man is no preacher; "What is they to preach?" he asks. "It's all plain enough. Word and flesh" (240). Yet as McCarthy's nature writing reminds us, as soon as we lose our blindness and begin to see and represent our environment, the border between "Word and flesh" starts to dissolve: our anthropocentric words cannot help but betray our embodied fleshiness while our flesh is marked by the words of surrounding discourses. *Outer Dark*, like "Whales and Men," reminds us that the words we use to distinguish and symbolize material difference cannot adequately capture the essence of our fluid existence, that "nomenclature is the very soul of secondhandness." McCarthy's bodies refuse to participate in such neat symbolic divisions: when Rinthy's child is taken away from her, her body responds by generating material, fluid reminders of her loss: "Already she could feel it begin warm and damp, sitting there holding her swollen breasts, feeling it in runnels down her belly until she pressed the cloth of her dress against it, looking down at the dark stains" (99). McCarthy's vision of the natural world — like the photography of Group f/64 — challenges and questions the symbolic boundaries and apparent borders between word and flesh, subject and society, photographer and environment, and illuminates instead a fluid connectivity between these ostensible binarisms: "Cut those trees and I bleed."

NOTES

1. K. Wesley Berry and Natalie Grant have also explored McCarthy's representations of the natural world; their concerns, however, are with McCarthy's southern fiction, in particular *The Orchard Keeper*.

2. "Whales and Men" is an unpublished screenplay that is part of the Southwestern Writers Collection in the Albert B. Alkek Library at Southwest Texas State University. Although the manuscript is not dated, it would appear that McCarthy wrote this screenplay in between *Blood Meridian* and *All the Pretty Horses*. At one point in the text, a character mentions "Lopez's book" in a reference to Barry Lopez's *Arctic Dreams* (published in 1986), so it is fair to assume that McCarthy was working on "Whales and Men" after the publication of *Blood Meridian* (1985). (Of course, the title of McCarthy's screenplay is itself an allusion to Lopez's *Of Wolves*

and Men [1978].) There is also a line from the manuscript, "Beware gentle knight," that finds its way into *All the Pretty Horses* (1992), so I would assume that — from this albeit flimsy evidence — "Whales and Men" was written between 1986 and 1991. I am indebted to Edwin T. Arnold for bringing this screenplay to my attention.

3. In "Beyond Ecology," Neil Evernden argues that the science of ecology is subversive precisely because it denies "the subject-object relationship upon which science rests" (93): "Where do you draw the line between one creature and another? Where does one organism stop and another begin? Is there even a boundary between you and the non-living world, or will the atoms in this page be a part of your body tomorrow? How, in short, can you make any sense out of the concept of man as a discrete entity?" (95).

4. Indeed, *Child of God* can be read as a parody, a rewriting, of the Thoreauvian project — although for Lester Ballard, of course, "civil disobedience" has been translated into something a little less civil.

5. See Adam Parkes's forthcoming essay for a more thorough discussion of McCarthy's "performative theory of identity" as it manifests itself in *Blood Meridian*.

6. *Blood Meridian*, like Faulkner's "The Bear," links ledgers to a discourse of European colonization and environmental destruction. Within this discourse, scalps become "receipt[s]" (98), and exploration of the natural world becomes synonymous with a self-perpetuating dance of violence driven by the demand for human flesh. Whereas Judge Holden strives for absolute "suzerainty" over the outrageous "pockets" of free life, Faulkner's Ike McCaslin speaks of mutual ecological interrelationships between the human and the natural worlds; he emphasizes stewardship of, not "inviolable" suzerainty over, the environment: "Because He told in the Book how He created the earth, made it and looked at it and said it was all right, and then He made man. He made the earth first and peopled it with dumb creatures, and then He created man to be His overseer on the earth and to hold suzerainty over the earth and the animals on it in His name, not to hold for himself and his descendants inviolable title forever, generation after generation, to the oblongs and squares of the earth, but to hold the earth mutual and intact in the communal anonymity of brotherhood" (246).

7. In *All the Pretty Horses*, Luis suggests that the horse exists outside the (symbolic) realm of the human: "among men there was no such communion as horses. . . . Rawlins asked him . . . if there was a heaven for horses but he shook his head and said that a horse had no need of heaven" (111). Indeed, one of the tragedies of this novel is that John Grady is put to work — and corrupted — by the frustrating task of breaking wild horses into manageable, economic parts that can be farmed by the hacienda. I develop these thoughts in "'The Hands of Yet Other Puppets.'"

10. Articulating the Cyborg
An Impure Model for Environmental Revolution
LOUIS H. PALMER III

ECOCRITICISM AND THE DECLINE
OF ENLIGHTENMENT PARADIGMS

In this essay, I take on one of the most vexing issues in the overlap between literary and environmental studies — the question of stakes. Although some might argue that literary scholarship is a field with little at stake, the turn in criticism to environmental advocacy raises the stakes considerably — to nothing less than, as we often repeat, the ultimate survival of life on Earth. My essay, which begins as a capsule history of modern philosophy and environmental thought and concludes with a new way of reading a canonical modernist text, comes out of a conviction that literary theory can be material and consequential in its outcome. I use Donna Haraway's cyborg model of subjectivity to intervene in the process of knowledge-construction in order to raise the stakes for literary studies by pursuing an essentially epistemological project — making new and strange the consequences of environmental dereliction.

Literary-environmental studies finds a tenuous perch on a bridge that not only spans the gap between disciplines but between entire paradigms of knowledge. On the one hand, ecocriticism touches upon texts closely aligned with the natural sciences, a paradigm based on empirical evidence and close observation. On the other hand, ecocritics traffic in the stuff of the humanities, probing discursive constructions of experience and ideology in the shifting seas of language and subjectivity. Nineteenth-century nature writing, characterized by romantic mystical concepts of a pure, wild, originary nature and the "organic" nature of the human subject, became environmental writing in the middle of the twentieth century by way of an infusion of ideas from the realm of natural science. The two leading writers of the early environmental movement, Aldo Leopold and Rachel Carson, were both scientists with talent and skill in descriptive language and rhetoric. Leopold and Carson were able to use their scientific backgrounds to write about personal experiences in a new way, supporting arguments for the value of nature in ways that were not (primarily) based on metaphysical claims to transcendence and spiritual kinship but were supported by scientific data and observation. To give one example, Leopold enhanced the notion of "connectedness" found in Thoreau and Muir by using a basic mechanical metaphor, suggesting the foolhardiness of removing parts and then expecting a machine to run as smoothly as before. In like fashion, Carson used empirical data to support observation to argue that the value gained by pesticide use wasn't worth the value lost by songbird extinction. Linking the value-laden language of the humanities, with its power to convince, to the material evidence of science, with its power to support, these writers were able to create a hybrid discourse that packed more of a punch than the old, idealistically based arguments, especially to a skeptical, modern audience.

In the postmodern, postindustrial age, however, humanitarians and scientists alike are looking critically at the Enlightenment bases of their structures of knowledge and are finding them lacking in explanatory power. Because of ecocriticism's relation to both scientific and humanistic paradigms, this development has created something of a crisis for literary-environmental scholars. Ironically, this critical movement, devoted to move literary study into the future, too often fights a rearguard action within the broader field of literary studies, clinging (or appearing to cling) to cherished notions that other humanities scholars have questioned or rejected outright. In advocating for Earth we often find ourselves in conflict with poststructuralist thinkers, whose focus on the discursive nature of all reality has discredited the essentialist arguments about pure "nature" that often underlie antidevelopment arguments.

At the same time, we support an economic and production system that floods the world media with images of consumption unimaginable to many of the world's human population. The massive planned economies of state socialism, the major opposition to commodity capitalism, have collapsed, leaving incredible environmental and human devastation in their wake, yet Marxist theorists in the West still tend to advocate humans-first policies that can make capitalism look environmentally friendly. Even cultural materialism, with its emphasis on the economic realm as the basis for knowledge-claims, leads back to some of the same questions that troubled Thoreau and Muir — how does one understand the intricacy and value of a natural system without resorting to a terrible reductivism?

With the advent of "theory" in the 1970s and 1980s, the premises of Enlightenment humanism have been progressively and painstakingly challenged. One of the points of challenge has been the model of the Subject, what used to be called Man. From a variety of perspectives — Derridean deconstruction, Althusserian political analysis, Lacanian psychology, Foucauldian discourse analysis — the concept of the Subject as stable, unified, coherent — all of the qualities suggested by the romantic/modernist term "organic" — have been broken down. How posthumanism understands subjectivity is very much under debate, but one way to describe the emerging model of the Subject would be something like a matrix, a point in a series of interconnecting strands attached to a variety of influences — cultural, racial, class-based, institutional, discursive, semiotic, historical, economic, material, genetic, somatic, and so on. If we imagine these strands to have coalesced into a node, a point of connection that is both unique and unstable, we approach a new model of the Subject, a term used because it suggests not only subject*ivity* (individual consciousness) but also subject*ness*, being subject to forces beyond the individual. This amorphous, emerging model is antiorganic in the romantic sense, opposed to the individual, unified, coherent Subject that has been the dominant model since the Enlightenment.

It is not that literary-environmental thinkers have not understood the implications of recent theoretical interventions. Two of the most perceptive contemporary environmental writers, Gary Snyder and Wendell Berry, have in different ways started to look at the implications of textualism and materialism. But Snyder's Buddhist-based wilderness advocacy and Berry's Christian-influenced home economics, brilliant as they are, still lie within the context of the Thoreau-Muir-Leopold tradition, a tradition based (in part) on Western Enlightenment epistemological structures undergirded by sexist and racist assumptions and by an ontology that is still basically metaphysical. One of the most enduring vestiges of Enlightenment thought is body/mind dualism, which has been transformed into a split between nature and culture in the American nature-writing tradition that begins with Emerson and Thoreau. By way of this model we have come to think of nature (usually with a capital N) as a pure, innocent, self-correcting, balanced system best preserved as wilderness with no contamination by culture, which is imagined as human-influenced, corrupt, polluting, destructive, and out of balance. Recent writers who have attacked the nature/culture dichotomy argue that it leaves us with untenable choices — a human-centered culture that will continue to squander resources, pollute, exploit, and cause extinctions, or a pure wilderness, where every trace of human presence is scrupulously erased, leaving no trace on nature's purity. Essayist Michael Pollan and poet Frederick Turner have both suggested that we adopt the figure of the garden to replace the unattainable and misleading model of wilderness. Pollan's *Second Nature* is an extended essay on the relationship of Americans to nature by way of the garden, interspersed with anecdotes about the author's own gardening experiences. Pollan advocates a pragmatic middle way between what he sees as the extremes of the developer and the environmentalist. As an editor of a prestigious New York magazine (*Harper's*) who commutes from a former farmhouse in rural Connecticut, he wants to have it both ways, and he succeeds in a way that few of us can afford to. At his house he describes a groomed flagstone path passing by a bog and a freshly mowed path through an overgrown meadow as examples of the best of both worlds, wild nature in balance (or at least at truce) with human control. This is his garden model, and in Pollan's perspective it trumps the wilderness because it mediates between the human and the natural without any claims for purity. But this perspective seems so insular, so comfortable, so unaware of the world outside the Northeast, that one has to question the portability of such a model. To corrupt an environmental bumper sticker, it's "think locally — act locally" and is about as productive in the larger scheme as Pollan's garden would be in Alaska or the Amazon.

Turner also advocates the garden as a model, basing his argument on readings in evolution and sociobiology, supported by reference to the usual suspects in the nature-writing tradition, the (male) romantics and Shakespeare. He points out that the first organisms, anaerobic bacteria, were also the first polluters. Their waste product so saturated the early biosphere that they were forced to follow the evolutionary imperative to adapt or die, so they learned to use the toxic substance — oxygen — and created nature as we know it, with its elaborate systems of balance and recovery. For Turner, nature is subsumed in culture; gardening joins music, cooking, and the family (!) as "American developments in the great mediators between nature and culture" (50). Like Pollan, he makes no bones about his anthropocentrism: "We are, like it or not, lords of creation" (50). From such a perspective the garden is a good model, with Man paternalistically cultivating and restraining nature (in both writers unproblematically "her") for the good of all. But it is also a rhetoric easily available for co-optation. One can imagine how an ideologue of the Wise Use persuasion could use the oxygen-as-pollution example.

Perhaps it is not surprising that white males such as Pollan and Turner can see the need for a new model to break the tyranny of the culture/nature dichotomy but that they fall back upon a very old one. White, heterosexual, able-bodied males are the most sharply defined identity form in the Enlightenment paradigm; they are the standard, the norm, the template. Never defined as other, never exiled to the hinterlands of subjectivity, why shouldn't such subjects believe in the effectiveness and centrality of Western models? Pollan and Turner are conservative in the root sense of the word, looking to replace current uncertainty with the comfortable reestablishment of older cultural institutions. They are also classic liberals in their attempts to mediate between extreme positions. But they do not look beyond the Enlightenment paradigm of subjectivity, even as they seek to break down the nature/culture dichotomy. "Man" is still the free, objective, solitary knower and doer, solemnly studying and cultivating the vast unruliness of the natural world. The challenges of poststructuralism and cultural materialism are also the challenges of multiculturalism and emerging models of subjectivity. One wonders what Pollan and Turner would make of a recent Native American novel, *Gardens in the Dunes*, where Leslie Marmon Silko develops an uncomfortable contrast between one traditional native model of gardening and that of the European-based colonists. Sticking to their Western, Eurocentric guns has impoverished Pollan's and Turner's arguments, so that they fail to ask important questions. One central question that the challenge to Enlightenment models raises is this: How can we develop new ways of knowing ourselves and our environment that will cause us to stop doing harm without falling back on essentialist or elitist models of the human in the world? One source of answers that provides an alternate model is socialist-feminist-biologist Donna Haraway's figure of the cyborg.

THE CYBORG MODEL

Cyborg studies has developed out of Haraway's initial intervention into a perspective that proposes that the violation of borders — disciplinary, figural, and material — is a necessary and laudatory practice. Haraway, a biologist by training, is a scientist who has absorbed the lessons of the antihumanist, or at least antitraditional, strands in the humanities. She is used to negotiating the boundaries between the sciences and the humanities. Her early work applied Thomas Kuhn's paradigm theory to biology. Her more recent work has attempted to integrate socialist politics with feminist thought to produce models for "a politics rooted in claims about fundamental changes in class, race and gender in an emerging system of capitalism; we are living in a movement from an organic, industrial society to a polymorphous, information system — from all work, to all play, a deadly game" ("Manifesto" 609). Haraway uses systems theory to criticize the idea of a pure or original state of innocence or essence and claims that we need to give up such trappings of male-dominated Western thought: "to recognize oneself as fully implicated in the world frees us of the need to root politics in identification, vanguard parties, purity and mothering" (618) and allows us to understand our part in the system as something more like integration or articulation into the environment — we become part of a cyborg, already attached, rather than free agents able to choose to help or hinder.

The figure of the cyborg is central to Haraway's "regenerative politics" because it is not innocent or detached or objective. For a contemporary model of the subject, it works because it looks at what we are, socially constructed organisms continually integrated with machines into a series of informational connections that replicate images of machine-human articulations, continuously reinforcing both the articulations between organic and inorganic and reproducing these relations in the form of new, socially constituted subjects. For a cyborg-subject deeply implicated in such an information system, the idea of a return to an originary or organic purity is absurd; to ask a contemporary female to be a traditional housewife is equivalent to asking her to be a medieval nun or a Roman matron.

Of course, Haraway's human cyborg model is more complicated than that suggested by the human-machine articulation. She also sees the figure of the cyborg as a human-animal mix. "The last beachheads of [human] uniqueness have been polluted if not turned into amusement parks — language, tool use, social behavior, mental events, nothing really convincingly settles the separation of human and animal. And many people no longer feel the need for such a separation" (606). The human-animal connections long stressed by environmental thinkers have been highlighted by evolutionary determinists and animal rights activists alike, resulting in a reduction of "the line between humans and animals to a faint trace re-etched in ideological struggle or professional dispute between life and social science. Within this framework, teaching modern Christian creationism should be fought as a form of child-abuse" (606).

The third boundary that is permeated by the cyborg model is one dear to the Western idealist tradition — "the boundary between the physical and the non-physical is very imprecise for us" (607). The twin advents of the cyber-world and the technology of miniaturization have made it impossible to perceive the difference between the informational and the material. How are the letters of this essay as I write them and they appear on a screen (Haraway calls this a "machine of sunlight" [607]) different from the letters as printed out onto a sheet of paper, from which you read them now? Which are more physical? More material?

What does it mean to become a cyborg, to blur these distinctions? The Western humanist tradition, from at least Descartes on, relies on the model of the "solitary knower" separate from the world, from others, from the objects of knowledge, as the epistemological base model, the starting point for all knowing. Instead of this unitary male knower, what if we substitute the figure of the cyborg, a human-animal of indeterminate sex (or sexes) connected and articulated to a system that both reflects and modifies it, plugged into flows of information from a variety of sources, environmental, bodily, and elsewhere? Ecological theory has taught us to see the interconnectedness of all natural systems, but it has preserved certain privileged concepts, such as that of individual autonomy, the uniqueness of human knowing, and the difference between the artificial and the natural. To adopt the cyborg model would be to give up our focus on the importance of the individual and that of the hierarchies of self/other by which we distinguish such individuality. The cyborg model is liberating in terms of its use of a biosystems or ecological model to understand subjectivity, but it destabilizes many of our most cherished and secure assumptions about what we are and where we live. It also destabilizes the nature/culture boundary, making it impossible to make claims about nature as a pure or originary state, another basic tenet that is an inheritance from the Enlightenment. In this interconnected figuration of the world, a concept of reality as merely textual or linguistic is as absurd as one that is merely natural. The stuff of language, like the stuff of nature, refuses to be reduced.

The figure of the cyborg can help us to find our way out of the impasse of the humanistic subject and the ideal state of nature without giving up the political commitment to produce a viable and living (if not pure or organic) world system. Haraway's argument for the cyborg is offered "for pleasure in the confusion of boundaries and for responsibility in their construction" (604). As cyborgs, we generate knowledges that are collective and horizontal, and we are above all implicated, articulated, connected. We can no longer keep refuge in our separation, our distance, our objectivity, our individuality. Thinking according to such tropes helps us to see who we are as part of a larger system rather than as transcendental and separate from where we are. Other species and cultures can no longer be seen as other. Neither can the environment. To go back to a figure that I used earlier, matrix can mean both a point of connection and the milieu where connection occurs.

THE EXAMPLE OF FAULKNER'S "THE BEAR"

I want to put aside for the moment the vertiginous effects of trying to think in the abstract about cyborg subjectivity and try to put it to use in a rather mechanical fashion, to attempt a cyborg reading of a piece of literature. I have chosen a literary-environmental chestnut, a canonized piece of fiction well ensconced in the traditions of both literary modernism and Enlightenment humanism: Faulkner's short story/novella "The Bear." For the "novel" Go Down Moses (1940), Faulkner merged several short stories about hunting that he had written in the 1930s, most notably the Ike McCaslin stories "Lion," "Delta Autumn," and "The Bear," and added a long section that served to connect the character of the young Ike found in these stories to the older man portrayed in "Delta Autumn," which became the following section in Go Down Moses. His immediate problem was how to connect an angry, bitter, racist old man with the sensitive nature-savant who renounces his plantation heritage after discovering evidence that his grandfather had fathered a daughter with a slave woman and subsequently fathered a child on the daughter, this rape-and-incest series creating a dual lineage of McCaslins, black and white. The major problem with reading *Go Down Moses* as a novel rather than as a short-story collection has been the question of thematic coherence. Daniel Singal summarizes it in this way: "When he did return to the book [after putting it aside for a few months in 1940], his approach underwent an enormous change. Not only was race displaced as the central focus by a new absorption with hunting and the wilderness, but the concern with overcoming stereotyped modes of vision by heightening the reader's perceptive capacities (always one of the essential aims of Modernist fiction) began to give way to the overt expression of moral sentiments" (275).

The division is thematic (race versus wilderness issues) but also stylistic ("telling" as opposed to "showing"). Most critics agree that Faulkner's later work represents a falling-off from the power of his earlier fiction, and Singal places this change right in the middle of *Go Down Moses*, during the writing of "The Bear." Singal's interpretive schema presents all of Faulkner's works as reflecting Faulkner's split psyche, which expresses itself in terms of a division between two aesthetics, modernist and Victorian. He sees *Go Down Moses* as straddling one of the more visible rifts between these two worldviews. Cleanth Brooks, on the other hand, maintains that "*Go Down Moses* has a good deal more over-all unity than a superficial glance might suggest" (244), going on to argue that the novel is unified by "the virtues that Faulkner feels are the bedrock of any civilization" (278), an interpretation that Singal would probably see as an expression of Faulkner's Victorian side. Brooks claims that "for most readers, 'The Bear' overshadows everything else in the book" (244), demonstrating the popularity of the story and the tendency of readers and critics at that historical moment (as of 1963) to read it on its own. Critical emphasis has changed in the thirty years since; today, much of what is written on "The Bear" tends to place it within the context of the larger work. If we try to get a handle on the story's reception history, it seems that the early-to-middle 1960s represented the high point in the story's cultural capital as an autonomous text. "The Bear" was widely anthologized and was published separately (with "Spotted Horses" and "Old Man") as part of Random House's *Three Famous Short Novels* in 1961. The high-water mark of this interpretive strategy was a 1964 Random House publication, *Bear, Man and God*, an edited volume that included the text, sources, earlier versions, and critical essays about the story. The volume offers a revealing snapshot of critical orthodoxy as of 1964 in its blithe assumption that seven approaches (biographical, background, canonical, cultural, interpretive, stylistic, and developmental) can "handle the totality of 'The Bear'" (116) and that "all major points of view are represented" (118). It also lets us see that new critical practice was somewhat more varied than we tend to give it credit for — there are, after all, seven approaches. What they all have in common is demonstrated by the collection's title, *Bear, Man and God*: the realms of the natural, the human, and the metaphysical are seen as a stable triangle, constant and interlinked to form an enduring structure, and Faulkner's story fits perfectly into such a schema, incorporating its elegiac idealization of "that doomed wilderness" (193), its focus on the ritual aspects of male initiation into a male society where "the best of all talking" (191) took place, and its long political/theological debate between the two McCaslin cousins, contrasting Ike's idealistic repudiation with Cass's concerned pragmatism.

"The Bear" certainly represents some of Faulkner's most evocative writing about nature. The diminishing wilderness, "whose edges were being constantly and punily gnawed at by men with plows and axes who feared it because it was wilderness, men myriad and nameless even to one another in the land where the old bear had earned a name, and through which ran not even a mortal beast but an anachronism indomitable and invincible out of an old dead time, a phantom, epitome and apotheosis of the old wild life which the little puny humans swarmed and hacked at in a fury of abhorrence and fear like pygmies about the feet of a drowsing elephant" (193) is presented as "doomed" in much the same way as Faulkner usually presented his Native American characters (the most prominent of whom was nicknamed Doom). The wild delta forest is represented by Sam Fathers in this story, a former slave who is half Native American and who serves as the boy Ike's initiator into the mysteries of the wild. The elegiac tone not only presents the wilderness as another Lost Cause but does so in terms equally as nostalgic. Despite the narrator's claims about the value of fellowship, whiskey, and talk among men, the boy's most important experiences are solitary moments far from the company of the others, where the presence of the bear (loaded with all of its semiotic baggage) provides an opening into a magical world. Compared to this, the actual conflicts with the bear, first with the two dogs, the feist and Lion, and its ultimate killing seem trivial (puny?) and busy. The twice-yearly hunting trips that the men take are not only opportunities for male bonding but vacations from the trivia of civilization, chances to engage the real issues of life and death in an anachronistic and nostalgic setting. When Major deSpain sells the woods to the timber interests and refuses to go back, Ike sees him as a diminished man:

> the boy looking down at the short, plumpish grey-haired man in sober fine broadcloth and an immaculate glazed shirt whom he was used to seeing in boots and muddy corduroy, unshaven, sitting the shaggy powerful long-hocked mare with the worn Winchester carbine across the saddlebow and the great blue dog standing motionless as bronze at the stirrup, the two of them in that last year and to the boy anyway coming to resemble one another somehow as two people competent for love or for business who have been in love or in business together for a long time sometimes do. (317)

Here we see the "Man"-nature-God triangle at its strongest; this is why Kenneth LaBudde understands the story as essentially primitivistic: "Civilization is evil. . . . Ike learned about God in the wilderness" (233).

The kind of cyborg reading that I want to suggest plays havoc with such a schema. The stable structure collapses when we see "Man" and nature as part of one metaorganism, and God is a difficult concept in a connected world where no one is separate or pure or unarticulated. The image of Major deSpain that Ike contrasts with the present one ceases to be culture (bad) versus nature (good) but becomes that of a cyborg horse-dog-gun-man, a combination of human, animal, and mechanism, surrounded by further connections and articulations — the woods, the bear out there, the other hunters — contrasted with a man in individual mode, unconnected and refusing to connect, except through the abstract forms of the papers in his hand and through the even more abstract economic transactions that have enabled the destruction of the forest. In a cyborg context, personal responsibility becomes not a metaphysical question of what God wants, the subject of Cass's and Ike's lengthy debate, but a material one of owning up to the benefits one is taking and to the sources of their connections. Ike's renunciation can be seen as an acknowledgment of the material connections of blood and property, an affirmation of "the earth mutual and intact in the communal anonymity of brotherhood" ("Bear" 257) rather than the detached and abstract "unmarked" connections of financial wealth and inheritance based on the twin injustices of slavery and property ownership. It is by way of the "unmarked" connection to the past that Ike defines his freedom-through-connection when Cass attempts to remind him of his "markedness," of his responsibility:

". . . the male, the eldest, the direct and sole and white and still McCaslin even, father to son to son —" and he: "I am free:" and this time [Ike] McCaslin didn't even gesture, no inference of fading pages, no postulation of the stereoptic whole, but the frail and iron thread strong as truth and impervious as evil and longer than life itself and reaching beyond record and patrimony both to join him with the lusts and passions, the hopes and dreams and griefs, of bones whose names while still fleshed and capable even old Carothers' grandfather had never heard: and he: "And of that too:". (299)

His connectedness, by way of the "frail and iron thread," is what supports his claim to freedom, his refusal to place value on patrimony and whiteness over the sorts of connections that his experiences in the wilderness had brought to the foreground for him, articulations to Sam and Old Ben and Boon. He rejects the "unmarked" abstract criteria that preserve dominance and privilege for a broader inheritance that affirms "the communal anonymity of brotherhood" (247). In "The Bear," according to such a reading, what dies when Lion and Old Ben and Sam Fathers and the wilderness itself all perish is a matrix, a series of vital and rich connections that leave Ike, as well as the bankers and lawyers and loggers, impoverished, whatever stances they take about their heritage.

Such a reading is at best provisional but indicates that writing about environmental-literary issues can make alternative choices and constructions, and like Ike, can choose not to continue to support structures of elitism, racism, and dualism that have proved to be plugs back into outworn ways of thinking. The idea of an impure scholarship comes from Edward Said's *Orientalism*, a work that helped to invent a new field, postcolonial studies, within literary studies. Said defines impure thinking as scholarship that resists "the common ways by which contemporary scholarship keeps itself pure" and foregrounds the "political, ideological, and institutional constraints" (13) that characterize disciplinary writing and enforce simplistic models and cause-and-effect habits of thought. I hope that literary-environmental thinkers can look beyond the borders of a discursive practice based primarily on Enlightenment humanism to find new models or paradigms that support hermeneutic practices that are less limited and constrictive. Limits and constraints also provide comfort and security, and to venture beyond the borders of the familiar can be terrifying and disorienting, emotions that can, in turn, produce panic, violence, and repression. Our history shows us that the explorers on the edge of the known world are often the sources of the most cruel and oppressive practices. Haraway is quick to demonstrate that cyborg models can also support an "informatics of domination." But in our search for a just, viable, and nontoxic future, we must not be limited by habits of mind that are based on structures of racial, national, class, and gender bias, however well hidden behind claims for liberty, equality, and fraternity. If, as Deleuze suggests, theory is a toolbox, we need not only to find new tools but new ways to use the old ones.

PART THREE

Rethinking Representation and the Sublime

11. Surveying the Sublime
Literary Cartographers and the Spirit of Place
RICK VAN NOY

One of the curiosities of the literature of American surveying and mapping is its reliance on the sublime. Since the sublime is concerned with an aesthetic and emotional response and surveying with a scientific one, the two would seem to be in conflict. The sublime deals with measureless emotion, while surveying precisely measures. The sublime implies something beneath the threshold of experience, what can't be mapped or limned. Yet when surveyors Henry David Thoreau and the first two directors of the U.S. Geological Survey, Clarence King and John Wesley Powell, went exploring and mapping the terra incognita, they repeatedly relied on the aesthetic of the sublime to communicate awe and reverence. How did the sublime and the map come together in an American literary cartography, and what are the consequences of the sublime as the dominant aesthetic that informed their American sense of place? [1]

Of course, surveyors do not "discover" the lands they travel through, but one of the powerful myths of exploration is that surveying takes place through seeing "new" land. According to this myth, as Simon Ryan has shown in *The Cartographic Eye*, explorers accurately and disinterestedly describe or map the new land that they see. Far from being an objective record of the natural world, the writing of these surveyors is generated by existing cultural and personal formations. While "discovery" disturbs a particular set of expectations, what is found through an examination of these literary cartographers is that discovery has also been anticipated, often according to the sublime.

An example from John R. Lambert, one of the surveyors for the Pacific Railroad (1853–1854) built under the direction of the War Department, will illustrate the place as predicted. Lambert enters the valley of the

Clarks Fork River, calling it "an aggregate of everything that is sublime and beautiful in scenery" (172).[2] Standing on the riverbank and looking up the valley, Lambert is taken in by the scene and its resemblance to these aesthetic "maps": "the view embraces all the elements of grandeur and beauty that can be imagined in mountain scenery, and in an extent which an artist would choose for a single picture" (173). The scene is as beautiful as a painting — nature is imitating art. The paradigm through which the land is discursively formed already exists, and contact is made within this matrix. Lambert continues to describe the picture being painted, only to pause: "it is almost sorrowful to reflect that very purpose of our explorations will soon dispel the 'enchantment that distance lends'" (173).

The mapping of the area and its potential consequences could harm the "enchantment" of it, as if measuring and surveying would make it less a work of art (in a curious conflation of nature and art) or a spellbound dream. The railroad will make the mountain crossings easier and the place more known and therefore, Lambert worried, less sublime. Instead, he wants to keep this space at such a distance that it can be held up in a "glowing blaze of light," full of supernatural glory. The sublime presented nature as omnipotent perfection, a sign of God's presence. To disturb or know that nature was to violate that sublimity and cause it to disappear.

The phrase the "enchantment that distance lends" seems to come from a poem by Scottish poet Thomas Campbell (1777–1844), "The Pleasures of Hope" (1799).[3] In the opening lines, Campbell refers to remote landscapes, ideal scenes of felicity that the imagination delights in contemplating. Campbell writes that what is "dim-discovered" is more pleasing than the past, since it resides in anticipation and hope. While Lambert most likely joined the survey to explore and map for the purposes of economic expansion and science, he also wished to see scenery in the "dim-discovered" light of the imagination. In a sense, he wants to leave it blank, as potential, a space awaiting further exploration. He faces what John Tallmadge calls the paradox that explorers eventually confront: "their discoveries destroy the very mysteries that allured them" (1178).

The problem with this sense of place is that it exists mostly in the mind of the explorer as abstract; viewed from afar, the place is not brought into any definition. This image of a blank and sublime space also celebrates two central myths of the American past — the free space to be explored by heroic individuals and the free, regenerative land that defines and enlarges the individual — but it limits the richness of the explorer's experience and also limits the place. Another problem with Lambert's sense of place is that it is seen only as it resembles previous aesthetic "maps," but they were not imminently portable in the arid West. What is needed is a more particularized understanding, an "enchantment" that involves a long history and experience of the place, not a "lingering" and "unmeasured" one. At the very least, one needs to understand the interior landscape from which one views the place.

Although the surveyors in this essay went about mapping space in a mathematical web constructed and maintained by positivism and scientific objectivity, they represented places according to an interior landscape consisting of discursive formations that both enabled and constrained their relationship to their environment. While these surveyors were measuring winding rivers and ragged mountain peaks and plotting nature into the coordinates of a Cartesian, geometrical space, they also represented what Jefferson called the "height of our mountains" (which, he suggests "has not yet been estimated with any degree of exactness" [20]), often according to the eighteenth- and nineteenth-century aesthetics of the sublime. While the map for them is first envisioned as a means to know and represent the unknown land, it is later seen as an incomplete form, incapable of accounting for their complex and diverse responses to nature. The map is especially deficient in depicting their internal geographies.

This essay will examine three mappers —Thoreau, King, and Powell— in order to map a history of responses to the western landscape in the nineteenth century. Thoreau's example will illustrate some relations between sublimity and mapping to be further developed in King and Powell. The land becomes less awesome and sublime to these writers, but it also becomes less of a symbol or abstraction, more particularized. Even though the sublime is tamed as cartographic methods progress, late-nineteenth-century writers shift the focus of the sublime from the feelings inside the perceiver to an aspect of the landscape itself, constructing something closer to the "spirit" of the place than a personal sense of it. It is not the map's (or the mapper's) fault that the land cannot be adequately represented but the land's resistance to being mapped. The land is seen less as blank potential, to be enchanted through distance ("a pleasure of hope" for Lambert), but more a place, revealed through close inspection. Especially for Powell, who couldn't get the "grand view" while constantly traveling through the Grand Canyon, contemporary maps, both aesthetic and cartographic, were inadequate to represent the kaleidoscopic forms in the arid West. The sublime for him came less from an unmapped wilderness than from a terrain with both human and geological marks all over it; his sublime required time and patience to cultivate an understanding, from several vantage points and perspectives, to interpret these signs. The sense of place embodied in Powell's decentered sublime, with its phenomenological feel for landscape, is an important counterbalance to the land as either private property or resource bank (or blank) — which the surveyor/map locates and validates. His sublime bears comparison with native stories that communicated a "spirit of place," a land charged with *numina*.

THOREAU'S ANTIMAP

The subject of maps appears frequently in Thoreau's *The Maine Woods*. The word "map" appears forty times in the text.[4] Thoreau finds that his map of the woods of Maine does not accurately represent what he sees. He says that one particular town, Passadumkeag ("where the water falls into the Penobscot above the falls" [323]), "did not look [as it did] on the map" (8). Instead, he finds politicians talking, as if he was still in Concord Square, and not the wilderness he expects.

In another instance, surveying the view on the way up Mount Katahdin, he writes about the reality of what he sees and the false appearance and inadequate preparation the map gave him: "From this elevation, just on the skirts of the clouds, we could overlook the country west and south for a hundred miles. There it was, the State of Maine, which we had seen on the map, but not much like that" (66). He has to remind himself and readers that "we are concerned now, however, about natural, not political limits" (66). Maps designate boundaries and provide an initial orientation, provide data for property and political limits, but can distort what is really there. The moment marks an epistemological shift — from one scale and reduced version of reality, the map, to the transcendental seer, who uses an entirely different scale or scheme.

If maps can present a false appearance of reality, at other times the maps Thoreau has with him are just plain wrong, and he expresses his frustration with them. They confound the names and geography: "we rowed a mile across the foot of Pamadumcook Lake, which is the name given on the map to this whole chain of lakes, as if there was but one, though they are, in each instance, distinctly separated by a reach of the river" (41). In one early instance, before his departure for Mount Katahdin, Thoreau perpetuates the errors created by maps. He traces Greenleaf's map of Maine to serve as his guide, discovering it to be a fraud: "a labyrinth of errors, carefully following the outlines of the imaginary lakes which that map contains" (15). Greenleaf's map has "imaginary lakes" because Greenleaf probably based it on one of the original plot maps, intended not as guides but as brochures for selling off the land.[5] When Thoreau traces Greenleaf's map, he perpetuates the mistakes and creates an even more perplexing "labyrinth of error." Thoreau's trip through the Maine woods will then allow him to fill in and correct these erroneous maps.

Toward the end of the "Ktaadn" chapter, something happens to shake his trust in maps even more seriously, so he would have us believe. During the summer of 1846, the writer/explorer tried to "scale" Mount Katahdin. He loses his way many times, and a storm prevents him from reaching the summit. His descent, however, leads to a discovery, for the slope that his map calls "Burnt Lands" is in fact a thick, young forest with fresh blueberries.[6] He has been on the trail of some moose when he comes across a "dense thicket," *"perhaps never seen by a white man before"* (69, emphasis added). Then a "full realization" comes to him: "this was primeval, untamed, and forever untamable *Nature*, or whatever else men call it" (68). This realization occurs not in the wild and alien landscapes he has just traversed but in a tame meadow. His passage is blocked by "non-human" nature, but the nonhumanity that he perceives is just that — a matter of perception more than a fact of the landscape. Just a page earlier he is "startled" to see the imprint of a man's foot and feels "how Robinson Crusoe felt in a similar case," but he then remembers that the group had come that way before. He seems to cherish the idea that he and his companions are first and wants to "unmap" the landscape of previous footprints and perception so he may provide his own.

Thoreau writes about a space that is, though called "Burnt Lands," somehow off the map. "It is difficult to conceive of a region uninhabited by man," he says, referring not only to humans' physical presence but also to the intrusion of our signs. He has brought our attention to what we *call* things (nature) but wants the space to be blank: "not even the surface had been scarred by man" (71). Here was something "unmapped": "no man's garden, but the unhandselled globe. It was not lawn, nor pasture, nor mead, nor woodland, nor lea, nor arable, nor waste-land" — all words to describe human places — but the "fresh" surface of the earth. "Man was not to be associated with it," he says, beginning to change his tone from surprise to something more like awe. It was not "Mother Earth" but a "place for heathenism and superstitious rites" — not for human-centered religions. "Talk of mysteries!" he continues, both excited and anxious about this natural world that seems devoid of human meaning: "Think of our life in nature, — rocks, trees, wind on our cheeks! the *solid* earth! the *actual* world! the *common sense! Contact! Contact! Who* are we? *Where* are we?" (70–71).

No map prepared him for this "solid earth" that he touches and experiences rather than the virtual one he anticipated through a two-dimensional simulacrum. On Katahdin he "discovers" the "inadequacy of maps in the face of wilderness" (Howarth, "'Where I Lived,'" 56) and a world that is almost prelinguistic, a notion he emphasizes through the negations in the passage and through the broken syntax and repeated questions. The "Burnt Lands" gave him a momentary sense of the strangeness of Earth, when perception was not mediated by the presence of human "maps." His disorienting cry entails a "violent subversion" to prior shapes of the world as a prelude to discovery (Robert Abrams 257). Thoreau seeks to deprive immediate reality of its preexisting structure and shape to experience "contact" with a world not of his own making.

The signs are everywhere, but Thoreau wants to "unmap" them. In pages leading up to the climax on Katahdin, Thoreau has called our attention to Prometheus, to Milton's *Paradise Lost*, and to *Robinson Crusoe*. He says that this is "that Earth of which we have heard" (70). Though he fears signs, he can't help but invoke them. A dialectic emerges in the passage between "mapping" and "unmapping" (or, as Lawrence Buell has observed, between emptying and filling — clearing the landscape but importing the sublime). The map for Thoreau serves as a metaphor of previous perceptions of the landscape, but it is also the means for imagining new cartographies. Thoreau effectively clears the space and map, even the linguistic signs, to make way for a new "discovery." Once he has no "map," he can experience the sublime.

In a college essay on the sublime, Thoreau quotes from Edmund Burke: "terror is in all cases whatsoever, either more openly or latently, the ruling principle of the sublime" (*Early Essays* 93). He continues to discuss

Burke's other elements of the sublime — mystery, power, and silence — only to reject terror as the basic element of the sublime in favor of reverence (Schneider 85). "I would make an inherent respect or reverence, which certain objects are fitted to demand, that ruling principle; which reverence, as it is altogether distinct from, shall it outlive, that terror to which [Burke] refers, and operate to exalt and distinguish us, when fear shall be no more" (*Early Essays* 96). "The infinite, the sublime, seize upon the soul and disarm it," he goes on to say, but do not "terrorize" it (96). As can also be seen in passages from King and Powell, compared to the sublime Burke describes, it seems a characteristic American trait to represent the awe and rapture of such experiences as primary.

Readings of the "Burnt Lands" passage often focus on two extremes, the one that elevates terror—Katahdin genuinely frightened him and he beat a path back to Walden Pond (Lebeaux 56)—or the ecocritical one that elevates awe (Marshall 230–231, O'Grady 39). Thoreau's early essay would seem to support the latter reading, but the occasion for the sublime experience has occurred because the place is supposedly unmapped or "unhandselled." What Thoreau really "maps" is the space of his mind, clearing it of perception. He actually journeys through a mapped landscape strewn with surveyors' ringbolts and branded logs but "unmaps" these signs to arrive at the point of contact he believes of New World "discoveries." After his metaphysical questions, Thoreau writes in the very next sentence: "Ere long we recognized some rocks and other features of landscape which we had purposely impressed on our memories" (*Maine Woods* 71). The quick recovery to a material object and to what was "impressed" in his mind tells us that the unmediated contact was something he willed. Thoreau maintained the notion that the Maine woods was a trackless and unmapped wilderness, a space and not a place.

KING'S IMPRESSIONIST MAP

Leaving Thoreau, after his climb of Mount Katahdin still marveling at the "wav[ing] virgin forest of the New World . . . unmapped and unexplored," let us turn to Clarence King, who explored and mapped that "new" territory. After graduating from the Sheffield Scientific School at Yale University in 1862 (the year Thoreau died) and serving as a field geologist (1863–1866) with Josiah D. Whitney's California State Geological

Survey, King sought federal funding to conduct a geological survey of the Great Basin region. With the backing of the War Department, King obtained congressional approval to create detailed maps and chart the resources for an area a hundred miles wide (through which the transcontinental railroad would run) along the 40th parallel between the Sierra Nevada and Rocky Mountains. King's *Mountaineering in the Sierra Nevada* was published as a complete text in 1872. The book describes King's life and impressions during his years as official surveyor on both the California and U.S. surveys (1864 and 1874, respectively).

King left the banks of the Colorado River with his friend John Gardiner in May 1866 to join Whitney's survey party in California. In his narrative, King begins to question his route and guide maps. As Gardiner lags behind, King starts to worry about their lack of water when places he had planned to drink from are not there: "springs which looked cool and seductive on our maps prov[ed] to be dried up and obsolete upon the ground" (34). Thirst and heat begin to dominate his imagination, producing a transformative vision of paradise:

> As we sat there *surveying* this unusual scene, the *white* expanse became suddenly transformed into a placid *blue* sea, along whose rippling shores were the *white* blocks of roofs, groups of spire-crowned villages, and cool stretches of *green* grove. A soft, vapory atmosphere hung over this sea; shadows *purple* and *blue*, floated slowly across it, producing the most *enchanting effect of light and color*. The dreamy richness of the tropics, the serene *sapphire* sky of the desert, and the cool, *purple* distance of the mountains, were grouped as by a miracle. It was as if Nature were about to repay us an hundred-fold for the lie she had given the topographers and their maps. (35, emphasis added)

What the map presents is not what the eye sees, but the eye also transforms what it sees into a delicious "miracle" and mirage. King's vision of a "placid blue sea" metamorphoses into a pastoral village through the act of interpretation. The desert is beguiling with these "ever changing illusions" and the "phantom lakes" pictured on maps, nowhere to be seen but everywhere to be "seen" (35). King's sea is no doubt a product of his geological knowledge, that the area was once a vast sea, but the rhetoric seems designed to de-homogenize the place, to "enchant" what was an otherwise blank desert or "white expanse" (akin to a blank map) with a "miracle," to color his canvas.

In his own experience with the inaccuracy of maps, Thoreau gets lost, empties the landscape of all familiar associations but awe, so he can experience "contact."[7] King aims not to empty the map but to revise it, to differentiate earth's surface with more color, light, and form, so he can experience his impressionistic mirage — something more human-made than sublime. "To search for the mountain springs laid down upon our maps was probably to find them dry," King writes, though one wonders if the pronoun "them" refers to springs or maps. These "maps" may indeed be dry, and they "afforded [him] little more inducement than to chase the mirages" (36). Any geographical order that may be "found" in the landscape must be taken as an impression and not from the map's precise relationships of length, height, and space.

After reaching his summit, Mount Tyndall, King looked at the stars while lying on a shelf of granite. Like Thoreau on Katahdin, King feels his "bones seeming to approach actual *contact* with the chilled rock" (79, emphasis added). Rather than map its exterior, King is sensing the rock, his bones approaching the same temperature as surfaces external to them. However, King's "contact" is mediated through how it seemed.

Though King's contact is more realist-impressionist than romantic-intuitive, he displays an allegiance to the transcendental strain in American literature, depicting his view from Mount Tyndall in terms of the romantic sublime with its sense of the indescribable. The total effect "*may not be described*; nor can I more than hint at the contrast between the brilliancy of the scene under full light, and the cold, deathlike repose which followed when the wan cliffs and pallid snow were all overshadowed with ghostly gray" (78–79, emphasis added). King's vistas confirm the sense of nature that he has brought with him into the mountains from his reading of Ruskin. While denying the possibility of true description, King is deft at word painting, and he employed not only Ruskin's sense of the Gothic and sublime but also his argument to improve freely on the topographical view to give a place's "true impression" (Lukens 26). Artists should not be bound "so much by the image of the place itself, as the spirit of the place" (Ruskin 4:22). Ruskin calls such a representation "useless" to engineers, surveyors, and geographers but yet capable of producing on the "far-away beholder's mind precisely the impression which the reality would have produced" (4:22). A topographical delineation of facts alone would fail to produce the sublime, for the mountains "speak quite another language."

The sublime is a way of apprehending what King sees by including it within a system of aesthetics. Though inexpressible, the sublime occupies a niche in a stable code. To say that the total effect "may not be described" is to invoke the topos (from Greek for "place") of the sublime and to absolve oneself of any deficiency in descriptive powers. But to deny that it can be described and then to describe it works in favor of the writer's authority: it constructs the explorer as "surmounter of linguistic, as well as geographical, obstacles" (Ryan 85). King's ineffability is followed by terms of absence: wan, pallid, gray. It is not the describer at fault but the land's failure to provide the recognizable differences from which the writer can operate. Still, the land is within King's system of representation and not a blank. The scene's absence is only viewed against the brilliant light, and even its blankness is a presence, a ghostly gray. It isn't a symbolic wilderness he wishes to describe but the spectrum of an atmospheric effect. Thoreau dispensed with "maps" to get to contact, while King is dependent on them: his contact is described through his impressionist "map."

Although it would seem that the "high" moments of his life occur atop summits (King's epigraph, *Altiora petimus*, or "we strive for higher things," would seem to support this), in the presence of the lower "life region" King seems closest to some kind of spiritual self-fulfillment. Ruskin has taught him that mountain peaks are supposed to be the sites of glory, but he feels more lighthearted (as opposed to light-headed at high altitude) and free when back in the shade of comforting trees. Mountain peaks should exalt the self, but it is lower, in the "sheltered landscape," that he feels "at home" (King 97). At the top of Mount Shasta, "[a]t fourteen thousand feet, little is left [of] me but bodily appetite and impression of sense. The habit of scientific observation, which in time becomes one of the involuntary processes, goes on as do heart-beat and breathing; a certain general awe overshadows the mind; but on descending again to the lowlands, one after another the whole riches of the human organization come back with delicious freshness" (269).

The heroic climb paradoxically leads to a quieting down of the ego until little is left but the physical senses and "general awe." Then the "human organization comes back" with renewed freshness, a "point of departure" King doesn't seem to understand, because it's not what he expected. The top of Tyndall is "inanimate" (97) while lower regions of Shasta provide the "spirit of life. The groves were absolutely alive like ourselves" (255). Of course, the lower regions are likely the places where King sat down to record his experiences. This is where language makes sense again, where he is able to concentrate space in the pages of his journal. It is where "here" takes on meaning in relation to "there."

While King was beginning to recognize a place, an embarrassing moment would occur to turn him away from such a notion. Another geologist, W. A. Goodyear, announced in the August 4, 1873, *Proceedings of the California Academy of Sciences* that King had missed "the real peak" in his 1871 account but rather climbed one next to Whitney. That would make King's second failed attempt at the highest mountain in California, for he was forced to turn back in 1864, the year he named Mounts Whitney and Tyndall. In his correction to the earlier edition of *Mountaineering* (and his response to Goodyear), King says in 1874 that he realized during his 1871 climb of the false Mount Whitney that the measurements taken with his instruments were off, but he attributed it "to some great oscillation of pressure due to storm" (291). The storm prevented him from seeing the "real" Mount Whitney with his eyes, so he relied on his map. When a sense of doubt overcame him, he "carefully studied the map" and established "beyond doubt the identity of the peak designated on the Map of the Geological Survey of California as Mount Whitney with the one I had climbed" (291). When King finally got to the real summit after Goodyear's paper in 1873, there in "*uncolored plainness,* stood the peak, where, in 1871, I had been led by the map, and my error perpetuated by the clouds" (298, emphasis added). Once again the spot on the map was an illusory mirage, and now King refuses to "paint."

Although he charged the error to the map, King declined to disparage the work of C. F. Hoffman, chief topographer of the survey. Hoffman's map was issued with the 1874 edition of *Mountaineering*, along with King's revision of the earlier chapter on Mount Whitney and his answer to Goodyear. In Hoffman's map, physical relief is expressed through elaborate brushwork, hachures, and shading. In their attempts to represent landforms, these maps were works of art in themselves. The system of contour lines for showing topography was only beginning. King's 40th parallel survey would be among the first. While the brushwork system is richer and has a more lifelike feel for landscape, the system of contour lines can better express distances, coordinates, and geologic data.

Guided with the more "picturesque" map but unable to see because of the storm (and hence verify what the map showed), King climbed the wrong mountain. King realized that he should have better trusted his instincts: "among the many serious losses man has suffered in passing from a life of nature to one artificial, is to be numbered the fatal blunting of all his senses" (296). Although his instruments and map should aid him, for King, these crucial senses can and should be more trusted.

By then King had been in the West for a decade. The peaks of the Sierra range had been named and were no longer "new." He was no longer in a chase to reach first summits; there were no more to be reached. As it so often does in *Mountaineering*, "intellectual and spiritual elevation" comes as he camps below the tree line. Here, "deep and stirring feelings come naturally, the present falls back into its true relation, one's own wearying identity shrinks from the broad, open foreground of the vision, and a calmness born of reverent reflections encompasses the soul" (302). Between the barren summits where maps can betray and the modern cities with their "smothering struggle of civilization," King senses his "true home" as he prizes the "simple, strengthening joy of nature" (293–294). King was finally "home on the range" — at least his own carefully defined "range," a hybrid of wilderness and home.

John O'Grady writes in *Pilgrims to the Wild* that King was a reluctant "pilgrim" because his unconscious kept the hostile, open space of the wild at bay. But how many of us are comfortable succumbing to wilderness, which is, by definition, a place where humans are not? King's text reflects how the awe-inspiring summits create an effect on him that cannot be measured or quantified and teach him the value of place over space — of a sheltered landscape versus an unbound one — even if his way of understanding place, as mapped and measured, is shaken. Like animals marking territory, humans carve up space to make a place, usually according to the experience of the shaper. We section off, inscribe, and name it. King's experiences with maps are emblematic of how that process eludes him yet remains: he wants to feel placed. If King's unconscious reveals anything to us through his texts, his return to images of campfire and enclosure reveals a desire to inhabit rather than view from above or quantify, as the map perspective locates and validates.

As King reflected on Mount Whitney after his 1873 ascent of the "real" peak, he wrote that it is "hard not to invest these great dominating peaks with consciousness," that is, project onto them a guardian spirit or some part of the interior landscape (304). King acknowledges the tendency to myth-make, for he watches it in his American Indian counterpart who intrudes upon his "hard, materialistic reality of Mount Whitney": "At last he drew an arrow, sighted along its straight shaft, bringing the obsidian head to bear on Mount Whitney, and in strange fragments of language told me that the peak was an old, old man, who watched this valley and cared for the Indians, but who shook the country with earthquakes to punish the whites for injustice toward his tribe" (306). King feels an "archaic impulse" take hold of him as the American Indian, "who must have subtly felt [King's] condition," sat down next to him and cast a "hawk eye" toward Mount Whitney.[8]

Though he doubts his counterpart's interpretation of the mountain's face, King claims he can "read" the American Indian's face, which has "written" upon it "a hundred dark and gloomy superstitions." Although King rejects the story of the mountain being an old man, he has himself represented the "spirit of place" throughout *Mountaineering*. As he watches him walk away, King considers the American Indian's "myth" for a moment, then proceeds to describe the mountain "as it really is . . . 14,887 feet high," scientifically quantified (306). The measurements of Mount Whitney determine how it will appear on the maps, but King's experiences with maps demonstrate how quantitative values don't tell the full story, nor do they bind him to place any better than the American Indian's "superstitions." Places are found on maps but also exist in a complicated layer of affiliation and imagination — what he earlier in *Mountaineering* called the "power of local attachment" (253). This is not something easy for the surveyor/scientist to admit, but in more than one instance King expresses the attraction nature has for him over and above scientific methodology: "No tongue can tell the relief to simply withdraw scientific observation, and let Nature impress you in the dear old way with all her mastery and glory, with those vague indescribable emotions which tremble between wonder and sympathy" (142). In acknowledging the realm of experience "no tongue can tell," King brings a high level of desire and sublimity to the surveyor's discourse. Places are named and contained by surveyors and mapmakers, but the mystery of a place must be projected by the writer.

A strong sense of anticlimax pervades the chapter he inserted for the 1874 edition that describes his attempt at "the real peak." From the monuments of stones at the top of Whitney, King discerns that he is at least the third party to reach its summit, "save Indian hunters" (302). He adds of the Euro-American ascents, "our three visits were all within a month" (302). But the magic and mystery he experienced on Tyndall are gone. Though he has named the peak, someone else has left a monument (that is, a history) on it. Whitney is not his, at least he can't lay imaginative possession to it, and he no longer feels the urge to tell about it: "I do not permit myself to describe details, for they have left no enduring impression, nor am I insensible of how vain any attempt must be to reproduce the harmony of such subtle aspects of nature" (304).

This is a shocking moment, a complete turnaround from an explorer who has carefully recorded his impressions of lingering sunsets and mountain scenes. But now the experience is no longer exhilarating because it is stale or because he is depressed over losing the glory of the first ascent. He no longer word-paints but proceeds to give a scientific explanation for the "atmospheric effect" at the top of summits, as if he is not representing its impression on him but rather its physical laws. Whitney has been explored and mapped, has been made into a place (as Euro-Americans would define it), but he is reluctant to make it his own. His humiliation seems to cause him to turn away from his aesthetic receptiveness and word-painting. Discoveries are constructed as visual events, the pleasure resulting from the fact that no Euro-American eyes have ever encroached upon the scene (Ryan 24). If that vision of the "new" is not available, then neither are the claims of "discovery." Perhaps more than the scientific embarrassment, Goodyear's discovery has made it impossible for King to develop either the sublime or his impressionistic vista.

King stands toward the end of a long line of exploration and mapping, a tradition that began for Europeans in the fifteenth century and one that he carried west. Maps facilitated the colonization and appropriation of space from native peoples, but they didn't help King feel appropriate to that space, and King closes the revised version of the "Mount Whitney" chapter of *Mountaineering* on this melancholic note. The Whitney experience and his embarrassment over it have clearly shaken him; he essentially repudiates his own book. He says now that Ruskin "helps us to know himself, not the Alps" and accuses him of "myth making." He says he feels the "liberating power of modern culture which unfetters us from self-made myths" (306). King now claims that the "varying hues which mood and emotion forever pass before [Ruskin's] mental vision mask with their illusive mystery the simple realities of nature, until mountains and their bold natural facts are lost behind the cloudy poetry of the writer" (305). King now chooses to see Whitney as "it really is" rather than according to the self-made myths or "hues" that he has given to his other mountain experiences or the animate spirit that the American Indian gives it. Among the three literary surveyors, John Wesley Powell developed a reverence resulting from knowing the terrain, not from knowing he was first.

POWELL'S MAP OF THE SUBLIME

As explorers, both Clarence King and John Wesley Powell were involved in the transformation of topography to place, but Powell's process ultimately differed from King's. For King, nature was a scene to be painted. For the mapmaker and scientific cataloger, even for the painter, mountain ranges, rivers, fossils, even Native Americans, might all be passive data to absorb. That view is static, usually gained from a bird's-eye view, but Powell's view was always changing, from heights, where he could look down on the space, to deep in the canyon, where his view was limited and changing.

The Exploration of the Colorado River of the West and Its Tributaries (1875) is an account of his 1869 through 1872 explorations of the last blank spot on unofficial maps of the continental United States, the Colorado River country. Powell's perspective changed with each turn of the river, and he was surrounded by its canyon's walls. Since he was always moving, so, too, was the landscape, seen to him as a motion picture rather than a static canvas of vast proportions — a single frame. Sound was part of this "kinesthetic effect: the constant roar of the river . . . the rush of the wind" (Tallmadge 1183). There was no one center to it, as there was a summit to a mountain, from which King could gaze on the still surroundings. Thoreau could measure the width, length, and depth of Walden Pond and map and locate its epicenter by moving around its stable presence, but the canyon country was a labyrinth that compelled a constant movement from one new point to another. In an 1895 revision to *The Exploration*, Powell writes about this constant change and its ultimate reward: a "sublime" prevision of "Paradise." "You cannot see the Grand Canyon in one view," he writes, "as if it were a changeless spectacle from which a curtain might be lifted" (397). To see it, you have to "toil from month to month through its labyrinths" (397). The Grand Canyon could not be seen from one view — a map, a painting, a text — it was not a changeless, monolithic spectacle. His enchanted paradise had to be earned and not seen through a single aesthetic.

Early in the expedition, Powell expressed confidence in his ability to "read" the canyon from one view: "All about me are interesting geologic records. The book is open and I can read as I run."[9] To presume the land is a text is to claim an ability to read it in ways useful for the exploration or to claim power over it. The idea of nature as a system of signs is part of the scientific method that exploration uses. But when the signs are difficult to read, the notion of the land as a decipherable "book" is put under some stress. Before completing his reading, Powell sees that all about him are "grand views" but then adds: "but somehow I think of the nine days rations and the bad river, and the lesson of the rocks and the glory of the scene are but half conceived" (263). Even when the canyon permitted a view or a truth, there was danger to worry about. The "grand view" is prevented by the dangers of the voyage and difficulty of seeing what lay ahead. Powell pushes on to get a better view, to check on the prospects to come, "but, arriving at the point, I can see below only a labyrinth of black gorges" (264).

The sublime was invoked to explain these failures of interpretation, but the sublime was not simply a construct that Powell imported with him. His sublime was a decentered one, gained from the shifting perspective in river courses rather than the view gained from high on summits. He could not gain the "grand view" or sympathetic "contact" with the canyon country. His was not the romantic sublime, nor was the Colorado River the Hudson. Instead of the romantic sublime, which according to Thomas Weiskel is an "egotistical sublime," foregrounding the human self and perceiving in one's own image and for one's benefit (48), Powell offered something closer to an ecological or decentered sublime, based on the self's relationship to what was beyond and outside it.

His conception that nature was sublime and operated independently from him enabled Powell to draw an important conclusion about nature: Powell's sense that nature wasn't to be seen from one "view" led to his radical conclusion that nature organized itself. In his scientific *Report on the Lands of the Arid Region of the United States* (1878), which drew on the material he developed for *The Exploration* (1875), Powell wrote that "divisional surveys should conform to the topography" (22). The terrain of the arid region should determine how settlement plots should be graphed, meaning that the long-used methods of government survey and mapping needed to be revised.[10] Powell recognized that nature organizes its own space, a position he took in a later essay he did for *Century* magazine in 1890, "Institutions for the Arid Lands," where he describes a river as a tree: "A dozen or a score of creeks unite to form a trunk. The creeks higher up divide into brooks. All these streams combined formed the drainage system of a hydrographic basin, *a unit of country well defined in nature*, for it is bounded above and on each side by heights of land that rise as crests to part the waters" (113, emphasis added). Natural formations, not surveyors, create the boundaries of space in the region, but note that Powell is bringing the sublime and the scientific together. Nature has its own "units," already well defined, though it also has a sublime force that "parts" its waters. Powell is bringing together the two codes, scientific ("hydrographic basins") and literary (the figure of a tree), to explain how nature operates. The sublime enabled him to explain nature's processes both as an interior landscape to be felt and as an aspect of nature's fundamental phenomena.

Powell concluded that the Grand Canyon was "the most sublime spectacle on earth" (*Exploration* 390).[11] As fact finder and data collector, he was not out to find the divine in nature, though as a writer it was an important tool. In the canyon country of the West, Powell was detecting not only the motion of the river but also the visible traces of nature's agency: geologic motion that was engraved in the rocks but whose forces were just below the threshold of consciousness or apprehension. "The wonders of the Grand Canyon cannot be adequately represented in symbols of speech, nor by speech itself," he said toward the end of *The Exploration*. Neither speech nor visual forms could fix the identity of the canyon country: "The resources of the graphic art are taxed beyond their powers in attempting to portray its features. Language and illustration combined must fail" (394). Discarding both visual and descriptive epistemologies, Powell turns to music: "It is the land of music. . . . The Grand Canyon is a land of song . . . the music of waters. The adamant foundations of earth have been wrought into a sublime harp, upon which the clouds of the heavens play with mighty tempests or with gentle showers" (394). It was a landscape of infinite variety and complexity, not to be known through one color, shape, or form. Powell rejects words and static maps to express the Grand Canyon and adopts music. If "maps" and language couldn't adequately represent the sense of place, perhaps music was a better form for capturing the sense of time, so detectable in the canyon's layers and audible in the river that cut it.

Though there was no one way of knowing the canyon, it did have a system, even if a musical one. For Powell, music may be an appropriate metaphor for understanding nature's processes, for it can be said to be more "natural" than either the literary or verbal arts. When he turned to *The Report*, Powell attempted to propose rather than impose a system for nature's use. He recognized that the rectilinear maps wouldn't do in the arid West, so he went on to suggest other "maps," both cultural and topographic. In the middle ground, where place is a process rather than fixed on the map or seen through a single aesthetic, Powell recognized the responsibility that ensues when we project language onto nature, ethical obligations generated by a writing or mapping of place.

Although Powell was committed to detecting the scientific characteristics of nature's forces and demarcations, he would sense some of the lack resulting from the scientific way of perceiving. Like King at the base of Mount Whitney and Thoreau in the forests of Maine with Joe Polis,[12] Powell sensed that Native Americans knew an aspect of the land for which he had no conception: "I have prided myself on being able to retain in my mind the topography of a country; but these Indians put me to shame. My knowledge is only general, embracing more important features of a region that remains as a map engraved on my mind; but theirs is particular. They know every rock and every ledge, every gulch and canyon, and just where to wind among these to find a pass, and their knowledge is unerring. They cannot describe a country to you, but they can tell you all the particulars of a route" (299–300).

Powell recognizes that he operates from the stance of the map reader, the bird's-eye view. Native Americans "cannot describe a country" because they do not describe it mathematically as the surveyor does or spatially as the cartographer would, nor do they draw on the scientific terms of geology or the aesthetic of the sublime. But the map-view cannot represent the crucial details, the trail along the little-known "gulch," or the rocks that may take one home. It orients in terms of vast distances, not in the sense of walking over the terrain. The Native Americans' knowledge of place results in one that is "unerring," a more "particular" spatialization of landscape. When Powell can't get the bird's-eye view, a surveillance or command of the territory, the landscape seems general, whereas to Native Americans, he thinks, the country is individuated. If the land is enchanted for them, it is gained through close association and living there, not from a faraway view or "pleasure of hope."

Though he also expresses confidence in being able to read the canyon, in many more places in *The Exploration* Powell acknowledges his own inability to "describe a country." Powell first experiences the sublime indescribability of the territory he can map and measure but not possess on June 17 in the Canyon of Lodore, which has "scenic interest" that is "even beyond the power of pen to tell" (163). About the navigation of dangerous rapids, Powell says, "It is not [possible] to describe the labor of such navigation" (255). As the journey progresses down the Colorado and Powell and his men become more fatigued and hungry as their rations nearly run out, his sense of sublime wonder and dread seems to increase. He says in an entry dated August 14: "At the very introduction it inspires awe. The canyon is narrower than we have ever before seen it; the water is swifter." (248). More than a mile deep in the canyon — deeper than most mountains are high, when measured from their base — the vantage point of a bird's-eye view, where Powell can survey and map (hence, *know* according to a map reader) the territory, is greatly diminished, and the canyon closes in. Powell acknowledges that is he in the realm of the "Great Unknown": "We have an unknown distance yet to run; an unknown river yet to explore. What falls there are, we know not: what rocks beset the channel, we know not; what walls rise over the river, we know not. Ah, well! we may conjecture many things" (247).

Powell is clearly building suspense, but he is also acknowledging the strange otherness and unknowability that the unmapped, unexperienced canyon has for him and his men. They couldn't have a way of knowing what was ahead, but Powell emphasizes the cumulative effect of this experience through the repetition of the main clause: "we know not." Some aspect of the known (falls, rocks, wall) is presented and then negated three times. As the walls close in so does the syntax, tightening and constricting, cutting off speculation in a three-syllable main clause. They can "conjecture" many things, but these are left unnamed after the empty expostulation: "Ah, Well!" When deep in the canyon, without the "grand view," Powell enters his sublime, which is associated not with what is clear and distinct but with what is vague and obscure. Ironically, Powell's scientific exploration aimed to make this unknown visible, representable, and perhaps tame, but this sublime sense of place is ambiguous, "vague and indescribable" as King writes it, and leads to conjecture rather than certainty.

After his thinking on the "knowledge" of Native Americans, Powell once again attempts to climb a summit "to obtain a view of the country." However, upon reaching the summit, he sees "once more the labyrinth of deep gorges that flank the Grand Canyon; in the multitude, I cannot determine whether it is itself in view or not" (300). After having spent months in the canyon, Powell is now not only unsure if he sees the Grand Canyon, but also unsure whether it can be seen.

Gaining a summit position has obvious benefits for Euro-American scientists: what other way can there be of gaining a "survey" of a particular space? To see the landscape unfold before one from an elevated view is to see as one views a map, omnisciently. But to move from the map to the landscape is to undergo an interpretive or "hermeneutic" shift (Ihde 67). Shifting from reading the map to reading the landscape itself requires a different mode of perception: one is no longer above that landscape but in it, and so the perceiver has to adjust his or her way of perceiving and understanding landscape. The landscape then becomes more a "labyrinth" than a "labyrinth of errors," seen from within rather than looking down or through the map.

Since he understood the difficulty in describing and "mapping" the canyon, when he turned to *The Report*, Powell proposed that the "maps" be revised. Neither the romantic sublime nor the Enlightenment grid nor pioneer expectations would do in the fragile country, so he suggested a new approach: commonwealths based around "sublime" watersheds.

For certain landscapes such as the Grand Canyon or the Yosemite Valley that King mapped, the sublime is the "map" for the surveyors encountering it and for those who came hence. As environmental historian William Cronon has written, the sublime led to preservation of America's first national parks: Yellowstone, Yosemite, and the Grand Canyon. However, for Cronon, the sublime was a formulaic and overused word, too focused on wilderness and too ignorant of indigenous people's view of the land, an enticing "flight from history," society, and responsibility (80). According to Bruce Greenfield, Thoreau's moment of discovery, when he stands in awe of a "pure" landscape in mystical wonder, detaches that landscape from the context that drove Europeans across the ocean and into unfamiliar countries (192). Many whites pushed aside the mythic interpretation of Native Americans to create a blank geographical space to move into — as if, without lines on paper, Native Americans' minds were also blank (Ryden 292). There can be no doubt of the function that maps performed for an expansionist government. However, these literary cartographers also sensed a strong ambivalence about their maps and the institutional project in which they were participating. Powell, especially, was able to look beyond the concerns and perceptions of the official government survey to include those of others, viewing the landscape through as many eyes and ways of knowing as possible.

Furthermore, sublimity has had many faces from Thoreau to Powell, and it was not the only response these surveyors brought to and took from these landscapes. The surveyors were also changed by their experiences, shaped by the places they encountered as they went about mapping them. These writers remind us that geologic developments are not static forms in the landscape; they have been "projected upon as they have been encountered, created as they were perceived, and reinterpreted as they were represented in literary texts," note Michael Branch and Daniel Philippon (2). What lies at the heart of their shifting experiences of landscape is that it may not be measured, molded, or mapped in any single, replicable way.

If the map produces a static landscape that can be managed from above, the sublime produces an active, resistant space and promotes humility: the sublime space is larger than the writer though he or she is a part of it. According to the aesthetic of the sublime, humans are not the masters of landscape but are included in the web of its mystery. Rather than produce knowledge, as the map does, the sublime beggars it. Though the sublime was indeed a cultural expression and the fashion of the time, in response to Cronon, Donald Worster offers a different interpretation of its widespread currency as a token for what surpasses the ordinary in human experience: "[the sublime] may be understood as an effort to recover and express those deeper feelings which in all sorts of cultures have linked the beauty of the natural world to a sense of wholeness and spirituality. The enthusiasm for [sublime] wilderness in America was undeniably a cultural fashion, but it also drew on that other-than-cultural hunger for the natural world that persists across time and space" (11).

Perhaps the sublime also drew on a reverence for the land: it manifests itself at the moments when these surveyors are relying more on immediate sensory experience and orienting themselves less on the basis of an abstract, mapped reality known through quantitative measurement, instrumentation, or other exclusively human involvement, when they participate in what David Abram calls the "more-than-human life-world" (217). In a sense, the sublime marks a shift away from a purely human set of signs to the animate earth. By assigning a positive, even if unmeasurable, value, the sublime marks a transition from space to place. These writers couldn't have the intimacy with place that Native Americans, living there for generations, possessed, but the sublime allows for the possibility of that relationship. It is a way of letting the landscape in rather than bound and set off. Writes John Elder, "Such repeated [sublime] responses [need not be seen as] a failure of imagination" or as a way of displacing landscapes outside the circle of culture "but rather [as] a gathering of vision and energy around particular natural objects and phenomena" (xix).

In invoking the sublime, these literary surveyors draw on a different interior landscape than the one they create in their scientific duties. If the map values the land for its pathways and resources, the sublime values it for its emotional richness. And while sublimity still draws something "useful" from the landscape, it is certainly an extraction that is less destructive. Through their example, they bring together the discourses of literature and science often at odds in contemporary discussions of the environment, so that they, and we, may better know their places. Like Clarence King, Clarence Dutton, one of the surveyors in Powell's party, had to apologize for such a "point of departure": "I have perhaps in many places departed from the severe ascetic style which has become conventional in scientific monographs. Perhaps no apology is called for. Under ordinary circumstances the ascetic discipline is necessary. Give the imagination an inch and it is apt to take an ell, and the fundamental requirement of the scientific method — accuracy of statement — is imperiled. But in the Grand Canyon district there is no such danger. The stimulants . . . are necessary here to exalt the mind sufficiently to comprehend the sublimity of the subjects" (xvi).

As surveyors with sensibility, they consistently "exalt" their readers' minds. Their scientific explanations arise out of descriptions that depart from the "severe ascetic style." Those descriptions are themselves often set in a narrative so readers might "discover" the place presented before them. To comprehend the "sublimity of the subjects," enthusiasm was as necessary to these literary cartographers' method as the scientific one, because they worked both to expand knowledge and enlarge the spirit.

All of us try to orient ourselves in our surroundings. Surveyors represent humanity's boldest attempt to pinpoint locations, to bring untrammeled space into some contours of definition, and to tie it all to the coordinate system that unifies the globe. In tracing their place in the world, they are preoccupied with a fundamental question about where we are (Thoreau shouts it on Katahdin), though they aren't equipped to answer unless they begin to combine theolodites with theology, cartography with literature.

Yet perhaps the very impotence that these surveyors write of, as registered in the sublime, carries important implications. Their sense that they can't "get it all in" leaves readers not with a "legacy of conquest" but with a kind of environmental humility or perhaps the decentered or ecological sublime of Powell. Within the difficulty of environmental representation lies an awareness not of mastering the environment but of entering it through a variety of forms, maps included, to realize the sense of place.

Among these three literary cartographers, Powell especially locates a middle ground between a set of familiar responses for surveyors: a subjective loss of self and "contact" on the one hand and a more objective mapping on the other; the desire to locate an unmediated and ahistorical sublime or blank spot on the map and a commitment to a detached, scientific discourse common to exploration narratives (the as it "really is" to both Thoreau and King). Powell writes about neither a depersonalized attention to place nor a sense of it that is infused with ecstatic enchantment and epiphany. In the former instance, the place fails to be individuated; in the latter, the writer loses a critical context from which to view the place and his or her position in it. What Powell was able to do, and what we might learn from him, is to cultivate mystery and enchantment in a place he came to know. For Powell, to know it was to know that it could not be completely known. Even though in Powell's time the height of the mountains could now be estimated with a higher degree of exactness, they retained their spirit. Through close inspection and the hard work necessary to begin to understand them, they can be seen less as blank, abstract space, to be projected upon, but already storied — already, in a sense, mapped.

NOTES

1. I use map (without quotation marks) to mean literally the piece of map with a spatial narrative, while also using "map" (with quotation marks) to talk about other cultural and personal landscapes we contain in our minds.

2. Others can summarize the difference between the terms better than I can, but generally, in aesthetics, the "sublime" refers to the nonhuman or infinite, the "beautiful" to the human or humanized, and the "picturesque" to something in between. However, Barbara Novak writes in *Nature and Culture* that the Hudson River School "telescoped the beautiful and the sublime into a single convention" (228). For an analysis of the various landscape aesthetic controversies and definitions, see Walter Hipple, *The Beautiful, the Sublime, and the Picturesque in Eighteenth-Century British Aesthetic Theory* (83–98).

3. The first few lines read: "Why do those cliffs of shadowy tint appear / More sweet than all the landscape near? —/ 'Tis distance lends enchantment to the view, / And robes the mountain in its azure hue. / Thus with delight we linger to survey / The promised joys of life's unmeasured way" (Campbell 1–2).

4. There are ten references to "map" in "Ktaadn," six in "Chesuncook," and twenty-four in "The Allegash and East Branch." Thoreau makes numerous references to the maps' inadequacy. They get the distances wrong: "The distance is nearly twice too great on the map of the Public Lands, and on Colton's Map of Maine" (*Maine Woods* 94). According to the scale of one map, a lake is one length, but according to someone who knows the place, it is much longer: "Measured on the map, Moosehead Lake is twelve miles wide at the widest place, and thirty miles long as it lies. The captain of the steamer called it thirty-eight miles as he steered" (165). At times, the places Thoreau travels through aren't even on the map: "We could not find much more than half of the day's journey on our maps" (280). This can cause frustration, but sometimes he manages to joke about the inaccuracy of his maps: "we went . . . through more than a dozen flourishing towns, with almost every one its academy; not one of which, however, is on my General Atlas. . . . The earth must have been considerably lighter to the shoulders of General Atlas then" (86).

5. In their introduction to a 1970 reprint of *Survey of Maine*, the curators of the Maine State Museum write that Greenleaf was a tireless promoter of Maine, spending a good deal of his time "procuring settlers" and supporting his "visionary promotional activities": "Greenleaf was, in a sense, a man captivated and obsessed by the potentialities of the Maine environment" (ii).

6. Thoreau's map may have been outdated as the lands may have been burned when they were mapped and the thicket was recovering and replenishing, or the alpine tundra may have had a "burnt" appearance to the namer and mapper. Whatever the case, Thoreau isn't quite prepared for what he sees.

7. A key difference is that the "lakes" King sees on maps may actually have been there at one time and weren't just drawn in to help sell the land. Many of the lakes in the region are dry, a phenomenon King the geologist could surely have predicted if he had read his Frémont and studied the drainage characteristics of the Great Basin.

8. Racism in *Mountaineering* is flagrant, "casual but constant" (Howarth xix). King's casual use of racial slurs — "greasers" and "tar-heads," for example — suggests "a bigotry consistent with his self-presentation as a genteel aristocrat" (Tallmadge 1179), but it was also a prejudice consistent with his way of classifying landscapes on his own terms. His prejudice against Native Americans is peculiar in light of his fascination with dark-skinned people. In 1878 he entered into a secret marriage with Ada Todd, a young African American from Brooklyn whom he supported under an assumed name; they eventually had five children. The strain of this double life and the failure of his business ventures landed him in an asylum. He died of tuberculosis in Phoenix on Christmas Eve, 1901. Such an ambivalence was partly due to King's mercurial nature and part a product of his day. For most surveyors/explorers, Native Americans were at once savages and guides — a hostile threat and a valuable source of information about the land. For example, despite his claim that "the Quakers will have to work a great reformation in the Indian before he is really fit to be exterminated" (60), King also sought out a tribe of Paiutes to settle a legal battle between two mining companies over possession of a silver-laden hill, needing them to verify place names that were found on the maps (Wilford 189). However, the general practice of the U.S. Geological Survey was to catalog and "survey" Native Americans as if they were elements in the landscape itself rather than acknowledge that they were skillful "surveyors" and mapmakers themselves. Lieutenant George M. Wheeler was instructed by the Army Corps of Engineers to obtain "everything relating to the physical features of the country, the numbers, habits, and disposition of the Indians who may live in this section" (quoted in Bartlett 338).

9. The nature-as-book metaphor was probably cliché by the time Powell used it, since it was no doubt exploited by Thoreau's famous "leaf" passages on the melting railroad bank in "Spring" and Whitman's "Leaves of Grass." Both use the pun to suggest that leaves of nature are like leaves of a book, implying an accessible natural order. However, Powell would have been reading the "pages" of geologic evolution, whereas Thoreau and Whitman were reading something more divine. Ernest Robert Curtis dates the first secular use of the term to before 1499, and

Barton Levi St. Armand suggests it goes back to Pliny, as it is implicit in the very idea of natural history. Sir Charles Lyell used it in his *Principles of Geology* (a book Powell would have been familiar with), but not optimistically. "The book of Nature is the book of fate," he said, and tells us not of the divine but of the end of the human species (quoted in St. Armand 36). In Powell's earliest account, one he wrote for W. A. Bell's *New Tracks in America*, which appeared in 1870 in England, he wrote that "the canyons of this region would be a book of revelations in the rock-leaved Bible of geology" (quoted in Darrah 21), suggesting that Powell thought the trip was apocalyptic or messianic.

10. Specifically, Powell's plan was to divide the map of the country into quadrangles, with smaller scales used for desert regions and larger ones, one mile to one inch, for more populated regions. The maps were to represent the shape of the land by contours, the classification of it (swamp, desert, and so forth) by colors, and important cultural features by lines and symbols (Wilford 214). According to an article in *National Geographic*, the 54,000-map project was completed a century later in 1991 (Miller 95).

11. Clarence Dutton, who worked under the Powell survey and according to some worked even harder to give an aesthetic principle to the canyon ("Though it was John Wesley Powell who effectively revealed the Grand Canyon, it was Clarence Dutton who gave it more modern understanding" [Pyne 33]), had written a decade before that the Grand Canyon "is the sublimest thing on earth. It is not alone by virtue of its magnitude, but by the virtue of its whole — its ensemble" (143). Dutton named his observation place Point Sublime.

12. In "The Allegash and East Branch," Thoreau discovers that Polis, his Native American guide, "does not carry things in his head, nor remember the route exactly, like a white man, but relies on himself at the moment. Not having experienced the need of the other sort of knowledge, all labeled and arranged, he has not acquired it" (185).

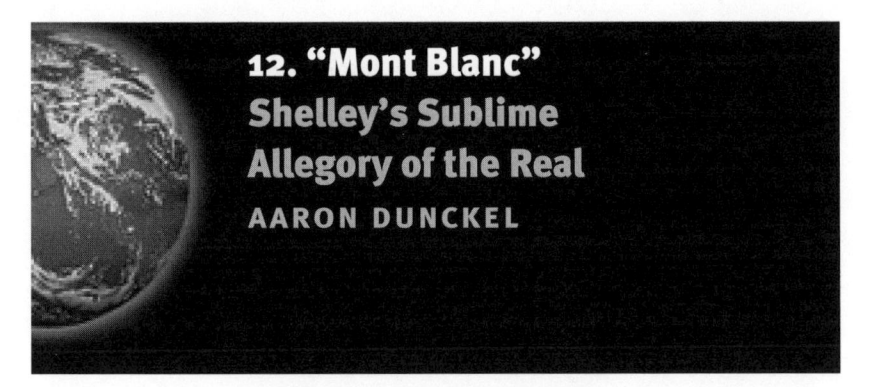

12. "Mont Blanc"
Shelley's Sublime
Allegory of the Real
AARON DUNCKEL

And what were thou, and earth, and stars, and sea,
If to the human mind's imaginings
Silence and solitude were vacancy?
— *Percy Bysshe Shelley, "Mont Blanc"*

These, the famous final lines of Percy Bysshe Shelley's "Mont Blanc" present a challenge for green approaches to Shelley's work. The "thou" here is Mont Blanc itself, the highest peak in Europe, which the poet views from a bridge over the Arve River in the Chamonix valley of southeastern France. The mountain is referred to generally throughout the poem as alien "Power" and has just been described (in lines 127–141) as completely remote from human contact. The direct address of this last apostrophe to the mountain reinforces a standard reading of the poem's ending question as rhetorical — a flourish that reestablishes the poet's control over his material. An example of this kind of reading is found in Donald H. Reiman and Sharon Powers's editorial gloss on these lines in the Norton Critical Edition of *Shelley's Poetry and Prose*: "The very power of the imagination to realize the nature of Power, so remote and foreign to all mortal experience, illustrates the supremacy of that imagination over the *silence and solitude* that threaten it. The poet is equal to Mont Blanc, for though the amoral Power can destroy him, only he can comprehend its meaning," (93). This is a view of the poet's relation to nature as agonistic, with the final triumph of the imagination over its other figured as incorporation: the alien "power" at last exists only as a function of the human imagination itself.

In this reading, "Mont Blanc" ends in presenting the critic who would claim Shelley for environmentalism with two problems: first, there is the common practice in Western intellectual tradition of representing nature as either a hostile other or an indifferent object (in this case, both); second, contradictorily, the antagonistic remoteness of the natural world is ultimately denied, and instead nature becomes merely an aspect of human subjectivity. The result is less like the Wordsworthian image of nature that we "half create and what perceive" than like Blake's Proverb of Hell: "where man is not nature is barren."[1]

Taken as rhetorical, Shelley's question thus becomes a doctrinal statement of transcendental idealism. Like Kant's account of the sublime, it affirms the primacy of the human in relation to overpowering nature by recourse to a paradoxical power of representation:

> In the immeasurableness of nature and the incompetence of our faculty for adopting a standard proportionate to the aesthetic estimation of the magnitude of its *realm,* we found our own limitation. But with this we also found in our rational faculty another non-sensuous standard, one which has that infinity itself under it as unit, and in comparision with which everything in nature is small, and so found in our minds a pre-eminence over nature even in its immeasurability. (*Critique* 111)

Kant's formulation here, involving the "rational faculty" rather than "the human mind's imaginings," may seem at first to be at some distance from Shelley's emphasis on the power of representation.[2] But Kant makes clear elsewhere that representation is precisely what is at stake in the sublime:

> For the beautiful in nature we must seek a ground external to ourselves, but for the sublime one merely in ourselves and the attitude of mind that introduces sublimity into the representation of nature. This is a very needful preliminary remark. It entirely separates the idea of the sublime from that of a finality of *nature* . . . because it does not give a representation of any particular form in nature, but involves no more than the development of a final employment by the imagination of its own representation. (93)

Ironically enough, Kant's concept of sublime representation is completely disconnected from any external referent. There are two "moments" in the Kantian sublime, which nevertheless become indistinguishable: there is the moment of experiencing a representation as purely aesthetic — separated from any "standard of sense" — and the subsequent moment of affective awareness of the import of this purely aesthetic experience.

These are indistinguishable because each is a central component of affect; the sublime is the very affectivity of affect. We experience a representation as sublime because we are able to represent it as such. One can go so far as to say that the experience of the sublime produces itself and is its own realization; it is autotelic, not unlike Wordsworth's "unfather'd vapour" in Book VI of *The Prelude* (527).

This comparison shows why Shelley's final question in "Mont Blanc" must be seen as rhetorical by readers in the vein of Reiman and Powers. It is useful to recall that by the early nineteenth century Mont Blanc was a supreme example of the sublime in nature and a European tourist's "must see." The inaccessible power of Mont Blanc, taken as the metaphorical embodiment of the sublime, would literally be nothing — certainly not sublime — unless available to affective representation. In denying that "silence and solitude" are "vacancy," Shelley affirms both the mountain's sublimity and the poet's imaginative power over it. It is sublime because Shelley is able to represent it as such, and in that very capacity for affective representation the poet, as it were, rises above the mountain.

But we should notice something odd about this reading. Why is it necessary, after all, to affirm the sublimity of an object that is patently sublime? The entire point of selecting Mont Blanc as poetic object from the standpoint of an effort at representation of the sublime is that such an affirmation is implied. Mont Blanc is almost by definition a sublime object. This redundancy hints that there is rather more anxiety in Shelley's final question than this kind of reading would suggest.

Connected to this is another, more obvious problem with Reiman and Powers's particular gloss on the question. If "silence and solitude" indeed do threaten the poet, it is certainly not because the "amoral power" may destroy him. To the contrary, everything indicates that the threat is not of impending doom but of an interminable distance, of a removal from human experience altogether. Silence and solitude are threatening as potentially vacant, not potentially deadly.[3] Listen to the almost obsessive insistence of some of the penultimate lines:

In the lone glare of the day, the snows descend
Upon that Mountain; none beholds them there,
Nor when the flakes burn in the sinking sun,
Or the star-beams dart through them: — Winds contend
Silently there, and heap the snow with breath

Rapid and strong, but silently! Its home
The voiceless lightning in these solitudes
Keeps innocently, and like vapour broods
Over the snow. . . . (131–139)

"Voiceless lightning" is of course lightning without thunder — so far away as to be completely unthreatening to human life but also unable to "speak" to those who would listen. The adjective "voiceless" repeats the concern with winds that have breath but are nevertheless silent (the adverb "silently" is used twice in one sentence to describe them).

In this context, Shelley's final question begins to appear less rhetorical and more earnest. If it is rhetorical, it is not so out of confidence in sublime experience but out of something approaching necessity, a required affirmation that the imagination indeed gives meaning — affect, to be more precise, which is the hallmark of the sublime — to an utterly remote nature. The issue seems not to be whether we are superior to nature because of this imaginative capacity but whether and how we can experience nature at all. The apostrophe itself can be read as an effort to establish contact with a being the nature of whose existence is unclear. It is only this kind of reading — understanding Shelley's "what were thou" in a literal sense — that thematically connects the otherwise rather tagged-on final three lines to the rest of a poem obsessed with marking the shifting distance between the mind and its environment.

My purpose in drawing this contrast between the conclusion of "Mont Blanc" and the Kantian sublime is not simply to develop a better reading of this problematic poem and thereby make it safe for ecocriticism. Rather, "Mont Blanc" raises issues about literary representation and our relationship to the natural environment that are of deep concern to ecocritical theory and our contemporary view of literary language. As a drama of an encounter between a human being and "the clear universe of things around" (40), "Mont Blanc" stages as an urgent question that, for reasons that are both political and emotional, is often taken as a given: can and should literature represent natural environments and the human experience within them? Unlike Kant, for whom representation reveals the limitlessness of human agency in the very face of limitless nature, Shelley's poem struggles with the distancing effect of representation from the natural environment it seeks to represent. The remainder of this essay is an attempt to sketch a theory of literary encounter with the natural world that does not rely on representation and to examine possibilities presented by other linguistic modes such as indication and (in a carefully defined sense) allegory. To do this, however, we cannot simply reject representation (which as I will shortly argue is a fool's game in any case) but must see how representation as such can be indicative or allegorical of something "beyond" the represented. My primary example will, of course, be "Mont Blanc," but to better understand what is at stake theoretically and politically, we must first take a detour from Shelley onto the postmodern ground on which contemporary ecocriticism works.

THE REAL WORLD: MIMESIS AND DEICTIC (DIS)ORIENTATION

Let me pose the question in a very broad way: is the role of literary language with respect to any environment essentially representational? That is, is its function to reenact, reproduce, sketch, or imitate, on the level of language, that which exists outside of language? Ecologically oriented critics may note with discomfort a nature/culture dualism inscribed in this question, but the question deserves serious attention in part just because language, as a system of signs, is of a manifestly different order than trees, birds, weather, or, for that matter, buildings, cars, and computers. Some ecocritics, like William Howarth, argue that there is no real duality: "Ecocriticism observes in nature and culture the ubiquity of signs, indicators of value that shape form and meaning. Ecology leads us to recognize that life speaks, communing through encoded streams of information that have direction and purpose, if we learn to translate the messages with fidelity" ("Some Principles" 77).

Thus, for Howarth, language — "signs," "encoded streams of information" — is a common element of both nature and culture. Yet despite this confidence in the universality of such "indicators of value," Howarth valorizes certain types of messages over others — at least when produced within culture. It turns out representation is a mode to be wary of.

Howarth mentions representation in the context of science rather than literature in order to contrast it with "deixis," or indication: "Ecocriticism, instead of taxing science for its use of language to represent (mimesis), examines its ability to point (deixis). . . . Through deixis, meaning develops from what is said or signed relative to physical space: I-you, here-there, this-that. Common as air or water, deixis expresses relative direction and orientation, the cognitive basis for description (Jarvella). In learning to read land, one can't just name objects but point to what they do" (80).

Recent cultural critiques of science, which among other things have attacked scientific representation's "truth function," provide an important context for Howarth's argument. Howarth has little use for these critiques in general, since for him they ignore or dismiss the reality of the natural world and its impact on culture, yet he is tacitly willing to concede their view of scientific representation. This concession is difficult to interpret unless we recall the ancient view, going back to Plato (Howarth's use of the term "mimesis" should put us in mind of the Greeks), that representation is inherently alienating. It puts a picture of a thing in place of the thing itself. Paradoxically, the more "true" and technically perfect the representation is, the more alienated from the original the reader or viewer becomes. The current state of the art in video simulation technology and virtual reality helps make the point very well: the closer the simulated experience comes to appearing "actual," the farther removed one is from real contact with the environment.

With this in mind, the motivation for Howarth's quick move from mimesis to deixis becomes clear: whereas mimesis implies alienation and objectification, deixis implies familiarization and the place of the subject in relation to objects. Mimesis encourages us to accept a dualistic conception of nature and culture, but we learn to live in the world through deictic acts of orientation. Orientation and "reading" or "translation" are conceived as two basic facets of the linguistic procedure by which we familiarize ourselves with our environmental home.

This may or may not be a fruitul way to understand scientific language from an ecocritical point of view, and Howarth is on the right track in emphasizing deixis, but it leaves literary language in an odd spot. The reason is that deixis in literature is necessarily "virtual." In his seminal analysis of the constitution of subjectivity in language, the linguist Emile Benveniste noted the relationship between the personal pronouns ("I," "you") and the deictic indicators ("this, here, now, that, yesterday, last year, tomorrow, etc."). These indicators "have in common the feature of being defined only with respect to the instances of discourse in which they occur, that is, depending upon the *I* which is proclaimed in the discourse" (226). We also learn that the personal pronouns have the peculiar linguistic feature of being nonreferential: "there is no concept 'I' that incorporates all the *I*'s that are uttered at every moment in the mouths of all speakers, in the sense that there is a concept 'tree' to which all the individual uses of *tree* refer. . . . *I* refers to the act of individual discourse in which it is pronounced, and by this it designates the speaker" (226).

I is thus the nodal point of discourse from which the orientational compass points of deixis radiate. This feature of language is among the things that make communication possible: we understand that *I* is appropriable by each speaker and that the point of reference for each deictic indicator is that speaker at the moment he or she is speaking.

Yet because *I* is a purely linguistic operator, it can be taken out of the immediate context of particular speakers — actual nodal points in space and time — and employed "virtually," as it is in literature. If deixis is only orienting in relation to a particular "point" of discourse, the act of removing that point from the actual landscape must be fundamentally disorienting — that is, unless we also provide a set of virtual compass points, a "world" to refer to, and especially a stable set of concepts to which *I* can refer in the absence of actual locus points of utterance. In short, to avoid sheer vertigo, the field of deictic orientation must also become a field of mimetic representation. In the literary landscape, it is only through mimesis that deixis can function as a means to orientation. The result is that deictic orientation now operates only in relation to the mimetic field. Therefore, by itself, the ability of language to "point" in no way guarantees the environmental familiarization sought by Howarth and a number of other ecocritics. In fact, deixis is precisely the linguistic modality that enables mimetic alienation. "Finding one's bearings" inside the field of representation entails losing touch (at least temporarily) with the world outside. This is not only the goal of virtual reality, it is the common sensation of getting "lost" in a novel. We are not lost *in* the novel — in fact we know exactly where we are — but lost *outside* of it.

One way to handle this fact about literary language is to follow a very long tradition, still deeply prevalent in our society, of regarding literature and associated narrative media like movies and television as pure escape. Readers of this essay are not likely to find this satisfactory since, on the one hand, it is one of the deepest faiths of our discipline in its socially and environmentally conscious modes that literature does reach beyond itself. On the other hand, it is often not possible to draw such strong distinctions between the mimetic and the real. An article that makes this case is Thomas de Zengotita's "The Gunfire Dialogues," published in the

July 1999 edition of *Harper's* magazine. Its argument is not unfamiliar: the intensity and synergistic quality of today's media have constructed an emergent culture in which the line between videotaped rehearsal of violence (the occasion of the essay is the school shootings in Littleton, Colorado) and the real thing becomes ever more fuzzy. De Zengotita's criticism of the Left is apropos here: "the media seem to them not material enough! They cling to old bread-and-circuses, opiate-of-the-people critiques. They learned nothing from O. J. and Di and Monica. They can't believe that virtual reality is *real*" (58). This is the by now familiar postmodern terrain, in which "the more enveloping and penetrating the stimulations and routines, the more uniform and centerless the settings of our lives . . . a vast plain of disengagement sustained by an economy devoted to simulations" (58). One example among many that could be added to de Zengotita's analysis is MTV's show *The Real World*, in which the "cast members" and the audience experience "reality" *because* the camera is rolling and sponsors are paying. The real *is* the simulated as well as vice versa.

One wants to just step outside. It is one of the truly salutary aspects of ecological criticism that it insists on an "outside" to the text. In a social world of mimetic synergy, the pressure of the nonhuman environment throws water in the face of our cultural solipsism. But how does literature open any route out? If literature is indeed fundamentally mimetic, doesn't this imply that we should, with Plato, ban it from our republic? If literature points beyond itself, it cannot do so in any immediate way but instead does so allegorically, as Plato himself recognized. That is to say, mimesis or representation must itself "point" to a referent that is not represented. This is by no means a simple idea, in part because this nonrepresented referent (whatever it is) is not simply "outside" the text — a "truth" of which literature is the "fiction."

A first step in thinking through a more authentic relationship to the environment through the medium of literature is not to insist on the "reality" of the experiences it represents but, paradoxically, to emphasize literature's fictionality and rigorously distinguish it from mimesis. Here is Paul de Man, who begins to appear a worthy source for ecocritics who are truly interested in the relation between nature and writing:

In a genuine semiology as well as in other linguistically oriented theories, the referential function of language is not being denied — far from it; what is in question is its authority as a model for natural or phenomenal cognition. Literature is fiction not because it somehow refuses to acknowledge "reality," but because it is not *a priori* certain that language functions according to principles which are those, or which are *like* those of the phenomenal world. . . . This does not mean that fictional narratives are not part of the world and of reality; their impact upon the world may well be all too strong for comfort. What we call ideology is precisely the confusion of linguistic with natural reality, of reference with phenomenalism. (*Resistance* 11)

De Man asks that we remain aware of the vertigo of fiction. I've noted that *I* is a purely linguistic operator. Fictionality marks the distance between any particular use of *I* and "I" in general as the central nodal point of any discourse. We know we are in the fictional because of that initial disorientation, prior to reorientation on the mimetic map (thus it is not the mimetic map itself that distinguishes the fictional). De Manian deconstruction insists on the primary disjunction between language and nature. We can conceive of nothing in nature like this linguistic *I*, because it is precisely this *I* that defamiliarizes us from the world around us. *I* marks the very possibility of fiction (what is generally called "point of view") and the beginning of our disentanglement from what de Man calls "ideology." While at first sight this may not seem particularly promising for an ecological perspective on literature (and de Man's criticism leads consistently away from such a perspective), one can see at least the cautionary value of insisting on literature as fiction.

Yet this is only a first step. Literary language, in de Man's view, tells us about nothing but "itself"; the breakdown in representation that he reveals at every turn returns us exclusively to language, as though once the "outside" cannot be viewed with clarity through language, it ceases to exist for language. De Man's limitation is not his view of literary language per se, but his view of the phenomenal world strictly as something to be known. What Slavoj Zizek says of Kant in his discussion of Kant's analytic of the sublime is equally true of de Man: "*it is Kant himself who still remains a prisoner of the field of representation*" (205). While de Man acknowledges that the "impact" of "fictional narratives . . . on the world may well be all too strong for comfort," he does not similarly acknowledge the reverse: the impact of "the world" on "fictional narratives." The irony here is that de Man's conception of the "phenomenal world" is firmly within the code of representation. That is, the world functions according to certain principles that would presumably be representable if only language were able to perform this task. In Kant, the inability of the mind to form a representation adequate to the sublime object inevitably returns us to ourselves — in de Man, an analogous linguistic process returns us to language.[4] But is it not possible to understand the role of the environment in both language and mind differently? Is there another way to conceptualize the sublime? At this point it might be helpful to relate a couple of allegories.

ALLEGORIES OF THE REAL

About a third of the way into "Mont Blanc" Shelley introduces a brief revision of Plato's allegory of the cave. It is a crucial point in the poem, since it is here that the poet tries to come to terms with his awareness of the separation of his imagination from the natural scene it has been endeavoring to represent. To grasp more completely what's at stake, though, let's start with a contemporary version of the allegory of the cave — call it the "allegory of the holodeck." In the television series *Star Trek: The Next Generation*, the holodeck is an image of the near-limit point of virtual reality. In the first episode of the series, the holodeck produces a simulation of primordial nature — a tropical rain forest — and through this reproduction of a natural environment inside the entirely humanoid-manufactured environment of the starship *Enterprise* displays to the television audience the holodeck's mimetic powers. There is thus an odd reversal in which the "natural" is the simulated and the artificial is the "actual." In Plato's story, we recall, the dwellers in the cave witness dim images, taking them for a reality that in fact is distant and inaccessible to them so long as they remain chained inside the cave. When one dweller manages to escape the cave, the light of the sun is at first so blinding that he cannot open his eyes. The light of the truth is vastly different from that of the dim fire that illuminates the cave. The crew of the *Enterprise*, on the other hand, may enter and leave the holodeck at will and are perfectly aware that their experiences on the holodeck are not real. What separates the holodeck from the rest of the ship is not, as in Plato, the respective intensity of experience in each locale but instead a difference in "content," as well as an unusual level of control displayed by the characters over the holodeck's internal environment (they are quite unchained).

But in fact the control one exercises on the holodeck is not that different from that employed elsewhere on the ship in that both rely on technological mastery. The difference between the actuality of the rest of the *Enterprise* and the virtuality of the holodeck is therefore rather more elusive, especially for the show's viewers (as opposed to the characters in the show), for whom science fiction is, of course, as "made-up" as anything the holodeck can simulate. The series accentuates this fact in later episodes, where instead of natural environments, the crew members usually use the holodeck to simulate scenes out of clearly recognizable fictional genres, from Arthurian romance to film noir. It is this "layering" of the fictional for the viewer as opposed to for the characters that as much as anything else marks the allegorical nature of the holodeck and suggests that the viewer inquire into the intended difference between two fictions. In Plato's allegory, both the cave and above ground are obviously symbolic: we are to accept the light of the sun as "more real" than the cave. The operating distinction of the allegory is one of affect: sunlight is brighter and more intense than firelight. But there is little affective difference between the holodeck and the rest of the *Enterprise* (there's nothing in theory to prevent characters from simulating the *Enterprise* itself on the holodeck).

What, then, distinguishes the two realms? The answer is: *nothing*. Certainly, the actual does not hold special claim to the real. In fact, the holodeck is invaded by the real almost every time it appears in the series in the form of glitches and malfunctions, just as on the ship as a whole. But because the holodeck is "doubly" fictional — a play within a play — it is capable of revealing a truth about the real that can be hidden by our "suspension of disbelief" with respect to the main decks of the *Enterprise*: in the Lacanian tradition developed by Zizek, the real exists as the symptom which is its index. On the holodeck, the image of perfect mimesis, the real is that which disrupts the smooth continuity of representation. We know we are in the presence of the real when mimesis breaks down — that is to say, the real is precisely that which is not represented but rather indicated by representation's failure. This is what happens on the "actual" *Enterprise* when its sensors fail to register or correctly interpret something in the ship's environment: a failure of representation. Of course, *Star Trek: The Next Generation* being a television series, these revelations of the real in the form of mimetic breakdown are always recuperated when the crew discovers what is "actually causing" the problem — that is, when they are able to produce an adequate representation of it and subsequently solve it through feats of spontaneous engineering. But also because it is a series, we are aware that these new representations will not be permanently adequate. The next time we enter the holodeck, we expect new symptoms to emerge that will require novel efforts at representation.

The limitation of the allegory of the holodeck as an allegory of the real is its presence in the ideological context of *Star Trek*'s drive, through science and technology, toward total representation. It is not even sublime in Kant's sense because there is no ultimate representational failure. Space is "the final frontier," but it is a frontier that will, like all frontiers, yield to exploration. Nevertheless, the allegory enables us to "see," albeit briefly, a real that is neither separable from our representations nor reducible to them. Shelley's version of the allegory of the cave — and its place within the context of "Mont Blanc" — presents an analogous possibility that also gives us an instructive ideological contrast. In a characteristic romantic gesture, Shelley's cave is that of "the witch Poesy" (44) — that is, similar to the holodeck, it is a retreat from the actual environment into a zone characterized by representation. But unlike the holodeck, where the real intrudes only surreptitiously and is not consciously desired by those inside, the speaker of the poem searches anxiously "among the shadows that pass by / Ghosts of all things that are, some shade of thee" (45–46). The "thee" is the ravine through which the Arve River flows, descending from the mountains. Things become complicated when we verify that the speaker is, at this moment, looking directly at this very ravine.

In fact, the speaker is completely surrounded by it. Not only is he immersed within its visual purview, but he is awash in the river's sound, accentuated by "echoing" "caverns" (30) that are kin to "the still cave" (44). The profoundly and confusingly intimate relationships here are already marked out in the poem's opening lines:

> The everlasting universe of things
> Flows through the mind, and rolls its rapid waves,
> Now dark — now glittering — now reflecting gloom —
> Now lending splendour, where from secret springs
> The source of human thought its tribute brings
> Of waters, — with a sound but half its own. (1–6)

It is impossible in these lines to keep "the mind" distinct from "the everlasting universe of things." At first the latter is a river that "flows through" the mind, but it turns out this mind has its own source that nevertheless contributes to the flow. In a final twist, the sound of this personal "tribute" is "but half its own" and so is still not entirely unique to the mind. The result is a picture of a human individual who, in his very subjectivity, is inseparable from his environment.

How, then, do we arrive at a point where the speaker finds himself groping among the shadows of a cave for an image of a thunderous presence that is part of his very being? Shelley tells us, somewhat enigmatically, that it is a direct *result* of the speaker's sensory immersion within the ravine:

Dizzy Ravine! and when I gaze on thee
I seem as in a trance sublime and strange
To muse on my own my separate phantasy,
My own, my human mind, which passively
Now renders and receives fast influencings,
Holding an unremitting interchange
With the clear universe of things around; (34–40)

It is the "interchange" itself — the passive "gaze" — that provokes the "trance" that is a manifestation of his "separate phantasy."[5] Here, in essence, is the fundamental and logically complicated difficulty (I am tempted to say "crisis," which is perhaps hyperbolic) of the human imagination as representer of its environment. As a creature of this environment, the human subject exists in passive, "unremitting interchange" with it, yet subjectivity — the insistence on "my own" — also demands a separation. The character of this subjective separation is "phantasy."

The "phantasy" is not a turning away from or forgetting of the ravine; on the contrary, the trance can only take place as a result of the speaker's experience within it. However, once the separation occurs, the ravine exists only, as it were, "in the poet's head" (the other burden of the "cave" metaphor) in the form of "ghosts," "shades," and "phantoms" (45–47). On the one hand, this bears a certain resemblance to the Kantian distinction between the phenomenal and noumenal realms — the insight that we can only experience the world through mental categories and never as it is "in itself." But the movement of Shelley's poem is much more dialectical: the speaker doesn't come to the ravine already removed from the environmental noumena by perceptual categories. This is a more pointed critique of representation than we find in Kant, but we also can therefore expect that the cave will not be the final image of the relationship between the speaker and the ravine.

Sure enough, at the end of the poem's second section (which encompasses lines 12–48), Shelley engineers an escape from the cave. Oddly, quite unlike Plato, it is not the speaker who escapes: instead it is the "phantoms" and "images" themselves. Although it is the speaker's "separate phantasy" that prompts these images' appearance, Shelley makes it plain once again that they are not a pure invention of the mind, since they return to the external world ("till the breast / From which they fled recalls them" [47–48]). But it is the last, ecstatic phrase of this section that demands our attention. Once the images of representation have fled, the speaker is able to affirm the existence of his immediate environment (the ravine) through a simple though astonished act of deixis — "thou art there!" (48). Two ideas emerge from this that significantly contrast with the allegory of the holodeck, while in a certain way affirming its basic insight. First is the fact that, in Shelley, representation itself is part of the real (which is not the same as saying that it is representative of it). The "cave of the witch Poesy" is indeed a retreat from the environment, but it is a retreat composed largely of the form and substance of that very environment. The holodeck, too, because necessarily created using the principles of physics, is part of its natural environment, but it is a retreat ideally fully controlled by its human creators. Shelley can make no such claim (and given his endorsement of his wife's powerful critique of such control in *Frankenstein*, conceptualized on the same trip during which Percy composed "Mont Blanc," it is doubtful he would want to).[6] As I've said, it is only when representation is disrupted on the holodeck that the presence of the real becomes manifest, but it is evident in "Mont Blanc" that representations are "ghosts of all things that are." The second, somewhat problematic, point is that in "Mont Blanc" we are at last made fully cognizant of the real through distancing. The speaker is able to point ("thou art there!") only once images of representation have fled. On the holodeck, by contrast, the revelation of the real is quite intimate.

THE THINGS WE POINT TO

There is much to be said for the theoretical and rhetorical value of insisting on the profound intimacy — in fact, the inseparability — of the environment in relation to ourselves from an ecological point of view. We live in a world where it is too easy to understand the natural world as existing "out there" and where we live as mostly "in here," while ecological damage all too often hits us where we live. I would not like to be construed as in any way criticizing this viewpoint. Yet as Shelley saw in this poem, at least, there is a particular value to recognizing the purely external aspects of the environment. It is this externality — a pure otherness — that enables if not a permanent release from, at least a deep questioning of cultural (perhaps even "multicultural") solipsism. This is what I would like to mean by "sublime."

The third part of "Mont Blanc" begins with another representational crisis, in which the speaker cannot decide if he is awake or asleep, that is once again relieved by a deictic act: "Far, far above, piercing the infinite sky, / Mont Blanc appears" (60–61). This is the first mention of the mountain, and it is followed by a long, "sublime" representation of its harshness and remoteness, which is nevertheless punctuated by claims for its beneficence. The mountain is represented as "rude, bare, and high, / Ghastly, and scarred, and riven" (70–71), while only a few lines later Shelley gives us this paean:

> The wilderness has a mysterious tongue
> Which teaches awful doubt, or faith so mild,
> So solemn, so serene, that man may be
> But for such faith with nature reconciled,
> Thou hast a voice, great Mountain, to repeal
> Large codes of fraud and woe; not understood
> By all, but which the wise, and great, and good
> Interpret, or make felt, or deeply feel. (76–83)

The contrast between these two perspectives on the mountain may seem to border on contradiction, but perhaps all it means is that Shelley, like many people native to alpine regions, sees the mountain as a god.

Certainly, Mont Blanc is for Shelley profoundly phallic (just as the ravine is vaginal and the cave, uterine). In Lacan, the phallus is the signifier without signification, the symbolic operator without content, and indeed the mountain has precisely these qualities: it has a "voice" yet is itself absolutely barren and empty. Ideally (like a god), its message is interpreted by a vaguely articulated priesthood ("the wise, and great, and good") who bring it to the people. The theistic and perhaps masculinist bent of this aspect of the poem is not to be discounted, but Shelley himself does not turn away from the mountain to the message or himself become its messenger: unlike Wordsworth, Shelley never becomes "nature's priest." Instead, he keeps his eyes trained on the mountain, noting its violence, its contributions to civilization, but particularly its remoteness. In doing so, he brings himself at last to the question with which I began this essay, which is to say he comes to a very appropriate question regarding a phallic object. While the mountain is no doubt an object of desire for the speaker, it does not become merely the repository for his fantasies. Instead, he wonders in what sense it could be said to exist without fantastic projection — that is, what is it *in itself*?

In what sense can the mountain be said to "exist"? Perhaps only in the sense that it "yet gleams on high" (127). Its very "thereness," as Keats said of the Grecian urn, teases us out of thought, and unlike Mount Everest for Sir Edmund Hillary, does not incite the speaker to the desire for conquest. Of course, as readers of this poem, we ourselves are not in the mountain's presence. Shelley's deixis is virtual — it is an allegory of pointing. Thus we do not come to "see" Mont Blanc, as perhaps we might think or allow ourselves to accept if Shelley had contented himself merely with representation (Mont Blanc as "symbol" is only a somewhat more sophisticated version of this). Perhaps the mountain does not exist. But other natural objects do, and we can point to them. Whether or not we are oriented in this way, we can acknowledge their discreteness, their fragile opacity to representation, as well as their relation to other objects. A poem like "Mont Blanc" helps us affirm, through the medium of literature, the existence of another world within our own, which we are part of and yet separate from. Perhaps this separateness is precisely what defines our responsibility toward it, as opposed to simply our undifferentiated self-interest in preserving our own species.

NOTES

1. Wordsworth, "Lines Written a Few Miles above Tintern Abbey," 107–108; Blake, *The Marriage of Heaven and Hell*, pl 10.14. It is a commonplace of criticism of "Mont Blanc" that Shelley rewrites and revises the Wordsworthian perspective on the relation between humans and nature expressed in "Tintern Abbey" and the "Intimations of Immortality" ode (see, for example, Wolfson and Manning 653, n.4).

2. In Mary Shelley's *History of a Six Weeks Tour*, Percy Shelley states that "Mont Blanc" "was composed under the immediate impression of the deep and powerful feelings excited by the objects which it attempts to describe; and, as an undisciplined overflowing of the soul, rests its claim to approbation on an attempt to imitate the untamable wildness and inaccessible solemnity from which those feelings sprang" (Wolfson and Manning 653, n.4).

3. For Kant, fear — or more precisely, "fearfulness without fear" — is an extremely important illustrative instance of the sublime response to nature (*Critique* 110).

4. One should not ignore de Man's own contribution to the study of Kant's sublime, "Kant's Materialism" in *Aesthetic Ideology*. Revealingly, in de Man's analysis, Kant is not talking about the human response to nature as such, but nature as it exists in "archetectonic" and linguistic systems.

5. Several years later, in *The Triumph of Life*, Shelley revisited this kind of experience, this time abandoning caves and darkness and allowing an image of the translucency of light itself to "clarify" the speaker's trancelike state:

> When a strange trance over my fancy grew
> Which was not slumber, for the shade it spread
>
> Was so transparent that the scene came through
> As clear as when a veil of light is drawn
> O'er evening hills they glimmer (29–33)

6. There is a fascinating instance of intertextuality between these two works that deserves more attention than I am able to give here. In *Frankenstein*, Victor has his decisive encounter with his creature on a glacial field on an ascent from the vale of Chamonix.

13. Vicarious Edification
Radcliffe and the Sublime

JAMES KIRWAN

One impulse from a vernal wood
May teach you more of man,
Of moral evil and of good,
Than all the sages can.

Sweet is the lore which Nature brings;
Our meddling intellect
Mis-shapes the beauteous forms of things: —
We murder to dissect.
—William Wordsworth, "The Tables Turned"

To commune with nature. To be alone with nature. This is perhaps the last great myth of unmediated experience. For when we say "alone with nature," this aloneness implies not merely a separation from whatever stands in contrast to nature, from everything that is marked by humanity, but also from the contingencies of the self, from that labyrinth of history, customs, transient or local motives, from, in short, the whole psychological morass that is the self as it is lived in the everyday. The experience of nature is, ideally, one of a being stripped bare as in an earlier age or another clime the individual might stand naked before God.

Consider the following reflection from an essay on landscape by the novelist Leslie Marmon Silko, made as she stands on the edge of a mesa in the southwestern United States: "So little lies between you and the sky. So little lies between you and the earth" ("Landscape" 94). How difficult it is to read this "you" as other than intensely singular. Simultaneously, however, it assumes an intersubjectivity, a commonality of experience. It is personal, even to the extent of claiming a position beyond personality, an appeal to our "buried life," and yet at the same time a public address: not "so little may lie," or even "so little will lie," but rather "so little lies." There is a standard of experience invoked here, even as that standard is rendered problematic by the doubt cast on the immediacy and therefore the potential universality of the experience.

The purpose of this essay is to suggest that what lies between us and the sky, what lies between us and the earth, is precisely and inescapably everything. Moreover, the barrier that separates us from nature is one that cannot be crossed quite simply because there is nothing on the other side: the very idea of our separation arises from our desire that there should be another side, for when were limits to the human ever evoked without the implicit suggestion that they might be transcended?

That nature is a human construct the function of which is to stand as an antithesis to human constructs is a thesis the general application of which I could not possibly hope to demonstrate in the space of an essay. I will rather confine my attention to a particular moment in literary history and a particular way of conceiving the naturalness of nature that, standing as it does at the origin of our modern attitude (West and East) toward this idea we call "nature," may serve both as an exemplar and, to some extent, an explanation of that attitude.[1] Specifically I will center my discussion on Ann Radcliffe's conception of the moral/religious import of the sublimity and the general philosophical background to that conception. That my thesis should be best illustrated by a literary treatment of the significance of nature is, of course, no accident. The very notion of nature's having a significance, in the sense of standing over against and thus offering, in the possibility of our communion with it, a way beyond the limitations of our individual humanity, is an essentially literary notion.

The novels of Ann Radcliffe (1764–1823) are generally regarded as definitive of the Gothic genre. She has also been described as "the landscape novelist of all time" (Monk 217). That much of what is characteristic in Radcliffe's descriptions of nature can be traced to Burke's theoretical account of the sublime is a fact routinely remarked in discussions of her work. What is less often noticed is that the role of the sublime in Radcliffe's novels, its emotional/dramatic weight, owes hardly anything to Burke but a great deal to a theme that runs throughout the discussion of the sublime in the eighteenth century. Burke, indeed, is remarkable among writers on the sublime for his neglect of this very theme: Kant, in 1790, referred to Burke as "the foremost author" of the empirical exposition of the sublime and did so by way of softening a criticism of his inadequacies, specifically Burke's failure to address sufficiently the causes and, more important, the moral implications of our capacity for the sublime (*Critique* 130). Before turning to the question of the relationship between scenery and virtue in Radcliffe's novels, it will be well to rehearse the development of this theme in the century of theorizing about the sublime that preceded their publication.

That there was felt to be a moral implication to sublimity can be seen even from the very terms in which the description of the psychological state itself developed from around the beginning of the eighteenth century. Early in the century, the prevailing theory of the grounds of sublimity was that, as John Dennis puts it, the joy arises "from our reflecting that we are out of danger at the very time that we see it before us" (Ashfield and de Bolla 37). (Significantly, however, he also describes how the soul is "transported" by "the consciousness of its own excellence . . . amazed by the unexpected view of its own surpassing power" [30].) [2] In 1739, however, Hume gave an account of the sublime grounded in a manner that foreshadows that dynamic that Kant was to find so morally significant: "It is a quality very observable in human nature," writes Hume, "that any opposition, which does not entirely discourage and intimidate us, has rather a contrary effect, and inspires us with a more than ordinary grandeur and magnanimity. In collecting our force to overcome the opposition, we invigorate the soul, and give it an elevation with which otherwise it would never have been acquainted" (433–434). Eight years later, John Baillie was advancing a theory containing most of Kant's fundamental points. According to Baillie, when an object is vast yet uniform "there is to the imagination no limits to its vastness, and the mind runs out into infinity, continually creating as it were from the pattern." The resulting "elevation" of the mind is due, Baillie continues, "to the mind's finding herself in the exercise of more enlarged powers, and hence judging higher of herself" (90). [3] This theory of sympathetic "expansion" is also to be found in Alexander Gerard, who holds that the mind "finds such a difficulty in spreading itself to the dimensions of its object, as enlivens and invigorates its frame: and having overcome the opposition which this ocasions, it sometimes imagines itself present in every part of the scene which it contemplates; and from the sense of this immensity, feels a noble pride, and entertains a lofty conception of its own capacity" (12). James Usher, whose theory of taste is generally Neoplatonic in tone, writes that "at the presence of the sublime, although it be always aweful, the soul of man seems to be raised out of a trance; it assumes an unknown grandeur; it is seized with a new appetite, that in a moment effaces its former little prospects and desires; it is rapt out of the sight and consideration of this diminutive world, into a kind of gigantic creation, where it finds room to dilate itself to a size agreeable to its present nature and grandeur" (Ashfield and de Bolla 147).

It is easy to see how this spatial metaphor might take on a moral tone — vertigo as magnanimity. In the authors mentioned above, the language slips easily from the intangible (the feeling) to the concrete (the image of expansion) to the abstract (morality). Which of the three, for example, does Hume intend when he speaks of how the contemplation of greatness "enlarges the soul" (432)? Others use the same metaphor, some merely to convey the quality of the experience, some apparently as if this notion of internal expansion actually had explanatory force. Baillie asserts that "every person upon seeing a grand object is affected with something which as it were extends his being, and expands it to a kind of immensity" (88). The explanatory emphasis is more marked in Gerard: "We always contemplate objects and ideas with a disposition similar to their nature. When a large object is presented, the mind expands itself to the extent of that object, and is filled with one grand sensation, which totally possessing it, composes it into a solemn sedateness, and strikes it with deep silent wonder and admiration" (12).

In Kant, this drama of the soul takes place in a landscape that is itself sublime. The "point of excess" toward which the imagination is driven in its attempt to comprehend the intuition of an object that is beyond its comprehension is, according to Kant, "like an abyss in which [imagination] fears to lose itself." Yet at the very moment the abyss opens beneath our feet, we find ourselves soaring above it: the attempt to comprehend imaginatively what exceeds the power of the imagination "reveals" to us the fact that there exists in the rational faculty a "non-sensuous standard, one which has . . . infinity itself under it as a unit, and in comparison with which everything in nature is small." In the experience the "forces of the soul" are raised "above the height of vulgar commonplace," the mind "feels itself elevated in its own estimate of itself on finding all the might of imagination still unequal to its ideas," and the subject "recognizes" that the "absolutely great" is located not without but within (*Critique* 106). Simply put, it is a pleasure, and an edifying one, to find every standard of sensibility falling short of the ideas of reason. Not, that is, because in doing so the imagination actually fastens upon something beyond the sensible but rather because the mind suddenly feels its ability to "thrust aside" all sensible barriers. It is this thrusting aside, this mental movement rather than the satisfaction of any end or interest, that, according to Kant, is "subjectively final" and thus makes the sublime a pleasure (94).

Indeed, from its very inception the concept of the sublime seemed inseparable from the notion of the dignity of the soul. Longinus had characterized it as "the echo of a noble mind" and declared the grandeur of the world to be evidence of the "noble ends" for which we were created (109, 146). In 1771, Sir Joshua Reynolds told his audience at the Royal Academy that it was impossible to conceive of "the most sublime ideas and the lowest sensuality" being united in the same mind (62). James Beattie, in a passage that anticipates Kant's own exposition of the moral import of the sublime, speaks of sublimity possessing the power to "raise our affections above the low pursuits of sensuality and avarice, and animate us with the love of virtue and honour," thus awakening in the mind such "great and good affections" as piety and patriotism (Ashfield and de Bolla 188, 190). Almost all writers on the sublime asserted that the experience of sublimity led one irresistibly to the idea of God. Joseph Addison wrote of how the sublimity of the ocean "naturally raises in [the] thoughts the idea of an almighty being, and convinces of his existence, as much as any metaphysical demonstration" (Addison and Steele 1:207). Shaftesbury had spoken of the "amazing depths . . . the abyss of Deity" (2:346), and many others held God to be, as Reid puts it, "of all objects the most grand" (496). Longinus himself had quoted from the Bible, and it was a commonplace to refer to Scripture for instances of the "true sublime" at its "highest" (111).

Though Kant can obviously not be taken as a direct influence on Radcliffe, it is his treatment of the sublime that best summarizes those trends in its discussion that underpin the novelist's writings. (There is a good deal less novelty in Kant's analysis than the majority of Kantians believe.) It is "a law (of reason)," according to Kant, "that we should esteem as small in comparison with ideas of reason everything which for us is great in nature as an object of sense"; whatever "renders . . . intuitable the supremacy of our cognitive faculties," that is, whatever "makes us alive to the feeling of this supersensible side of our being," will be in harmony with this "law" (Critique 106). Yet as a matter of fact, not everyone appears to appreciate the sublime, or at least not everyone will find that it is inspired by what Kant believes should, reasonably, inspire it. Kant accounts for such different perceptions of what is sublime, or different judgments, from the same vantage point, of objects that may inspire the feeling of sublimity, in terms of the subject's deference to the "moral law":

> The pleasure in the sublime in nature, as one of rationalizing contemplation, lays claim [like the pleasure in objects of taste] to universal participation, but still it presupposes another feeling, that, namely, of our supersensible sphere, which feeling, however obscure it may be, has a moral foundation. But there is absolutely no authority for my presupposing that others will pay attention to this, and take a delight in beholding the uncouth dimensions of nature. . . . Nevertheless, having regard to the fact that attention ought to be paid upon every appropriate occasion to this moral birthright, we may still demand that delight from everyone; but we can do so only through the moral law, which in its turn, rests upon concepts of reason. (149)

The sublime, then, according to Kant, presupposes another feeling, which has a "moral foundation." To feel the sublime, and not merely terror, we must be susceptible to certain ideas: we only feel sublimity insofar as our reason exercises a dominion over our sensibility, "letting it look out beyond itself into the infinite, which for it is an abyss." For this reason, Kant says, only the individual who has developed moral ideas will experience the sublime — the untutored will merely experience terror. A stormy ocean, he writes, is only sublime if we bring to it a "rich stock of ideas," enabling the mind to abandon sensibility (which would react with horror) for "ideas involving higher finality" (92).

It is, moreover, a matter of common observation, according to Kant, that "a feeling for the sublime is hardly thinkable unless in association with an attitude of mind resembling the moral" (120). He is quite categorical in insisting that sublimity is not an original product of culture, not something "introduced in a more or less conventional way into society" (116). Rather its foundations lie in a person's "native capacity" for feeling moral ideas, a product of our moral birthright. Hence, he concludes, our judgment on the sublime always implies the necessity of others' agreement, and just as we say someone who does not appreciate beauty has no taste, so we say that someone unaffected by the sublime has no feeling. Indeed, later he expands on the observation by declaring that "to take an *immediate interest* in the beauty of *nature* . . . is always the mark of a good soul" (274–275).

It may fairly be said that by the end of the eighteenth century the notion that the sublime was edifying had become orthodox. When Wordsworth in 1798 advised his readers to "close up those barren leaves; / Come forth, and bring with you a heart / That watches and receives," a great weight of fertile leaves on the nature of the wisdom to be so passively acquired already lay behind the sentiment and its likely reception. There was, of course, some dissent from this orthodoxy even within theoretical writings that positioned themselves in other respects alongside the works of the writers reviewed above. Moreover, it remained possible for individuals even in the early part of the following century to echo, with some complacency, the kind of judgment Johnson had made fifty years earlier when he asserted that the sight of bustling Fleet Street was superior to anything "Nature" could offer (Boswell 1:285). Indeed, the excesses of the new breed of sublime-enthusiasts, *précieux* of nature, might render the passing of such judgments a positive pleasure (see Monk 212–227). The degree to which this orthodoxy, extended to encompass the spectacle even of nonsublime nature, had solidified into a truth of human nature by the end of the nineteenth century can best be judged not from the effusions of those, such as Ruskin, who had continued to give it explicit voice but rather from the way in which Wilde's paradoxes in "Decay of Lying" play off its status as a common assumption. That the notion is tenaciously with us at the start of the twenty-first century would scarcely be worth remarking were it not for the fact that it has become such common currency, has become so intrinsic a part of the very meaning of the word "nature," as to pass unnoticed as a specific belief. Elmore Leonard might almost be deliberately setting out to illustrate Kant's assertion that a feeling for nature is always the mark of a good soul when in *Killshot* he has a particularly unpleasant sociopath rhetorically ask, "What was there to love about [nature]? Nature was just *there*, outside, wherever there wasn't something else" (211). Accustomed as we are to the idea of concentration camp staff relaxing to Mozart, faced with the undeniable fact of the Nazis' predilection for the charms of landscape, we hurry to reassure ourselves with the reflection that, after all, this was nature converted by the eye of the beholder to kitsch.

There are two possible ways in which nature might be conceived as the vehicle of an edifying revelation, both of which are given voice in the eighteenth century. At the very start of that century, Shaftesbury had observed that beauty is never in form but rather always lies in design, so that whenever we are moved by an object what we are really admiring is "Mind, or the effect of Mind" (2:405). In the historical context, this "Mind" is ambiguous, and its ambiguity points at once to both possible explanations for the truth that nature is supposed to contain. Most probably Shaftesbury intended the reader to understand this "Mind" to mean God, "Mind" being one of the many daring/reticent circumlocutions that a deist such as Shaftesbury might use. The view implied by this interpretation is given clear expression by David Hartley when he contrasts the ultimately childish and trivial influence of art to that "far superior" beauty of nature, which leads us to "humility, devotion, and the study of the ways of providence" (2:249). We have already met with the other possible reading of Shaftesbury's "Mind" in the almost purely psychological account of the effect of the sublime by Kant, who explicitly rejected the notion that the nature or even the existence of the deity could be inferred from the spectacle of matter. ("Psychological" is, however, a description that Kant would certainly have balked at, and, indeed, the extent to which his account relies on an appeal to the transcendental is still a matter of contention.) [4]

An account along the lines of Kant's — that is, one that sees the power of nature lying not in its being a revelation of the Creator's handiwork but rather in its capacity, as a stimulus of unique authenticity, to call forth what is fundamental within the individual — is far more likely to be found sympathetic by the majority of those who might now reflect on the question. Shaftesbury can afford, as it were, to view nature simply as a medium, since the sense of transcendence inspired by the aesthetic will find its fulfillment in what was, for him, the more stable reality of the deity: that deity whose glory, infused into nature, *is* the aesthetic. In our more secular world (secular in the sense that even the religious are less likely than they once were to reach for God as as an immediate explanation of phenomena) nature is unlikely to be seen in an explicitly theological framework; the nature lover, we feel, loves nature for itself — though, as we shall see, the very idea of nature as a revelation implies something equally absolute. Nature once stood for God; now it stands for whatever stands for God.

Within the context of eighteenth-century deism, in which the fundamental and improving truths of human existence were held to be available to the individual through introspection alone, the distinction between the two ways in which nature can be held to perform a revelatory function becomes considerably less decisive. In the case of Radcliffe, for example, it is not possible to tell whether the contrast she draws between the authentic religious sense her characters derive from the contemplation of nature and false, superstitious piety is a matter of deist convictions or, more simply, anti-Catholicism. It is not, however, necessary to decide this question, since what makes Radcliffe interesting in the present context is not simply the notion of the moral import of the sublime that she shares with the aestheticians of her period but rather the way in which, in Radcliffe, the role of the sublime in the psychological economy of the eighteenth century (so similar to the role of nature in general today) becomes a matter of representation.

If we turn to Radcliffe's acknowledged masterpiece, *The Mysteries of Udolpho* (1794), we soon discover that a sensitivity to the sublime is, indeed, a clear index of moral feeling, the sure sign of a superior soul. When it is reported that the heroine Emily's fear of precipices is mixed with "admiration, astonishment, and awe," while the facile Madame Montoni "only shuddered" (1:170), it might almost be a direct gloss on Kant's assertion that it is a capacity for moral ideas that separates a perception of sublimity from a feeling of mere horror. It is the countess, "whose vacant mind, overcome by the langour of idleness, would neither suffer her to be happy herself, nor to contribute to the happiness of others," who positively turns her back on the sublimity of nature (2:151):

[The countess] retired to an apartment on the modern side of the château, which was fitted up with airy elegance: and as the windows opened upon balconies that fronted the sea, she was there saved from a view of the horrid Pyrenees. Here, while she reclined on a sofa, and, casting her languid eyes over the ocean, which appeared beyond the wood-tops, indulged in the luxuries of ennui, her companion read aloud a sentimental novel on some fashionable system of philosophy, for the countess was herself somewhat of a philosopher, especially as to infidelity. . . . The Lady Blanche, meanwhile, hastened to indulge, amidst the wild wood-walks around the château, her new enthusiasm, where, as she wandered under the shades, her gay spirits gradually yielded to pensive complacency. (2:147)

Emily's father, the wise St. Aubert, tells her that "virtue and taste are nearly the same; for virtue is little more than active taste," and Emily, reflecting on rumors of Valancourt's corruption, asks herself if it is "possible that a mind so susceptible of whatever is grand or beautiful, could stoop to low pursuits, and be subdued by frivolous temptations?" (2:257). Of Valancourt, we are told that the "ardour for whatever is great and good in the moral world, as well as in the natural one, displayed itself in his infant years" (1:120). It is Madame Cheron, devoid of both sensibility and true moral character, who utters such heresies as "there is no accounting for taste" and "what has a man's face to do with his character?" (1:115). We are specifically told that the languid countess's tastes are divorced from action; she may almost faint at a story of "fictitious sorrow," but "her countenance suffered no change when living objects of distress solicited her charity, and her heart beat with no transport to the thought of giving them instant relief" (2:171).

It is no coincidence that religious infidelity is mentioned in connection with the countess for, as in the theorists quoted earlier, in Radcliffe a capacity for feeling sublimity readily merges with religious feeling. Often this is merely implicit, as when we are told that Emily, in contemplating the sublime, "seemed to have arisen into another world, and to have left every trifling thought, every trifling sentiment, in that below: those only of grandeur and sublimity now dilated her mind, and elevated the affections of the heart" (1:167). Sometimes, however, the connection is quite explicit: it is one of Emily's earliest pleasures, we learn, to ramble in nature, particularly the mountains "where the silence and grandeur of solitude impressed a sacred awe upon her heart, and lifted her thought to the GOD OF HEAVEN AND EARTH" (1:6). The convent education of Blanche affords Radcliffe much scope for enlarging on and refining this theme. Blanche, reflecting on how this education has deprived her of an experience of landscape, asks herself,

> "How can the poor nuns and friars feel the full fervour of devotion if they never see the sun rise or set? Never till this evening did I know what true devotion is; for never before did I see the sun sink below the vast earth." . . . Blanche's thoughts arose involuntarily to the Great Author of the sublime objects she contemplated, and she breathed a

prayer of finer devotion than any she had uttered beneath the vaulted roof of a cloister. (2:143, 146)

The sublime here becomes a specifically unmediated experience of the transcendental, a conflation of that opposition, so crucial to the era, between natural and revealed religion. It is a revelation that, like Wordsworth's conception of poetical truth, does not stand upon external testimony but is "carried alive into the heart by passion," a truth "which is its own testimony" (Preface 136):

> Her eyes were filled with tears of awful love and admiration and she felt that pure devotion, superior to all the distinctions of human systems, which lifts the soul above this world, and seems to expand it into a nobler nature — such devotion as can, perhaps, only be experienced when the mind, rescued for a moment from the humbleness of earthly considerations, aspires to contemplate His power in the sublimity of His works, and His goodness in the infinity of His blessing. (Radcliffe 48–49)

This immediacy of conviction, that is, the self-guaranteeing or self-authenticating nature of the experience of transcendence in sublimity, was, however, recognized, even in the heyday of the sublime, as a source of moral ambiguity. Dennis, in writing of how, in the sublime, "the soul is amazed by the unexpected view of its own surpassing power," revealingly reflects that "greatness of mind is nothing but pride well regulated" (Ashfield and de Bolla 30). The question is, of course, how well regulated this pride might be, given that the sublime would appear at first sight to be the most obvious instance in the aesthetic realm of feeling overwhelming all other faculties of the mind.

The very immediacy, the conviction of authenticity, in the sublime arose from the fact that it was, almost by definition, transporting and irresistible. Longinus had described how sublimity in poetry "exerts an irresistible force and mastery, and [gets] the upper hand with every hearer" (100). Reynolds describes it as that which "impresses the mind at once with one great idea; it is a single blow," an effect that "so overpowers and takes such possession of the whole mind, that no room is left for attention to minute criticism" (62, 242). It took no very great effort of imagination to see how closely allied such an effect might be to that enthusiasm that was, for the age, the chief enemy of both reason and morality. Dennis, for example, who described the sublime as a "pleasing rape upon the soul," defines it as "nothing else but a great thought, or great thoughts moving the soul from its ordinary situation by the enthusiasm which naturally attends them" (45–47). Even after the derogatory meaning of the word "enthusiasm" was firmly established, writers continued to use it to characterize the experience of sublimity, though usually with a preliminary caution to the reader to the effect that the "enthusiasm" under discussion was not to be confused with that "enthusiasm" that might be conceived to proceed from an overheated and distempered imagination and to imply superstition or madness. Shaftesbury, for example, characterizes the sublime as enthusiasm, with the proviso that we take it as a "plausible enthusiasm, a reasonable ecstasy" (2:400–401). Reid, too, explicitly links sublimity with enthusiasm: "What we call sublime in description, or in speech of any kind, is a proper expression of the admiration and enthusiasm which the subject produces in the mind of the speaker. If this admiration and enthusiasm appears [*sic*] to be just, it carries the hearer along with it voluntarily, and by a kind of violence rather than by cool conviction: for no passions are so infectious as those which hold of enthusiasm" (496). The question of what will appear "just" to any particular subject is, of course, a vexed one. It requires a very optimistic view of human potential to sustain the belief that "thinking with the blood" is a state that deserves cultivation.

According to Kant, every strenuous feeling that excites the consciousness of overcoming a resistance and leaves behind an impression of the mind's strength and resoluteness (even in the case of anger, desperation, or impetuous action) is aesthetically sublime (*Critique* 125). Where is the morality in this?[5] The treatment of the theme of the "Great Man" by Voltaire and Fielding is evidence of contemporary unease over equating grandeur or abstract force with virtue. In aesthetic theory, too, the potential conflict of the impressive and the edifying was sometimes recognized. Burke, for example, notes that the dog, while amiable and useful, is in no way sublime; it is rather the wolf, by virtue of its very "unmanageable fierceness," that is suitable for "grand descriptions and similitudes" (66–67). In a similar vein, Hugh Blair writes that while virtue is "the most natural and fertile source of . . . moral sublimity," nevertheless "on some occasions, where virtue either has no place, or is but imperfectly displayed, yet if extraordinary vigour and force of mind be discovered, we are not insensible to a degree of grandeur in the character; and from the splendid conqueror, or the daring conspirator, whom we are far from approving, we cannot withhold our admiration" (35). (Samuel Richardson was to lament that he had met with more admirers of Lovelace than of Clarissa.) Beattie, distinguishing between admiration and approval, asserts that "the test of sublimity is not moral approbation, but that pleasurable astonishment wherewith certain things strike the beholder" (Ashfield and de Bolla 183). Baillie, after noting that such qualities as the desire for conquest or fame are sublime, claims that "the sublime, and virtue, are quite different things," and that when "sublime passions" are virtuous, they are so "by association and accident" (93–95).

That the sublime is an aesthetic and not a moral category, a matter purely of the blind certainties of taste and not, as Kant would have it, a "rationalizing contemplation," is a truth that steals, almost unwittingly it seems, upon Radcliffe's text. (Austen was, of course, later consciously to pick apart — in *Love and Friendship*, *Northanger Abbey*, and *Sense and Sensibility* — this complex of the moral, erotic, and aesthetic so successfully blended by Radcliffe; indeed, in the *Italian*, Radcliffe herself significantly loosens the connection between the sublime and the moral.) Emily's love for Valancourt is, for example, influenced by scenic considerations: "The grandeur and sublimity of the scenes amidst which they had first met had fascinated her fancy, and had imperceptibly contributed to render Valancourt more interesting by seeming to communicate to him somewhat of their own character" (1:92). Later Emily, considering the "depravities" reported of Valancourt, reflects that they are not, after all, inconsistent with the "warmth and impetuosity" of his character (2:188). As if to illustrate Burke's comparison of the relative sublimity of the dog and the wolf, there are the following descriptions of Emily's sinister captor Montoni and one of his cronies:

> [Sometimes] the deep workings of his mind entirely abstracted him from surrounding objects, and threw a gloom over his visage that rendered it terrible; at others, his eyes seemed almost to flash fire, and all the energies of his soul appeared to be roused to some great enterprise. Emily observed these written characters of his thoughts with deep interest and not without some degree of awe, when she considered that she was entirely in his power. . . . As they mounted their horses, Emily was struck with the exulting joy expressed on the visage of Verezzi, while Cavigni was gay, yet with a shade of thought on his countenance;

and as he managed his horse with dexterity, his graceful and commanding figure, which exhibited the majesty of a hero, had never appeared to more advantage. Emily, as she observed him, thought he somewhat resembled Valancourt in the spirit and dignity of his person. (1:195, 307)

This undermining of the connection between the sublime and the moral is not, however, simply a matter of objects that inspire the feeling of sublimity yet from which the beholder would wish to withhold moral approval. The very existence of the sublime could be interpreted, as it was by Kant, merely as in itself evidence of the moral capacity of the beholder, regardless of the nature of the object — though how one can "admire" without "admiring" is a difficulty that Kant himself does not solve. (Alive as Kant was to the potential for self-deception in such a conflation of virtue with taste as Radcliffe's St. Aubert proposes, he was unable to resist the temptation of the idea that our spontaneous feelings might be indicative of our better selves, though he sought to avoid the specific conflation in question by asserting, unconvincingly, that the sublime was not a matter of taste.) More important than this with regard to the ambiguity of the sublime is that, as we have seen, distinguishing between the ascent to a state of "divine complacency" and the descent into the delirium of enthusiasm was a particularly difficult task — especially given that the only guarantee that it is reason or disinterest that is dominating sensibility (as it should in the sublime), rather than merely a strong interest of sensibility (pride) dominating a weaker one (fear), is the subject's own spontaneous inner conviction that this is the case. The delirium of enthusiasm is also the result of spontaneous inner conviction; fanatics and lunatics, too, subscribe to truths that are their own testimonies.

Sublimity and enthusiasm are, indeed, precariously balanced in the *Mysteries of Udolpho*. Music, we are told, inspires in Emily an "excess of tenderness and regret" that can rise to a degree "scarcely endurable"; there are times, indeed, when "if it had not suddenly ceased, she might have lost her reason" (1:288–289). The sublime is, moreover, explicitly linked to superstition. Reporting a discussion between the baron and the count on the possibly supernatural origin of certain phenomena, Radcliffe remarks that, though the count, who tends to a natural explanation, "had much the superiority of the baron in point of argument," it is the baron, with his supernatural account, who persuades most of their audience by virtue of "that love, so natural to the human mind, of whatever is able to *distend its faculties with wonder and astonishment*" (2:220, emphasis added). Blanche, finding herself inclining to the baron's side, must make a conscious effort to "forget the superstitious tales she had been told in her convent." Emily, who has been warned against the dangers of enthusiasm by her father on his deathbed, nevertheless also finds she must "[blame] herself for suffering her romantic imagination to carry her so far beyond the bounds of probability, and [determine] to endeavour to check its rapid flights lest they should sometimes extend into madness" (2:11). In the event of possibly real danger, she finds that "her imagination was inflamed, while her judgment was not enlightened, and the terrors of superstition again pervaded her mind" (2:40).

To inflame the imagination and make the terrors of superstition pervade the mind might, however, be a statement of Radcliffe's own method, for despite the resolutely natural cast of her *expliqués*, the main point of interest for the reader, the quality that keeps the pages turning, is a suspense that depends upon the threat/promise of the supernatural. The wise explicit cautions against superstition that the text contains and the implicit condemnation of it signaled by its prevalence among (invariably) half-witted servants can be misleading. *The Mysteries of Udolpho* is a novel, not an essay on the sublime, and when it cautions us against allowing feeling to overwhelm good sense it is placing itself, from a rhetorical point of view, in line with that popular form of pornography of the time — treatises on the dangers of masturbation (see Wagner 17–21).

Radcliffe gives the sublime to us in two basic ways: through the heroine's response to what is sublime and through the dangers, real or imagined, with which the heroine is faced. It is hardly surprising, therefore, that a certain confusion (as we saw with the portrayal of Montoni) creeps in between the imaginary *imaginary* danger that is the basis of the sublimity of the descriptions of the landscape and the imaginary *real* danger that confronts the heroine. That Emily shares the tastes to which the novel also appeals perforce produces the paradoxical situation that she can respond to "real" danger as to the sublime. A prisoner of Montoni, with the prospect either of a forced marriage to "a man who possessed neither her affection nor esteem" or whatever punishment "Italian revenge" may dictate, she finds this prospect mingling with the "equally gloomy, and equally terrible" prospect of the mountains and forests through which she is passing in a manner strongly reminiscent of the very pleasure that attended her first encounter with the alpine landscape (1:228). The paradox is, however, an appropriate one, for what we are dealing with here, what in fact we have been dealing with all along, is not an experience either of fear or, indeed, of nature but rather the representation of such an experience.

This last is a key point and instructive with respect to my broader theme of the revelatory role that nature, conceived of as a suprahuman reality, has come to play for us. The very significance of the sublime lay in its immediacy, in the irresistible power of the direct experience of the overwhelming: it was this character that would enable it to convey a revelation — either of God or, at least, of the nobility of the soul — that was, in Radcliffe's words, "superior to all the distinctions of human systems." What the success of Radcliffe's work shows is that a whole generation could entertain this notion, even as they entertained the feeling in a way — vicariously — that the notion itself precluded. The enthusiast for the sublimity of Radcliffe's landscapes, uplifted and edified before the spectacle of nature, really stood in a hall of mirrors.

This last is almost self-evident today: the passage of time must perforce render conspicuous the horizons of a literary work, the limits at which the self-awareness of the author and original audience ended. (It is the discernment of these limits that is the experience we call finding a thing "dated.") There appears now to be little natural in Radcliffe's or the eighteenth century's response to nature. Despite what is often remarked about the obsolescence of philosophical systems when compared with the relative timelessness of art, philosophy tends to date far less readily than fiction, if only because with the majority of philosophers, no matter how clear the thought itself, we cannot reconstruct what it *felt like* to entertain that thought.

It is no more than a coincidence, though a happy one for my purposes here, that neither the great writer of the sublime, Radcliffe, nor the great writer on the sublime, Kant, had any direct experience of the sublimities they described. It is well known that Radcliffe had never seen the landscapes whose sublimity she celebrated and so very obviously succeeded in communicating — if one can speak of "communicating" in such a scenario. For details she relied heavily on contemporary travel writing, the works of Rousseau, and such painters as Salvator Rosa and Claude

Lorrain, though the almost hallucinatory intensity of these landscapes is her own. Similarly Kant, in his chapter "The estimation of the magnitude of natural things requisite for the idea of the sublime," gives two examples: the pyramids of Egypt and Saint Peter's Basilica in Rome (*Critique* 98–99). Leaving aside the fact that neither of these is a natural feature, we may note that Kant had, of course, seen neither of them, and indeed he cites Savary's *Lettres sur l'Égypte* (1787) as his source for the emotional effect of the former. Later, when discussing the standard example of the Alps, his avowed source is Saussure's *Voyages dans les Alpes* (1779, 1786) (115–116). In his earlier *Observations*, he writes, with disarming ingenuousness, that "the sight of an Egyptian pyramid, as Hasselquist [*Reise nach Palä stina in den Jahren* (1762)] reports, moves one far more than one can imagine from all the descriptions" (49).

The link between the sublime, even the sublime of natural phenomena, and representation was established at the very origin of the eighteenth century's interest in sublimity: Longinus's *On the Sublime*, it must be remembered, was avowedly a work not about nature but about a certain poetical style. In 1747 Baillie wrote that "as the sublime in writing is no more than a description of the sublime in nature, and as it were a painting to the imagination what nature herself offers to the senses, I shall begin with an inquiry into the sublime of natural objects" (88). This interchangeability, or identity, of the object and its representation is also adopted by Burke, though he reverses Baillie's ordering. According to Burke, the highest degree of the emotions caused by the sublime, that is, astonishment, belongs specifically to "the great and sublime in *nature*" (57). Yet he illustrates obscurity (darkness) with quotations from Milton and the Bible, and, indeed, forgetting instances of the direct experience of darkness entirely, goes on to argue the superiority of poetry over painting in respect to communicating obscurity. The next source of the sublime that he deals with — power — begins with a consideration of animals but soon switches to their description in Job. Likewise, the power of the deity is represented through appropriate biblical, and even classical, passages. "Privation" (vacuity, darkness, solitude, and silence) is illustrated by Virgil. The same appeal to literary examples is to be found in the discussions of the other sources, or effects, of sublimity that Burke lists: magnificence, light, intermitting sound, the cries of animals, and even smells and tastes. The case of difficulty — exemplified by reflection on the force necessary to construct Stonehenge — presupposes human agency and therefore falls outside nature. (Nature as the work of God would properly fall under power.) Terror, vastness, infinity, succession, uniformity, loudness, and suddenness are not, however, represented by representation (57–87). It should be noted that Burke, unlike Baillie, does not hold poetry to be an imitative art in any simple sense; the business of poetry, as of rhetoric, he asserts, is "to affect rather by sympathy than imitation; to display rather the effect of things on the mind of the speaker, or of others, than to present a clear picture of the things themselves" (172). The sublime style, in particular, is "strong expression" rather than "clear expression"; it describes a thing not "as it is" but "as it is felt" (175).

This distinction could provide an admirer of Radcliffe's sublimity with a ready answer to the challenge that the experience of the sublime in her work is, at a conservative estimate, thirdhand: that since the sublime is a matter of the thing "as it is felt," then whatever can communicate this feeling is itself sublime, that is, the feeling of the thing "as it is felt" is the essence of the experience. This experience, however, can no longer claim to be the direct revelation of some external "nature"; rather, it has taken on its own psychological/moral life, and, as is notorious in the very case under discussion, it is impossible not to feel that such an independent life is a barrier between the beholder and what we might consider to be the reality of nature, which has become an affectation that forestalls the possibility of "direct experience."

Yet if the experience of the sublime in the eighteenth century turns out to be a cultural construct, an all but enclosed circuit from which a real encounter with nature is excluded, does not the very supposition of such a state of affairs presuppose the possibility of a real encounter with nature, an encounter unencumbered with prejudgments about "how it is felt"? (It is so easy now to see how the eighteenth-century mind revolved within a compass of a narrow conception of cause and effect, of character and motives; or at least it seems easy to discern the limits of this compass within the conception we designate "the eighteenth-century mind.") Can it make sense, after all, to speak of artificiality if there is nothing to stand as a contrast with it, to speak of a hall of mirrors unless there is a world, or at least the possibility of a world, beyond? If there is a limit there must be another side to this limit, something on the other side of the so much that stood between the enthusiast for the sublime and the mountain itself or indeed the "so little" that stands, for Silko, between "us" and the sky and earth; there must be something on the other side that enables us to speak of a border and its dimensions and enables us to invoke the notion that it is only a border, a space that can be crossed. The distance is crucial, of course. It makes no sense to speak, as Thoreau did, of "contact" unless there is a space to be traversed. Moreover, it is necessary that the revelation, the truth, should come from without, that we should feel sure that what we are experiencing is a transcendence of that limited self that sought the contact.[6]

We no longer use "nature," as it was used in the eighteenth century, as a synonym for "reality," nor do we find in the spectacle of the nonhuman world a revelation of the ways of providence. Yet nature remains for us a fundamental reality and, as such, a source of secular grace: our unmediated experience of the world, the background against which the true self will emerge, our Eleusinian mysteries, our presence of whatever stands for God. The general "truths" people may deduce from their experiences always have about them the air of interpretation, the suspicion of the refractions of personal motives and limitations; with nature alone is it simply sufficient to bring "a heart that watches and receives." We might ask "How did you find Paris?" and mean what was your Paris like, or did you like the kind of things Paris is customarily considered uniquely to offer, but it would seem absurd to ask the same question about Lake Windermere or the Grand Canyon.

Between the end of the seventeenth century and the end of the nineteenth century religion proper was forced to confront, in western Europe at least, an onslaught of scepticism, in various forms, that, where it did not actually destroy faith, perforce brought into sharp relief the difficulty of faith; the extraordinarily profound implications for the individual's mental economy of belief in propositions about the world that are at once fundamental and yet which, by their very nature, lie beyond the reach of the standard of verification that the individual necessarily applies to every other aspect of reality.[7] That sublimated religious feeling, which the aesthetic during a slightly later period increasingly came to provide, has never had to encounter a comparable spirit of Enlightenment. The creeping heresy of differences in taste, as well as the inescapably manufactured nature of art objects (or, in the case of nonobject art, the individual intention for something to be art and the collective agreement that the intention is fulfilled), prevents art from becoming, for the majority at least, the source of any "spontaneous wisdom," despite the best efforts of those who form and sustain artistic canons. The aesthetic response to nature is another matter; it has become, in Radcliffe's phrase, "superior to all the distinctions of human systems." Even when, as in Radcliffe's case, the response to nature appears, in retrospect, to have been merely a mood generated by certain desires circulating within just such a human system — in this case, the literary sublime — we are more likely to invoke a reality of nature to stand as a contrast than to see in it a symptom of the truth I have striven to convey here: that just as there are forms of art that become dated there are forms of nature that do the same, and this because our nature is always as much a construct as our art, because our nature is a form of art.

We wish nature to stand over against the contingencies of time and place, or even the limitations of human being, to be something that will redeem us from these limitations. Two hundred years ago Kant sought to find some guarantee of the validity of the intimation of transcendence that the experience of nature gave, yet ultimately he found nothing but a spontaneous inner conviction, registered as aesthetic feeling, that such was the case. Such a spontaneous inner conviction, a feel of the rightness or truth of a thing, taking the form of pleasure and uplift, was precisely the experience that Radcliffe communicated to her readers. In Silko, we encounter a more modern contention; we are complex, fallen creatures separated from the earth and sky. But this means nothing unless it leads us to imagine the possibility of not being separated from the earth and sky, unless we find the notion of such a union in some way meaningful.

It is impossible to take Wordsworth's advice to shut up our books and turn to nature, for what we will find on the other side of this border between books and nature is that very self that we thought would, at this point, lie behind us. Human beings never can shut up their books, in the sense of escaping human culture. What we call "nature" is ineluctably a story, one we have known since childhood, and the knowing of it since childhood is another story. It is, indeed, the literary, the very site, now traditional, of the celebration of nature that must always reveal this — that, in the long run, we are never alone with nature and that it is the desire that this should not be so that makes it so. The little that lies between us and the sky and the earth is everything in us that fosters the illusion that nothing may lie between us and the sky and the earth.

It is a measure of the weight of the literary tradition dealt with here that I should find myself catching, in the closing sentences, the strains of an elegy upon a lost nature. The intention of this essay, however, has rather been to suggest that there never was or could be a nature of this kind to lose — except as a matter of faith.[8]

NOTES

1. The notion of the spectacle of nature as a revelation of the divine, both within Neoplatonic and early Patristic writings, is dealt with at length in Kirwan (*Beauty* 27–48). It is, however, what the modern notion of the significance of nature does not have in common with these writings that is my present theme. While these earlier works no doubt might be adduced as remote influences on our modern notions, the fact that the latter are not purely a Western phenomenon makes it perhaps wiser to see these ancient texts as manifestations of an enduring psychological tendency rather than as directly causal.

2. Addison, for example, describes our pleasure in the terrible as similar to our feelings upon viewing a "dead monster": "the more frightful appearance they make, the greater is the pleasure we receive from the sense of our own safety" (Addison and Steele 3:298). Du Bos makes this same feeling of security the grounds of "the attractiveness of spectacles proper for exciting great emotions" (1:10–12).

3. Like Kant, Baillie makes sublimity an action of the mind rather than a property of objects: the mind, he writes, "sublimes" objects (91).

4. See Kirwan "'Claim,'" passim.

5. Burke, too, had described the sublime as "manly" and the beautiful, or merely languid, as "feminine" (36–37). Schiller later makes a similar distinction between two types of beauty — a melting beauty and an energizing beauty (111–113). The effect of the former, according to Schiller, is relaxing, though this may lead to a certain degree of effeminacy and enervation; the effect of the latter is bracing, though this may result in savagery and hardness. A combination of the two, he believes, is required to achieve a harmony of being (113, 116–119). But in Burke and Kant the emphasis is definitely on the superiority ("manliness") of the sublime — Kant cites as examples of manly sublimity of soul the waging of war (providing civilians are respected) and decries the effeminacy that comes from prolonged peace (*Critique* 112–113). Later, Schelling will speak of the sublime (which he restricts to art) as a source of "heroic resolve" and a means of "cleansing" oneself of pettiness, cowardice, weakness, and intellectual flaccidity (87–90). It is not surprising that Adorno should claim that Kant, by "situating the sublime . . . in a dimension of power," betrayed himself into an "unmitigated complicity with domination" (284). For Adorno, the sublime is an ideological expression; he describes it as a "reflex of the bourgeois delusion of grandeur, of the social preoccupation with quantities and record bests and also of bourgeois hero worship" (103–104). (Though, paradoxically, he also attributes a positive value to the impact of abstract magnitude as a reminder of the limits of human domination

[375].) Huhn has described the sublime as "the justification of domination and violence" and the making of "domination pleasurable and violence beautiful" (269). This thesis, while a useful response to the recent positing of the sublime (in, for example, Crowther and Lyotard) as somehow aestheticaly and morally superior to the beautiful, nevertheless perhaps overstates the case and is, in Huhn's case at least, based on the untenable premise that there is no subreption involved in the experience of the sublime.

6. For the parallels between this situation and the way in which we invest literature with value, see Kirwan (*Literature* 153–165). For a more general discussion of this theme in relation to the aesthetic per se, see Kirwan (*Beauty* 97–98, 155 n.27).

7. The greatest saints are, of course, traditionally the greatest doubters. However, it may fairly be said that before the period under discussion, consciousness of the acute difficulty of religious faith was not, in general, a province of the laity.

8. I wish to thank Steven Rosendale for his valuable suggestions toward the improvement of this essay.

CONTRIBUTORS

ANDREA BLAIR is an assistant editor at Louisiana State University Press and is currently editing anthologies on Jessie Fauset and Catherine Maria Sedgewick.

MICHAEL P. BRANCH is associate professor of English at the University of Nevada, Reno (UNR), and teaches courses in nature writing and American literature and codirects UNR's graduate program in literature and the environment. He is a cofounder and past president of the Association for the Study of Literature and Environment (ASLE) and is current book review editor of *ISLE: Interdisciplinary Studies in Literature and the Environment*. He has written more than seventy articles, chapters, and reviews on nature writing and environmental literature and is coeditor of *The Height of Our Mountains: Nature Writing from Virginia's Blue Ridge Mountains and Shenandoah Valley* (1998), *Reading the Earth: New Directions in the Study of Literature and Environment* (1998), and *John Muir's Last Journey: South to the Amazon and East to Africa* (2001). His current work includes *Reading the Roots: American Nature Writing Before Walden* (forthcoming).

ALISON BYERLY is professor of English and acting provost at Middlebury College, where she teaches an English/environmental studies course, "Visions of Nature." Her book, *Realism at Risk: Aesthetics and Representation in Nineteenth-Century Fiction*, was published in 1997. In addition to publications in the field of Victorian fiction, she has contributed essays on Lewis Thomas and artist-naturalist Cathy Johnson to *American Nature Writers*, edited by John Elder (1996). She is also the author of "The Picturesque Aesthetic and the National Park System," in *The Ecocriticism Reader* (1996). The current essay is part of a book project entitled *Going Nowhere: Virtual Travel and Victorian Culture*.

AARON DUNCKEL is visiting assistant professor of English at the University of Wisconsin, Oshkosh, where he teaches courses on literary theory, English literature, and composition. Concurrently with ongoing work on the theory of the sublime, Dunckel is completing a book on the history of the concept of romanticism in nineteenth- and twentieth-century literary criticism.

HELENA FEDER teaches in the English department at the University of California, Davis, where she is currently in the doctoral program. Her research focuses on the theoretical possibilities of wilderness.

ELEANOR HERSEY studies twentieth-century American literature and popular culture at the University of Iowa. Her current research examines recent film adaptations of novels written by Lucy Maud Montgomery, Willa Cather, and Edith

Wharton. Her articles have appeared in *Legacy: A Journal of American Women Writers*, *Journal of Popular Film and Television*, and *Studies in Popular Culture*.

JAMES KIRWAN is professor of philosophy at Kobe City University, Japan, and is the author of *Literature, Rhetoric, Metaphysics: Literary Theory and Literary Aesthetics* (1990) and *Beauty* (1999). His current research focuses on taste, literary theory, and eighteenth-century literature.

JAMES D. LILLEY's essays, reviews, and interviews have appeared in the *Southern Quarterly*, *Interdisciplinary Studies in Literature and Environment*, *MELUS*, and the *Mississippi Review*. He is editor of *Cormac McCarthy: New Directions* (forthcoming). Lilley is the 2001 recipient of Princeton Environmental Institute's Ford Graduate Prize in the Environment, and he is currently working on a Ph.D. dissertation at Princeton University, "Race and Removal," which explores how the literature of the emerging U.S. nation influenced, and was influenced by, the politics of American Indian removal and African colonization.

LOUIS H. PALMER III is assistant professor of English at Castleton State College in Vermont. His recent work focuses on discourses of race in the southern Gothic. He has written and presented on a variety of regional and Gothic literatures and serves as Gothic chair for the Popular Culture Association.

STEVEN ROSENDALE is assistant professor of English at Northern Arizona University, where he teaches courses on American naturalism, modernism, and American nature writing. His publications include essays on naturalism in the journal *Genre* and in *Political Moments in the Classroom*, edited by Margaret Himley (1997). His current research project, a book titled *City Wilderness: Political Ecology on the American Literary Left*, examines the historical and ideological links between Left literary culture and environmentalism in the United States.

GORDON SAYRE, associate professor of English at the University of Oregon, is the author of *"Les Sauvages Americains": Representations of Native Americans in French and English Colonial Literature* (1997) and editor of *American Captivity Narratives* (2000). He enjoys hiking and climbing in the Oregon mountains, and his recent research has focused on mountaineering and U.S. Forest Service policy.

SCOTT SLOVIC is professor of literature and the environment at the University of Nevada, Reno, where he served as founding director of the Center for Environmental Arts and Humanities from 1995 to 2001. The author of numerous articles on environmental literature, he has also written, edited, or coedited eight books, most recently *Getting Over the Color Green: Contemporary Environmental Literature of the Southwest* (2001). He served as founding president of the Association for the Study of Literature and Environment (ASLE) from 1992 to 1995 and currently edits ASLE's journal, *ISLE: Interdisciplinary Studies in Literature and Environment*. In addition, he edits the Credo Series for Milkweed Editions and the Environmental Arts and Humanities Series for the University of Nevada Press.

JAMES TARTER is an assistant professor of English at Lewis-Clark State College in Lewiston, Idaho, teaching courses in environmental studies, multiethnic literature, and Native American literature and working in the Native American Bridge Program. He is currently finishing a book titled *Locating Environmental Justice in Contemporary American Fiction*. Recently, he has published essays on environmental justice in *Reading Under the Sign of Nature*, edited by John Tallmadge and Henry Harringon (2000), and in *Environmental Justice Politics, Poetics and Pedagogy* (forthcoming).

RICK VAN NOY is assistant professor of English at Radford University, where he teaches technical writing, composition, environmental literature, and American literature. While traveling from New Jersey to Colorado to Washington to Ohio and now in Virginia, he became increasingly interested in the sense of place and the ways people shape and give value to their varied landscapes. He has also worked as a technical writer for surveyors and engineers. His current research includes a book titled *Surveying the Interior* and an article on the literary nonfiction of John McPhee.

BIBLIOGRAPHY

Abram, David. *The Spell of the Sensuous*. New York: Vintage, 1996.

Abrams, M. H. "Structure and Style in the Greater Romantic Lyric." In *Romanticism and Consciousness: Essays in Criticism*, ed. Harold Bloom. New York: Norton, 1970.

Abrams, Robert E. "Image, Object, and Perception in Thoreau's Landscapes: The Development of Anti-Geography." *Nineteenth Century Literature* 46:2 (1991): 245–262.

Addison, [Joseph], and [Richard] Steele. *The Spectator*. Ed. Gregory Smith. 4 vols. London: W. M. Dent, 1945.

Adorno, Theodor. *Aesthetic Theory*. Trans. C. Lenhardt. 1970. Reprint, London: Routledge and Kegan Paul, 1984.

Aiken, Susan Hardy, Ann E. Brigham, Sallie A. Marston, and Penny Waterstone, eds. *Making Worlds: Gender, Metaphor, Materiality*. Tucson: University of Arizona Press, 1998.

Alinder, Mary Street. *Ansel Adams: A Biography*. New York: Henry Holt, 1996.

Allen, Paula Gunn. "The Feminine Landscape of Leslie Marmon Silko's *Ceremony*." In *The Sacred Hoop: Recovering the Feminine in American Indian Traditions*. Boston: Beacon Press, 1986.

Alston, Dana, ed. *We Speak for Ourselves: Social Justice, Race and Environment*. Washington, D.C.: Panos Institute, 1990.

Altick, Richard. *The Shows of London*. Cambridge: Harvard University Press, 1978.

Ashfield, Andrew, and Peter de Bolla. *The Sublime: A Reader in British Eighteenth-Century Aesthetic Theory*. Cambridge: Cambridge University Press, 1996.

Austin, Regina, and Michael Schill. "Black, Brown, Red and Poisoned." In *Unequal Protection: Environmental Justice and Communities of Color*, ed. Robert D. Bullard. San Francisco: Sierra Club, 1994.

Baillie, John. "An Essay on the Sublime." In Ashfield and de Bolla, *The Sublime*.

Bakhtin, Mikhail. *Rabelais and His World*. Trans. Hélene Iswolsky. Bloomington: Indiana University Press, 1984.

Bammer, Angelika, Minrose Gwin, Cindi Katz, and Elizabeth Meese. "The Place of the Letter: An Epistolary Exchange." In Aiken et al., *Making Worlds*.

Bartlett, Richard A. *The Great Surveys of the West*. Norman: University of Oklahoma Press, 1962.

Basso, Keith. *Wisdom Sits in Places: Landscape and Language among the Western Apache*. Albuquerque: University of New Mexico Press, 1996.

Bate, Jonathan. "Living with the Weather." *Studies in Romanticism* 35 (1996): 431–447.

———. *Romantic Ecology: Wordsworth and the Environmental Tradition*. London: Routledge, 1991.

Baudrillard, Jean. *Selected Writings*. Ed. Mark Poster. Stanford, Calif.: Stanford University Press, 1988.

Baym, Nina. *Woman's Fiction: A Guide to Novels by and about Women in America, 1820–70*. 2nd ed. Urbana: University of Illinois Press, 1993.

Behdad, Ali. *Belated Travellers: Orientalism in the Age of Colonial Dissolution*. Durham, N.C.: Duke University Press, 1994.

Bénard de la Harpe, Jean-Baptiste. "Journal du Voyage de la Louisiane fait par le sieur Bénard de la Harpe et des découvertess qu'il a fait dans les parties de l'Ouest de cette colonie." In *Découvertes et Etablissements des François dans l'Ouest et le Sud de l'Amérique Septentrionale*. Ed. Pierre Margry. Vol. 6. Paris: D. Jouaust, 1878.

Benton, Ted, ed. *The Greening of Marxism*. New York: Guilford Press, 1998.

Benveniste, Emile. *Problems in General Linguistics*. Trans. Mary Elizabeth Meek. Miami Linguistics Series 8. Miami: University of Miami Press, 1971.

Berry, K. Wesley. "The Lay of the Land in Cormac McCarthy's *The Orchard Keeper* and *Child of God*." *Southern Quarterly* 38:4 (2000): 61–77.

Berry, Wendell. *Another Turn of the Crank*. Washington, D.C.: Counterpoint Press, 1995.

———. *The Unsettling of America: Culture and Agriculture*. New York: Avon, 1977.

Bhabha, Homi K. "Dissemination: Time, Narrative, and the Margins of the Modern Nation." In *Nation and Narration*, ed. Homi K. Bhaba. London: Routledge, 1990.

Blair, Hugh. *Lectures on Rhetoric and Belles Lettres*. 1783. Reprint, London, 1825.

Blake, William. *The Complete Poetry and Prose of William Blake*. Ed. David V. Erdman. Garden City, N.Y.: Anchor/Doubleday, 1982.

Bloom, Harold. "Elegiac Conclusion." In *Falling into Theory: Conflicting Views on Reading Literature*, ed. David H. Richter. Boston: Bedford/St. Martin's, 2000.

Blunt, Alison, and Gillian Rose. Introduction to *Writing Women and Space: Colonial and Postcolonial Geographies*, ed. Alison Blunt and Gillian Rose. New York: Guilford, 1994.

Booth, Michael. *Victorian Spectacular Theater 1850–1910*. Boston: Routledge, 1981.

Boswell, James. *Life of Johnson*. 2 vols. 1791. Reprint, London: J. M. Dent and Sons, 1960.

Boyle's Thames Guide. London: G. Boyle, 1840.

Branch, Michael P., and Daniel J. Phillipon, eds. *The Height of Our Mountains: Nature Writing from Virginia's Blue Ridge Mountains and Shenandoah Valley*. Baltimore: Johns Hopkins University Press, 1998.

Brantlinger, Patrick. *Rule of Darkness: British Literature and Imperialism, 1830–1914*. Ithaca, N.Y.: Cornell University Press, 1988.

Brooks, Cleanth. *William Faulkner: The Yoknapatawpha Country*. New Haven, Conn.: Yale University Press, 1963.

Bryant, Bunyan, ed. *Environmental Justice: Issues, Policies and Solutions*. Washington, D.C.: Island, 1995.

Buell, Lawrence. *The Environmental Imagination: Thoreau, Nature Writing, and the Formation of American Culture*. Cambridge: Belknap Press of Harvard University Press, 1995.

Bullard, Robert D., ed. *Confronting Environmental Racism: Voices from the Grassroots*. Boston: South End Press, 1993.

———. *Unequal Protection: Environmental Justice and Communities of Color*. San Francisco: Sierra Club, 1994.

Bullard, Robert D., and Glenn S. Johnson, eds. *Just Transportation: Dismantling Race and Class Barriers to Mobility*. Gabriola Island, B.C.: New Society Publishers, 1997.

Burke, Carolyn, and Jane Gallop. "Psychoanalysis and Feminism in France." In *The Future of Difference*, ed. Hester Eisertein and Alice Jardine. New Brunswick, N.J.: Rutgers University Press, 1985.

Burke, Edmund. *A Philosophical Enquiry into the Origin of Our Ideas of the Sublime and the Beautiful*. 1757, 1759. Ed. James T. Boulton. Reprint, Notre Dame, Ind.: University of Notre Dame Press, 1968.

Butler, Judith. *Bodies that Matter: On the Discursive Limits of "Sex."* New York: Routledge, 1993.

———. *Gender Trouble: Feminism and the Subversion of Identity*. New York: Routledge, 1990.

Butterick, George F. "The Mysterious Vision of Susan Howe." *North Dakota Quarterly* 55 (1987): 312–321.

Buzard, James. *The Beaten Track: European Tourism, Literature, and the Ways to "Culture" 1800–1918*. Oxford: Clarendon Press, 1993.

Cabeza de Vaca, Álvar Núñez. *Adventures in the Unknown Interior of America*. 1542. Trans. and ed. Cyclone Covey. Reprint, Albuquerque: University of New Mexico Press, 1998.

Campbell, Thomas. *The Poetical Works*. New York: Crowell, 1851.

Cantwell, Robert. *Alexander Wilson: Naturalist and Pioneer*. Philadelphia: Lippincott, 1961.

———. *The Land of Plenty*. New York: Farrar and Rinehart, 1934.

Casey, Edward S. *The Fate of Place: A Philosophical History*. Berkeley: University of California Press, 1997.

Churchill, Ward. "Radioactive Colonization: Hidden Holocaust in Native North America." In *Struggle for the Land: Indigenous Resistance to Genocide, Ecocide and Expropriation in Contemporary North America*. Monroe, Maine: Common Courage Press, 1993.

Churchill, Ward, and Winona LaDuke. "Native America: The Political Economy of Radioactive Colonialism." *Journal of Ethnic Studies* 13 : 3 (1985): 123–136.

Clark, Ronald W. *Benjamin Franklin: A Biography*. New York: Random House, 1983.

Coleridge, Samuel Taylor. *The Poems of Samuel Taylor Coleridge*. Ed. Ernest Hartley. 1912. Reprint, London: Oxford University Press, 1951.

Conway, Jill Ker, Kenneth Keniston, and Leo Marx. *Earth, Air, Water, Fire: Humanistic Studies of the Environment*. Amherst: University of Massachusetts Press, 2000.

Cooper, Susan Fenimore. *Rural Hours*. 1850. Ed. Rochelle Johnson and Daniel Patterson. Athens: University of Georgia Press, 1998.

Covey, Cyclone. Preface to *Adventures in the Unknown Interior of America*, by Álvar Núñez Cabeza de Vaca. 1542. Trans. and ed. Cyclone Covey. Reprint, Albuquerque: University of New Mexico Press, 1998.

Creeley, Robert, and Susan Howe. "Four-Part Harmony: Robert Creeley and Susan Howe Talk It Out." *Village Voice Literary Supplement*, April 1994, 21–22.

Cronon, William. "The Trouble with Wilderness; or, Getting Back to the Wrong Nature." In Cronon, *Uncommon Ground*.

———, ed. *Uncommon Ground: Toward Reinventing Nature*. New York: W. W. Norton, 1995.

Crowther, Paul. *The Kantian Sublime: From Morality to Art*. Oxford: Clarendon Press, 1989.

Culler, Jonathan. *The Pursuit of Signs: Semiotics, Literature, and Deconstruction*. Ithaca, N.Y.: Cornell University Press, 1981.

Darrah, William Culp. "The Exploration of the Colorado River in 1869." *Utah Historical Quarterly* 15 (1947): 9–18.

Davidson, Michael. *Ghostlier Demarcations: Modern Poetry and the Material Word*. Berkeley: University of California Press, 1997.

Dell, Floyd. *Upton Sinclair*. New York: George Doran, 1927.

Deloria, Vine, Jr. *God Is Red: A Native View of Religion*. Golden, Col.: Fulcrum, 1994.

de Man, Paul. *Aesthetic Ideology*. Ed. Andrzej Warminksi. Minneapolis: University of Minnesota Press, 1996.

———. *The Resistance to Theory*. Minneapolis: University of Minnesota Press, 1986.

Dennis, John. *The Grounds of Criticism in Poetry*. London, 1704.

Description of Banvard's Panorama of the Mississippi and Missouri Rivers.
Extensively Known as the "Three-Mile Painting." London: W. J. Golbourn,
Leicester Square, 1848.

de Zengotita, Thomas. "The Gunfire Dialogues: Notes on the Reality of
Virtuality." *Harper's*, July 1999, 55–58.

Di Chiro, Giovanna. "Nature as Community: The Convergence of Environment
and Social Justice." In *Uncommon Ground: Toward Reinventing Nature*. New
York: W. W. Norton, 1995.

Dickens, Charles. *David Copperfield*. Oxford: Clarendon Press, 1978.

———. *Great Expectations*. Ed. Angus Calder. London: Penguin, 1980.

———. *Our Mutual Friend*. Oxford: Clarendon Press, 1978.

*Dickens's Dictionary of the Thames; from Its Source to the Nore. By Charles Dickens
the Younger*. London: J. Smith, 1895.

Du Bos, Abbé [Jean Baptiste Dubos]. *Critical Reflections of Poetry, Painting
and Music with an Inquiry into the Rise and Progress of the Theatrical
Entertainments of the Ancients*. 1719. Trans. Thomas Nugent. 3 vols. Reprint,
London, 1748.

DuPlessis, Rachel. *The Pink Guitar: Writing as Feminist Practice*. New York:
Routledge, 1990.

Dutton, Clarence E. *Tertiary History of the Grand Canyon*. 1882. Reprint, Santa
Barbara, Calif.: Peregrine, 1977.

Elder, John. Foreword to *The Height of Our Mountains*, ed. Michael P. Branch and
Daniel J. Philippon. Baltimore: Johns Hopkins University Press, 1998.

Electronic Text Center, University of Virginia Library. <http://etext.lib
.virginia.edu/>.

Eliot, George. *Adam Bede*. Ed. Stephen Gill. London: Penguin, 1980.

———. *The Mill on the Floss*. Ed. Gordon S. Haight. Boston: Houghton Mifflin,
1861.

"Encounter at Farpoint." *Star Trek: The Next Generation*. Dir. Corey Allen. Fox.
1987.

Enzensberger, Hans. "A Critique of Political Ecology." In *The Greening of
Marxism*, ed. Ted Benton. New York: Guilford Press, 1998.

Evernden, Neil. "Beyond Ecology: Self, Place, and the Pathetic Fallacy." In
Glotfelty and Fromm, *The Ecocriticism Reader*.

———. *The Social Creation of Nature*. Baltimore: Johns Hopkins University
Press, 1992.

Faulkner, William. "The Bear." *Go Down, Moses*. New York: Vintage International,
1990.

———. *Go Down Moses*. New York: Random House, 1942.

———. *Three Famous Short Novels*. New York: Random House, 1961.

Finch, Robert, and John Elder, eds. *The Norton Book of Nature Writing*. New York: W. W. Norton, 1990.

Fitter, Chris. *Poetry, Space, Landscape: Toward a New Theory*. Cambridge: Cambridge University Press, 1995.

Ford, Paul Leicester. *The Many-Sided Franklin*. 1898. Reprint, Freeport: Books for Libraries, 1972.

Garrard, Greg. "Radical Pastoral?" *Studies in Romanticism* 35 (1996): 449–465.

Gerard, Alexander. *An Essay on Taste: To which is now added Part Fourth, Of the Standard of Taste, with Observations Concerning the Imitative Nature of Poetry*. Edinburgh, 1780.

Glotfelty, Cheryll. "Introduction: Literary Studies in an Age of Environmental Crisis." In Glotfelty and Fromm, *The Ecocriticism Reader*.

Glotfelty, Cheryll, and Harold Fromm, eds. *The Ecocriticism Reader: Landmarks in Literary Ecology*. Athens: University of Georgia Press, 1996.

Goodman, Nelson. *Ways of Worldmaking*. Indianapolis, Ind.: Hackett Publishing Company, 1978.

Grant, Natalie. "The Landscape of the Soul: Man and the Natural World in *The Orchard Keeper*." In *Sacred Violence: A Reader's Companion to Cormac McCarthy*. El Paso: Texas Western University Press, 1995.

Greenfield, Bruce. *Narrating Discovery: The Romantic Explorer in American Literature, 1790–1855*. New York: Columbia University Press, 1992.

Greenleaf, Moses. *Survey of Maine*. 1829. Reprint, Augusta: Maine State Museum, 1970.

Grinde, Donald A. *Ecocide of Native America: Environmental Destruction of Indian Lands and Peoples*. Santa Fe, N.M.: Clear Light, 1995.

Guidebook to Mr. Washington Friend's Grand Tour of Five Thousand Miles in Canada and the United States of America. Nottingham, Eng.: Stafford and Co., n.d.

Hall, Kathy. "Impacts of the Energy Industry on the Navajo and Hopi." In Bullard, *Unequal Protection*.

Haraway, Donna. "A Cyborg Manifesto." In *Postmodern American Fiction: An Anthology*, ed. Paula Geyh et al. New York: W. W. Norton, 1998.

———. "The Promises of Monsters: A Regenerative Politics for Inappropriate/d Others." In *Cultural Studies*, ed. Lawrence Grossberg et al. New York: Routledge, 1992.

———. "Situated Knowledges: The Science Question in Feminism and the Privilege of Partial Perspective." *Feminist Studies* 14 (1988): 575–599.

Hardy, Thomas. *The Mayor of Casterbridge*. Ed. Martin Seymour-Smith. New York: Penguin, 1985.

———. *Tess of the D'Urbervilles*. London: Penguin, 1978.

Hartley, David. *Observations on Man, His Frame, His Duties, and His Expectations*. 2 vols. London, 1749.

Hemingway, Andrew. *Landscape Imagery and Urban Culture in Nineteenth-Century Britain*. Cambridge: Cambridge University Press, 1992.

Herbert, Christopher. *Culture and Anomie: Ethnographic Imagination in the Nineteenth Century*. Chicago: University of Chicago Press, 1991.

Hicks, Granville. *The Great Tradition*. 1933. Rev. ed. New York: Biblio and Tannen, 1967.

———. *Small Town*. New York: Macmillan, 1946.

Hicks, Granville, and Richard Bennett. *The First To Awaken*. New York: Modern Age Books, 1940.

Hipple, Walter J. *The Beautiful, the Sublime, and the Picturesque in Eighteenth-Century British Aesthetic Theory*. Carbondale: Southern Illinois University Press, 1957.

Hofrichter, Richard. *Toxic Struggles: The Theory and Practice of Environmental Justice*. Philadelphia: New Society, 1993.

Hovet, Grace Ann, and Theodore R. Hovet. "Tableaux Vivants: Masculine Vision and Feminine Reflections in Novels by Warner, Alcott, Stowe, and Wharton." *American Transcendental Quarterly* 7 : 4 (December 1993): 335–356.

Howarth, William. Introduction to *Mountaineering in the Sierra Nevada* by Clarence King. New York: Penguin, 1989.

———. "Some Principles of Ecocriticism." In Glotfelty and Fromm, *The Ecocriticism Reader*.

———. "'Where I Lived': The Environs of *Walden*. In *Approaches to Thoreau's Walden and Other Works*, ed. Richard J. Schneider. New York: MLA, 1996.

Howe, Susan. *The Birth-mark: Unsettling the Wilderness in American Literary History*. Hanover: Wesleyan University Press, 1993.

———. *Frame Structures: Early Poems 1974–1979*. New York: New Directions, 1996.

———. "An Interview with Susan Howe." With Lynn Keller. *Contemporary Literature* 36 : 1 (1995): 1–34.

———. "Speaking with Susan Howe." With Janet Ruth Falon. *Difficulties* 3 : 2 (1989): 28–42.

Huhn, Thomas. "The Kantian Sublime and the Nostalgia for Violence." *Journal of Aesthetics and Art Criticism* 53 (1955): 269–275.

Hulme, Peter. *Colonial Encounters: Europe and the Native Caribbean, 1492–1797*. London: Routledge, 1992.

Hume, David. *A Treatise of Human Nature*. 1739. Ed. L. A. Selby-Bigge. Reprint, Oxford: Clarendon Press, 1967.

Huxtable, Ada Louise. *The Unreal America: Architecture and Illusion*. New York: New Press, 1997.

Hyde, Ralph. *Panoramania! An Exhibit at the Barbican Art Gallery, Nov 3 1988 – Jan 15 1989*. London: Barbican, 1988.

Ihde, Don. *Technology and the Lifeworld: From Garden to Earth*. Bloomington: Indiana University Press, 1990.

An Illustrated Description of the Diorama of the Ganges. London, 1850.

ISLE: Interdisciplinary Studies in Literature and Environment 8 : 1 (winter 2001).

Jefferson, Thomas. *Notes on the State of Virginia*. 1787. Ed. William Peden. Reprint, New York: W. W. Norton, 1954.

John Johnson Collection of Printed Ephemera. Diorama Box 1, Diorama Box 3. Bodleian Library, Oxford.

Johnson, Barbara. "Apostrophe, Animation, and Abortion." In *Feminisms*, ed. Diane Price Herndl and Robyn Warhol. New Brunswick, N.J.: Rutgers University Press, 1991.

Johnson, Rochelle, and Daniel Patterson. Introduction to *Rural Hours*, by Susan Fenimore Cooper. Ed. Rochelle Johnson and Daniel Patterson. Athens: University of Georgia Press, 1998.

Jussim, Estelle, and Elizabeth Lindquist-Cock. *Landscape as Photograph*. New Haven, Conn.: Yale University Press, 1985.

Kant, Immanuel. *The Critique of Judgement*. 1790. Trans. James Creed Meredith. Reprint, Oxford: Clarendon Press, 1952.

———. *Observations on the Feeling of the Beautiful and the Sublime*. 1764. Trans. J. T. Goldthwaite. Reprint, Berkeley: University of California Press, 1965.

King, Clarence. *Mountaineering in the Sierra Nevada*. 1872. Ed. Francis Farquhar. Reprint, Lincoln: University of Nebraska Press, 1997.

Kirwan, James. *Beauty*. Manchester, Eng.: Manchester University Press, 1999.

———. "'The Claim to a Nobler Motive': Morality, Reason, and the Sublime in Kant." In *Debats theoriques et mise en forme esthetique*. Paris: Champion, forthcoming.

———. *Literature, Rhetoric, Metaphysics: Literary Theory and Literary Aesthetics*. London: Routledge, 1990.

Kline, Mary-Jo. *A Guide to Documentary Editing*. Baltimore: Johns Hopkins University Press, 1987.

Kolodny, Annette. *The Land Before Her: Fantasy and Experience of the American Frontiers, 1630–1860*. Chapel Hill: University of North Carolina Press, 1984.

———. *The Lay of the Land: Metaphor as Experience and History in American Life and Letters*. Chapel Hill: University of North Carolina Press, 1975.

Kristeva, Julia. *Revolution in Poetic Language*. 1974. Trans. Margaret Waller. Reprint, New York: Columbia University Press, 1984.

Kroeber, Karl. *Ecological Literary Criticism: Romantic Imagining and the Biology of Mind*. New York: Columbia University Press, 1994.

LaBudde, Kenneth. "Cultural Primitivism in William Faulkner's 'The Bear.'" In Utley, Bloom, and Kinney, *Bear, Man, and God.*

LaDuke, Winona. "A Society Based on Conquest Cannot Be Sustained: Native Peoples and the Environmental Crisis." In *Toxic Struggles: The Theory and Practice of Environmental Justice*, ed. Richard Hofrichter. Philadelphia: New Society, 1993.

Lambert, John R. "Report of the Topography from the Mississippi River to the Columbia." In *Reports of Explorations and Surveys to Ascertain the Most Practicable and Economic Route for a Railroad from the Mississippi River to the Pacific Ocean.* Vol. 1. Washington, D.C.: Nicholson, 1855.

Lawson-Peebles, Robert. *Landscape and Written Expression in Revolutionary America.* Cambridge: Cambridge University Press, 1988.

Lazer, Hank. *Opposing Poetries: Readings.* Evanston, Ill.: Northwestern University Press, 1996.

Lebeaux, Richard. *Thoreau's Seasons.* Amherst: University of Massachusetts Press, 1984.

Lefebvre, Henri. *The Production of Space.* 1974. Trans. Donald Nicholson-Smith. Reprint, Cambridge, Mass.: Blackwell, 1997.

Leonard, Elmore. *Killshot.* Harmondsworth, Eng.: Penguin, 1990.

Leopold, Aldo. *Round River: From the Journals of Aldo Leopold.* Ed. Luna B. Leopold. London: Oxford University Press, 1972.

———. *A Sand County Almanac and Sketches Here and There.* 1949. Reprint, New York: Oxford University Press, 1989.

Le Page du Pratz, Antoine-Simon. *Histoire de la Louisiane, contenant la Découverte du ce vaste pays, sa Description géographique, un Voyage dans les Terres, l'Histoire Naturelle; les Mœurs, Coutumes & Religion des Naturels, avec leurs Origines; deux Voyages dans le Nord du nouveau Mexique, dont un jusqu'à la Mer du Sud.* 3 vols. Paris: De Bure, Veuve Delaguette, et Lambert, 1758.

———. *The History of Louisiana, or of The Western Parts of Virginia and Carolina: Containing a Description of the Countries that lie on both Sides of the River Mississippi: With an Account of the Settlements, Inhabitants, Soil, Climate, and Products.* London: T. Becket, 1764. Ed. Joseph Treagle. Reprint, Baton Rouge: Louisiana State University Press, 1975.

———. *The Journey of Moncacht-apé, an Indian of the Yazou Tribe, across the continent, about the year 1700.* Ed. and trans. Andrew McFarland Davis. Worcester: Charles Hamilton, 1883. Reprint, Tacoma, Wash.: Ye Galleon Press, 1966.

Lilley, James D. "'The Hands of Yet Other Puppets': Reading Repetition and Figuring Freedom in Cormac McCarthy's *All the Pretty Horses*." In *Myth,*

Legend, Dust: Critical Responses to Cormac McCarthy, ed. Rick Wallach. New York: St. Martin's Press, 2000.

Lokash, Jennifer. "Shelley's Organic Sympathy: Natural Communitarianism and the Example of Alatsor." *Wordsworth Circle* 28 (1997): 177–183.

Longfellow, Henry Wadsworth. *Henry Wadsworth Longfellow: Poems and Other Writings*. Ed. J. D. McClatchy. New York: Library of America, 2000.

Longfellow, Samuel. *Life of Henry Wadsworth Longfellow*. 1891. Vol. 1. Reprint, New York: Greenwood, 1969.

Longinus. *On the Sublime*. In *Classical Literary Criticism*. Ed. T. S. Dorsch. Harmondsworth, Eng.: Penguin, 1965.

Lopez, Barry Holstun. *Arctic Dreams: Imagination and Desire in a Northern Landscape*. New York: Charles Scribner's Sons, 1986.

———. *Of Wolves and Men*. New York: Touchstone, 1978.

Love, Glen A. "Revaluing Nature: Toward an Ecological Criticism." *Western American Literature* 25:3 (1990): 201–215.

Luckin, Bill. *Pollution and Control: A Social History of the Thames in the Nineteenth Century*. Bristol and Boston: Adam Hilgar, 1986.

Lukens, Erick Jon. "Shaping California : Landscape and Literary Form in Clarence King, Frank Norris and Raymond Chandler." Ph.D. diss., Princeton University, 1995.

Lutwack, Leonard. *The Role of Place in Literature*. Syracuse, N.Y.: Syracuse University Press, 1984.

Lyotard, Jean-François. *Lessons on the Analytic of the Sublime*. Trans. Elizabeth Rottenberg. Stanford, Calif.: Stanford University Press, 1994.

Ma, Ming-Qian. "Articulating the Inarticulate: Singularities and the Counter-method in Susan Howe." *Contemporary Literature* 36 (1995): 466–489.

MacKenzie, Alexander. *Journal of a Voyage to the Pacific*. New York: Dover, 1995.

Marshall, Ian. *Story Line: Exploring the Literature of the Appalachian Trail*. Charlottesville: University of Virginia Press, 1998.

Mather, Cotton. *The Christian Philosopher*. 1721. Ed. Winton U. Solberg. Reprint, Urbana: University of Illinois Press, 1994.

McCarthy, Cormac. *All the Pretty Horses*. New York: Vintage International, 1992.

———. *Blood Meridian: Or the Evening Redness in the West*. New York: Vintage International, 1992.

———. *Child of God*. London: Picador, 1989.

———. *The Crossing*. New York: Vintage International, 1995.

———. *The Orchard Keeper*. New York: Random House, 1965.

———. *Outer Dark*. New York: Vintage International, 1993.

———. *Suttree*. New York: Vintage, 1986.

———. "Whales and Men." Unpublished screenplay. Southwestern Writers Collection, Albert B. Alkek Library, Southwest Texas State University.

McDowell, Linda, and Joanne P. Sharp. Introduction to *Space, Gender, Knowledge: Feminist Readings*, ed. Linda McDowell and Joanne P. Sharp. London: Arnold, 1997.

McKusick, James. "Coleridge and the Economy of Nature." *Studies in Romanticism* 35 (1996): 375–392.

McNamee, Gregory. "Wild Things: Forget Deconstruction —Today's Hippest Literary Critics Have Gone Green." *Utne Reader*, November–December 1997, 14–15.

Meisel, Martin. *Realizations: Narrative, Pictorial, and Theatrical Arts in Nineteenth-Century Britain*. Princeton, N.J.: Princeton University Press, 1983.

Mellor, Anne, and Richard E. Matlak, eds. *British Literature 1780–1830*. Orlando, Fla.: Harcourt Brace, 1996.

Miles, Josephine. *Pathetic Fallacy in the Nineteenth Century: A Study of Changing Relation between Object and Emotion*. New York: Octagon, 1976.

Miller, Peter. "John Wesley Powell: Vision of the West." *National Geographic* 185:4 (1994): 89–114.

Momaday, N. Scott. *The Man Made of Words*. New York: St. Martin's Press, 1997.

Monk, Samuel. *The Sublime: A Study of Critical Theories in XVIII-Century England*. 1935. Reprint, Ann Arbor: University of Michigan Press, 1960.

Morton, Timothy. *Shelley and the Revolution in Taste: The Body and the Natural World*. New York: Cambridge University Press, 1994.

———. "Shelley's Green Desert." *Studies in Romanticism* 35 (1996): 409–430.

Muir, John. *John Muir's Last Journey: South to the Amazon and East to Africa; Unpublished Journals and Selected Correspondence*. Ed. Michael P. Branch. Washington, D.C.: Island, 2001.

———. *A Thousand-Mile Walk to the Gulf*. 1916. Ed. William Frederic Badè. Reprint, San Francisco: Sierra Club, 1991.

Museum of London Collection. Dioramas, Panoramas Box A1; Dioramas, Panoramas Box A2; Dioramas, Panoramas Box A3; Oversized Panoramas/ Dioramas C1.

Nabhan, Gary Paul. *Cultures of Habitat: On Nature, Culture and Story*. Washington, D.C.: Counterpoint, 1997.

Naylor, Paul Kenneth. "Where Are We Now in Poetry?" *Sagetrieb* 10:1–2 (1991): 29–44.

Nearing, Scott, and Helen Nearing. *The Good Life: Helen and Scott Nearing's Sixty Years of Self-Sufficient Living*. New York: Shocken, 1970.

Nelson, Robert M. *Place and Vision: The Function of Landscape in Native American Fiction*. New York: Peter Lang, 1993.

New, Caroline. "Man Bad, Woman Good? Essentialism and Ecofeminism." In *Space, Gender, Knowledge: Feminist Readings*, ed. Linda McDowell and Joanne P. Sharp. London: Arnold, 1997.

Novak, Barbara. *Nature and Culture: American Landscape and Painting, 1825–1875*. New York: Oxford University Press, 1980.

Oerlemans, Onno. "Romanticism and the Metaphysics of Species." *Wordsworth Circle* 28 (1997): 136–147.

Oettermann, Stephan. *The Panorama: History of a Mass Medium*. Trans. D. L. Schneider. New York: Zone Books, 1997.

O'Grady, John P. *Pilgrims to the Wild*. Salt Lake City: University of Utah Press, 1993.

Oliver, Kelly. *Reading Kristeva: Unraveling the Double-bind*. Bloomington: Indiana University Press, 1993.

Ousby, Ian. *The Englishman's England: Taste, Travel, and the Rise of Tourism*. Cambridge: Cambridge University Press, 1990.

Parini, Jay. "The Greening of the Humanities." *New York Times Magazine*, (October 29, 1995), 52+.

Parkes, Adam. "History, Bloodshed, and the Spectacle of Identity in *Blood Meridian*." In *Cormac McCarthy: A Collection of Critical Essays*, ed. James D. Lilley. Albuquerque: University of New Mexico Press, forthcoming.

Perelman, Bob. *The Marginalization of Poetry: Language Writing and Literary History*. Princeton, N.J.: Princeton University Press, 1996.

Phillips, Dana. "History and the Ugly Facts of Cormac McCarthy's *Blood Meridian*." *American Literature* 68:2 (1996): 433–460.

Pite, Ralph. "How Green Were the Romantics?" *Studies in Romanticism* 35 (1996): 356–373.

Plotnik, Arthur. *The Elements of Editing: A Modern Guide for Editors and Journalists*. New York: Macmillan, 1982.

Pollan, Michael. "The Idea of a Garden." In *Green Perspectives*, ed. Walter Levy and Christopher Hallowell. New York: Harper Collins, 1994.

———. *Second Nature: A Gardener's Education*. New York: Atlantic Monthly Press, 1991.

Powell, John Wesley. *The Exploration of the Colorado River and Its Canyons*. Canyons of the Colorado 1895. Reprint, New York: Penguin, 1987.

———. "Institutions for the Arid Lands." *Century* 40 (1890): 111–116.

———. *Report on the Lands of the Arid Region of the United States, with a More Detailed Account of the Lands of Utah. With Maps*. 1878. Intro. and ed. T. H. Watkins. Reprint, Harvard: Harvard Common, 1983.

Pratt, Geraldine. "Geographic Metaphors in Feminist Theory." In Aiken et al., *Making Worlds*.

Pratt, Mary Louise. *Imperial Eyes: Travel Writing and Transculturation*. Boston: Routledge, 1992.

Pughe, Thomas. "Revision and Vision: Cormac McCarthy's *Blood Meridian*." *Revue Française D'Études Américaines* 62 (1994): 371–382.

Pyne, Stephen J. *How the Canyon Became Grand: A Short History*. New York: Penguin, 1998.

Quammen, David. E-mail to Scott Slovic. May 28, 1998.

Radcliffe, Ann. *The Mysteries of Udolpho*. 1794. 2 vols. Reprint, London: J. M. Dent, 1931.

Raleigh, Sir Walter. "The Discovery of the Large, Rich, and Beautiful Empire of Guiana." In *Selected Writings*. Harmondsworth, Eng.: Penguin, 1986.

Reich, Charles A. *The Greening of America*. New York: Random House, 1970.

Reid, Thomas. *Essays on the Intellectual Powers of Man*. 1785. In *The Works of Thomas Reid*. Ed. William Hamilton. 2 vols. Reprint, Edinburgh: Machlachlan and Stewart, 1872.

Reynolds, Sir Joshua. *Discourses on Art*. 1797. Ed. Robert R. Wark. Reprint, London: Collier-Macmillan, 1966.

Rich, Adrienne. *Blood, Bread, and Poetry: Selected Prose 1979–1985*. New York: W. W. Norton, 1986.

Rideout, Walter. *The Radical Novel in the United States, 1900–1954: Some Interrelations of Literature and Society*. Cambridge: Harvard University Press, 1956.

Rose, Gillian. *Feminism and Geography: The Limits of Geographical Knowledge*. Minneapolis: University of Minnesota Press, 1993.

Rossanda, Rossada. "Die Socialistischen Länder: Ein Dilemma des westeuropean Linken." *Kursbuch* 30 (1973): 175–187. Quoted in Enzensberger, "Critique," 36.

Roszak, Theodore. *Person/Planet: The Creative Disintegration of Industrial Society*. New York: Doubleday, 1978.

Ruskin, John. *Modern Painters*. 5 vols. New York: Dutton, 1906.

Ryan, Simon. *The Cartographic Eye*. Cambridge: Cambridge University Press, 1996.

Ryden, Kent. *Mapping the Invisible Landscape: Folklore, Writing, and the Sense of Place*. Iowa City: University of Iowa Press, 1993.

Said, Edward. *Orientalism*. New York: Routledge, 1982.

Sayre, Gordon M. *"Les Sauvages Américains": Representations of Native Americans in French and English Colonial Literature*. Chapel Hill: University of North Carolina Press, 1997.

Scarry, Elaine. *The Body in Pain: The Making and Unmaking of the World*. New York: Oxford University Press, 1987.

Schelling, F. W. J. *The Philosophy of Art*. 1859. Trans. D. W. Stott. Reprint, Minneapolis: University of Minnesota Press, 1989.

Schiller, Friedrich. *On the Aesthetic Education of Man: In a Series of Letters*. 1795. Trans. E. M. Wilkinson and L. A. Willoughby. Reprint, Oxford: Clarendon Press, 1967.

Schneider, Richard J. *Henry David Thoreau*. Boston: Twayne, 1987.

Scholes, Robert. *The Rise and Fall of English: Reconstructing English as a Discipline*. New Haven, Conn.: Yale University Press, 1998.

Shaftesbury, Earl [Anthony Ashley Cooper]. *Characteristicks of Men, Manners, Opinions, Times*. 3 vols. [London], 1711.

Sharpe, Leslie T., and Irene Gunther. *Editing Fact and Fiction: A Concise Guide to Book Editing*. Cambridge: Cambridge University Press, 1994.

Shaviro, Steven. "'The Very Life of the Darkness': A Reading of *Blood Meridian*." *Southern Quarterly* 30 : 4 (1992): 111–120.

Shelley, Mary Wollstonecraft. *History of a Six weeks' tour through a part of France, Switzerland, Germany and Holland with letters descriptive of a sail around the Lake of Geneva, and of the glaciers of Chamouni*. London: T. Hookham, C. & J. Ollier, 1817.

Shelley, Percy Bysshe. *Shelley's Poetry and Prose*. Norton Critical Edition. Ed. Donald H. Reiman and Sharon B. Powers. New York: W. W. Norton, 1977.

Silko, Leslie Marmon. *Ceremony* (1977). Reprint, New York: Penguin, 1986.

———. *Gardens in the Dunes*. New York: Simon and Schuster, 1999.

———. "Landscape, History, and the Pueblo Imagination." In *Antaeus: On Nature*, ed. Daniel Halpern. London: Collins Harvill, 1989.

———. *Yellow Woman and a Beauty of the Spirit*. New York: Simon and Schuster, 1996.

Sinclair, Upton. *American Outpost: A Book of Reminiscences*. New York: Farrar and Rinehart, 1932.

———. *The Journal of Arthur Stirling*. New York: D. Appleton, 1903.

———. *The Jungle*. New York: Doubleday Page, 1906.

———. *The Lost First Edition of Upton Sinclair's* The Jungle. Ed. Gene DeGruson. Atlanta: St. Lukes, 1989.

———. *Plays of Protest*: "The Naturewoman," "The Machine," "The Second-story Man," "Prince Hagen." New York: M. Kennerly, 1912.

Singal, Daniel. *William Faulkner: The Making of a Modernist*. Chapel Hill: University of North Carolina Press, 1997.

Slovic, Scott. "Reaching Out to the Great Unwashed: Ecocritics, Environmental Writers, and Their Audience(s)." American Literature Association Symposium. Puerto Vallarta, Mexico. December 1998.

———. *Seeking Awareness in American Nature Writing*. Salt Lake City: University of Utah Press, 1992.

Smith, Anne-Marie. *Julia Kristeva: Speaking the Unspeakable*. Modern European Thinkers. Sterling, Va.: Pluto, 1998.

Snyder, Gary. *A Place in Space: Ethics, Aesthetics and Watersheds*. Washington, D.C.: Counterpoint, 1995.

———. *The Practice of the Wild*. San Francisco: North Point Press, 1990.

———. *The Real Work: Interviews and Talks 1964–1979*. San Francisco: New Directions, 1980.

Solberg, Winton U. Preface and introduction to *The Christian Philosopher*, by Cotton Mather. Ed. Winton U. Solberg. Urbana: University of Illinois Press, 1994.

Soper, Kate. "Greening Prometheus: Marxism and Ecology." In Benton, *The Greening of Marxism*.

Spaulding, Jonathan. *Ansel Adams and the American Landscape*. London: University of California Press, 1995.

St. Armand, Barton Levi. "The Book of Nature and American Nature Writing: Codex, Index, Contexts, Prospects." *Interdisciplinary Studies in Literature and the Environment* 4:1 (spring 1997): 29–41.

Stevens, Michael E., and Steven B. Burg. *Editing Historical Documents: A Handbook of Practice*. Walnut Creek, Calif.: AltaMira, 1997.

Stewart, Veronica. "The Wild Side of *The Wide, Wide World*." *Legacy* 11:1 (1994): 1–16.

Swados, Harvey. *A Radical's America*. Boston: Little and Brown, 1962.

Swan, Edith. "Laguna Symbolic Geography in Silko's *Ceremony*." *American Indian Quarterly* 12:3 (summer 1988): 229–249.

Sweet, Timothy. "Economy, Ecology and *Utopia* in Early Colonial Promotional Literature." *American Literature* 71:3 (September 1999): 399–425.

Tallmadge, John. "Western Geologists and Explorers: Clarence King and John Wesley Powell." In *American Nature Writers*. Vol. 2. Ed. John Elder. New York: Charles Scribner's, 1996.

Taylor, Walter Fuller. "The Jungle." In *Literary History of the United States*, ed. Jonathon Spiller. New York: Macmillan, 1953.

Thompson, David. *David Thompson's Narrative, 1784–1812*. Toronto: Champlain Society, 1962.

Thoreau, Henry David. *Early Essays and Miscellanies*. Ed. Joseph Moldenhauer and Edwin Moser, with Alexander C. Kern. Princeton, N.J.: Princeton University Press, 1975.

———. *The Maine Woods*. Ed. Joseph Moldenhauer. Princeton, N.J.: Princeton University Press, 1972.

———. *Walden*. In *The Portable Thoreau*, ed. and intro. Carl Bode. New York: Penguin, 1981.

Tompkins, Jane. Afterword to *The Wide, Wide World*, by Susan Warner. 1850. Reprint, New York: Feminist Press, 1987.

———. *Sensational Designs: The Cultural Work of American Fiction, 1790–1860*. New York: Oxford University Press, 1985.

The Tour of the Thames; or, the Sights and Songs of the King of Rivers. London: John Kendrick, 1849.

Trollope, Anthony. "Tourists Who Don't Like Their Travels." In *Travelling Sketches*. Ed. Asa Briggs. New York: Arno Press, 1981.

Turner, Frederick. "Cultivating the American Garden." In Glotfelty and Fromm, *The Ecocriticism Reader*. ·

United Church of Christ Commission for Racial Justice. *Toxic Wastes and Race in the United States: A National Report on the Racial and Socio-Economic Characteristics of Communities with Hazardous Waste Sites*. New York: United Church of Christ, 1987.

Up the River from Westminster to Windsor. A Panorama in Pen and Ink. Illustrated with Eighty-One Engravings and a Map. London: Hardwicke and Bogue, 1876.

Utley, Francis Lee, Lynn Z. Bloom, and Arthur F. Kinney, eds. *Bear, Man, and God: Seven Approaches to William Faulkner's "The Bear."* New York: Random House, 1964.

Vail, Jeffrey. "'The bright sun extinguish'd': The Bologna Prophecy and Byron's 'Darkness.'" *Wordsworth Circle* 28 (1997): 183–192.

Vaughan, Alden T. Introduction to *New England's Prospect*, by William Wood. Ed. Alden T. Vaughan. Amherst: University Massachusetts Press, 1977.

Villiers de la Terrage, Marc, ed. *"L'Etablissement de la Province de la Louisiane, Poème Composé de 1728 à 1742 par Dumont de Montigny." Journal de la Société des Américanistes* (1931): 273–440.

Wagner, Peter. *Eros Revived: Erotica of the Enlightenment in England and America*. London: Collins, 1990.

Walkowitz, Judith. *City of Dreadful Delight: Narratives of Sexual Danger in Late-Victorian London*. Chicago: University of Chicago Press, 1992.

Warner, Susan. *The Wide, Wide World*. 1850. Reprint, New York: Feminist Press, 1987.

Weaver, Jace, ed., *Defending Mother Earth: Native American Perspectives on Environmental Justice*. Maryknoll, N.Y.: Orbis Books, 1996.

Weiskel, Thomas. *The Romantic Sublime: Studies in the Structure and Psychology of Transcendence*. Baltimore: Johns Hopkins University Press, 1976.

White, Richard. "'Are you an Environmentalist or Do You Work for a Living?': Work and Nature." In Cronon, *Uncommon Ground*.

Wilford, John Noble. *The Mapmakers*. New York: Vintage, 1981.

Wilson, Alexander. *The Culture of Nature: North American Landscape from Disney to the Exxon Valdez*. Cambridge: Blackwell, 1992.

Wolfson, Susan. "'Romantic Ideology' and the Values of Aesthetic Form." In *Aesthetics and Ideology*, ed. George Levine. New Brunswick, N.J.: Rutgers University Press, 1994.

Wolfson, Susan, and Peter Manning, eds. *The Romantics and Their Contemporaries*. Vol. 2A of *The Longman Anthology of British Literature*, ed. David Damrosch. New York: Longman, 1999.

Women and Geography Study Group. *Feminist Geographies: Explorations in Diversity and Difference*. Harlow, Eng.: Longman, 1997.

Wood, William. *New England's Prospect*. 1634. Ed. Alden T. Vaughan. Reprint, Amherst: University of Massachusetts Press, 1977.

Woolf, Virginia. *Collected Essays by Virginia Woolf*. Vol. 2. London: Hogarth, 1966.

———. *A Room of One's Own*. San Diego, Calif.: Harvest, 1981.

Wordsworth, William. *Oxford Author's Selected Poems*. Ed. Stephen Gill. London: Oxford University Press, 1984.

———. Preface to the 1850 edition of *Lyrical Ballads*. In *The Prose Works of William Wordsworth*. Ed. W. J. B. Owen and Jane Worthington Smyser. Vol. 1. Oxford: Clarendon Press, 1974.

———. *William Wordsworth: A Critical Edition of the Major Works*. Ed. Stephen Gill. London: Oxford University Press, 1984.

Wordsworth, William, and Samuel Taylor Coleridge. *Lyrical Ballads 1798*. Ed. W. J. B. Owen. 2nd ed. Oxford: Oxford University Press, 1969.

Worster, Donald. "The Wilderness of History." *Wild Earth* 7 : 3 (winter 1997): 9–13.

Zamir, Shamoon. "Literature in a 'National Sacrifice Area': Leslie Silko's *Ceremony*." In *New Voices in Native American Literary Criticism*, ed. Arnold Krupat. Washington, D.C.: Smithsonian Institution Press, 1993.

Zizek, Slavoj. *The Sublime Object of Ideology*. New York: Verso, 1989.

INDEX